Language and Legal Judgments

Integrating research methods from linguistics with contemporary legal argumentation theory, this book highlights the complexities of legal justification by focusing on the role of value-laden language in argument construction and use. The combination of linguistic analysis and the pragma-dialectic approach to legal argumentation yields a new way of perceiving and understanding the phenomenon of evaluation, one that offers theoretical and practical gains. Analyzing a vast corpus of judicial opinions from the US Supreme Court and Poland's Constitutional Tribunal, the book paints a clear picture of complex linguistic choices made by judges to assess and support arguments in the justifications of their decisions. The book will be of interest to scholars in law, linguistics and rhetoric as well as to judges and practicing lawyers engaged in the art of argumentation.

Stanisław Goźdź-Roszkowski is Associate Professor and Head of Department of Specialized Languages and Intercultural Communication at the University of Łódź, Poland.

Law, Language and Communication

This series encourages innovative and integrated perspectives within and across the boundaries of law, language and communication, with particular emphasis on issues of communication in specialized socio-legal and professional contexts. It seeks to bring together a range of diverse yet cumulative research traditions in order to identify and encourage interdisciplinary research.

The series welcomes proposals – both edited collections as well as single-authored monographs – emphasizing critical approaches to law, language and communication, identifying and discussing issues, proposing solutions to problems, offering analyses in areas such as legal construction, interpretation, translation and de-codification.

Series Editors

Anne Wagner is Professor of Legal Semiotics and Research Professor at Centre de Recherche Droits & Perspectives du Droit, équipe René Demogue, Lille University, France. She is the Editor-in-Chief of the *International Journal for the Semiotics of Law* (Springer) and President of the International Roundtables for the Semiotics of Law. She has been awarded the National Research Grant for her research career. Her main research interests include semiotics, verbal and non-verbal sign system analyses, language and law, legal culture and heritage, legal translation, legal terminology, and legal discourse studies.

Vijay K. Bhatia, formerly Professor of English, City University of Hong Kong, is now Adjunct Professor at Chinese University of Hong Kong, and Visiting Professor at the Hellenic American University, Athens (Greece). He is also the founding President of the Languages for Specific Purposes and Professional Communication Association for Asia-Pacific. His research interests include Critical Genre Analysis, academic and professional discourses in legal, business, newspaper, and promotional contexts; ESP and Professional Communication; simplification of legal and other public documents; intercultural and cross-disciplinary variations in professional genres.

Titles in the series

Ambiguity in EU Law
A Linguistic and Legal Analysis
Sofiya Kartalova

Fair Trial Rights and Multilingualism in Africa
Perspectives from Comparable Jurisdictions
Catherine S. Namakula

Language and Legal Judgments
Evaluation and Argument in Judicial Discourse
Stanisław Goźdź-Roszkowski

For more information about this series, please visit:
www.routledge.com/Law-Language-and-Communication/book-series/LAWLANGCOMM

Language and Legal Judgments

Evaluation and Argument in Judicial Discourse

Stanisław Goźdź-Roszkowski

Routledge
Taylor & Francis Group
LONDON AND NEW YORK

First published 2024
by Routledge
4 Park Square, Milton Park, Abingdon, Oxon OX14 4RN

and by Routledge
605 Third Avenue, New York, NY 10158

Routledge is an imprint of the Taylor & Francis Group, an informa business

British Library Cataloguing-in-Publication Data
A catalogue record for this book is available from the British Library

ISBN: 9781032366906 (hbk)
ISBN: 9781032366920 (pbk)
ISBN: 9781003333302 (ebk)

DOI: 10.4324/9781003333302

Typeset in Galliard
by Deanta Global Publishing Services, Chennai, India

Contents

About the author *vi*
Preface *vii*

PART I
Introduction **1**

1 Evaluation: What is it, and why does it matter? 3

2 Evaluation, argumentation and the justification of judicial decisions 16

PART II
Evaluative language patterns as a persuasive device **33**

3 Evaluating processes and propositions 37

4 Evaluating status and sites of contention 69

PART III
Uncovering evoked and less obvious evaluative meanings **99**

5 Value-based lexis and argument in morally sensitive issues 101

6 Evaluative language: The model of critical discussion and strategic manoeuvring 128

7 Pulling the strands together 163

Index *171*

About the author

Stanisław Goźdź-Roszkowski is Associate Professor and Head of the Department of Specialised Languages and Intercultural Communication, University of Łódź (Poland). His recent scholarly work focuses on the intersection of corpus and functional linguistics, argumentation theory and rhetoric. He has published and lectured extensively on the use of evaluative language in judicial discourse from a comparable perspective.

Preface

In the popular stereotype, judicial discourse should be objective and rational, devoid of any linguistic expressions of evaluation, especially those related to evaluative attitudes. Ideally, in their decisions and justifications, judges should confine themselves to communicating facts and propositional information related to the decision-making process. Judges are expected to draft their decisions in a way that reflects the application of relevant legal norms to the facts of the case, suppressing signs of their subjectivity. However, this view of evaluation as incongruent with the ideal of unbiased and objective adjudication is far from the reality of judicial decision-making processes. Ever since the legal realist movement of the 1920s and the emergence of the strategic model and attitudinal model (Segal & Spaeth 2002), it has become accepted that the ideologies and values of justices play a role in how disputes are decided.[1] Indeed, judges' personal values and ideologies leave a discernible imprint on formal judicial prose. The idea that judges should communicate only in the impersonal tones of a detached and dispassionate professional is challenged in Justice William J. Brennan's influential essay 'Reason, Passion, and "The Progress of the Law"',[2] in which he argues that 'this internal dialogue of reason and passion' is essential to the 'vitality' of the decision-making process. Laura Krugman Ray observes that judicial opinions can 'employ a variety of rhetorical strategies to justify a position or persuade a reader that the majority has erred' (2002: 233). The interrelatedness between the rhetorical strategies used by judges and the pervasive evaluative language found in judicial decisions that are the main subject of this book.

While evaluation has attracted increasing attention in linguistics and linguistically informed research over the past two decades, few studies recognize the inherently argumentative nature of judicial discourse, nor incorporate the theoretical insights and analytical tools developed in legal argumentation

1 This is true, even if, as Posner (2008) suggests, the role of subjectivity in judicial decision-making may have been somewhat exaggerated by the early advocates of legal realism.
2 William J. Brennan, Jr. was one of the longest-serving (16 October 1956 –20 July 1990) and most influential justices in the history of the US Supreme Court.

theory (Feteris 2017; Dahlman & Feteris). Even fewer take into account the uniquely strategic nature of justification (also referred to as opinion writing) as a distinct type of judicial writing and how its strategic nature imposes constraints on how judges express assessments and take stances. Language, in general, and evaluative language, in particular, becomes the primary tool for judges who must balance the mandatory need to justify the reason for their decision with an almost equally imperative need to persuade various audiences that their choices are sound. Even when full of linguistic detail, most linguistic studies of evaluation in judicial discourse have relatively little explanatory power. Such studies often lack a pragmatic or rhetorical perspective; they do not clarify *why* evaluative items are used in legal justification nor how they contribute to the realization of judges' argumentative and strategic goals. On the other hand, argumentation scholars tend to focus on assessing the merits of legal argumentation based on certain norms of rationality – norms which serve as a basis for establishing whether an argument is sound and reasonable. Argumentation scholars seldom pay attention to the specific linguistic resources used by judges to construct their arguments, and they often analyze instances of argumentative propositions outside of the linguistic contexts that shape those propositions. Among the extant surveys of judicial linguistics and argumentation theory, few bring the two disciplines together to show how methods from linguistics and legal argumentation studies can complement and enrich each other The present book attempts to demonstrate how integrating linguistic and argumentative insights, discourse, genre information and other contextual phenomena, in combination with the statistical exploitation of data, will vastly improve our study of the justification of judicial decisions. My underlying assumption is that the evaluative function is one of the most basic and important functions of language. I argue that evaluative language and judicial argumentation are always interwoven in the justifications of court decisions. Judicial justification is an institutionalized form of discourse communication in which evaluation itself is the core information communicated.

This book adopts a comparative approach because its aim is to shed new light on the extent to which evaluation and evaluative strategies should be treated as specific to justification as a text genre and on how the concrete expressions of evaluation are unique to each given legal culture. One of my premises is that evaluative language is inherent in any act of justification but that its actual expression depends on what is allowed or disallowed within the institutional, meaning also the national and linguistic, context of the opinion. These institutional constraints will vary, given the profound impact of the common law and civil law traditions which lie at the heart of how different judicial institutions operate and which, in turn, have shaped the genre of judicial opinion. It is important to stress here that my comparison does not aspire to be comprehensive nor exhaustive. Given the multifarious and multi-faceted nature of evaluation as a linguistic phenomenon, not to mention the complexities of adjudication when approached from the perspective of two different legal traditions, no single researcher could carry out a systematic and in-depth comparison, even of justifications from two distinct legal cultures. To make this study feasible, the scope of the analyses had to be delimited to a realistic compass. The United States, in particular its Supreme Court, serves as a common point of reference for many comparative studies today, as the epitome of the common law tradition. Some of the decisions of the US Supreme Court, especially those related to human rights issues, such as access to marriage for same-sex couples or women's reproductive rights and so on, receive intense international media attention. Further, it is not uncommon for Polish judges, in their own opinions, to rely on arguments made by US Supreme Court justices.[3] In a paper published in 2007, Lech Garlicki, a leading expert on constitutional law and a judge of the Constitutional Tribunal (1993–2001) and the European Court of Human Rights (2002–2012), wrote that the '[tribunal] represents one of the best-established constitutional jurisdictions among the "new democracies" of Europe (2007: 57). Nine years later, the rule of law crisis in Poland had set in, eventually undermining the tribunal's position and credibility (Sadurski 2019).[4] Nevertheless, the tribunal's adjudication remains an important source of constitutional argumentation in the civil law tradition in Poland.

The findings documented in this book come from analyses which exploit the strong connections between judicial arguments and the language in which they are made. Any reasoning is, naturally, expressed with words that carry argumentative content. As Martin Hinton correctly observes 'just as reasoning begets argumentation through language, so language, through argumentation, begets greater reason'. (2021: 217). Defining argument or argumentation is a formidable task in itself, a source of a heated debate among argumentation theorists. According to one definition, conflict and disagreement should be accepted as inherent in argumentation, as '[a] conflict may occur when there is disagreement or doubt about any of the steps in, or the conclusion of, the "reasoning"' (Baumtrog 2018: 90). When doubt and disagreement occur,

3 For example, Poland's Supreme Court in the justification of its decision in case no. II KK 337/17 on refusal to provide services on the grounds of freedom of conscience and religion refers to arguments made by the US Supreme Court in *Masterpiece Cakeshop, Ltd. Et al v. Colorado Civil Rights Commission*.

4 The rule of law crisis in Poland is associated with the overhaul of the Polish judicial system launched soon after Poland's right wing party Law and Justice (PIS) won the general election in 2015. The Constitutional Tribunal was the first court that came into direct conflict with the new government and the parliamentary majority over the appointment of its judges. After assuring its control over the Constitutional Tribunal (by adopting legislative measures widely questioned by leading scholars and lawyers in Poland and abroad), the government moved on to restructure other judicial institutions, notably the National Council of the Judiciary and the Supreme Court, undermining their independence. The changes to the judicial system in Poland have led to an ongoing conflict with the European Union, which argues that the independence of the judiciary is embedded in the rule of law, and any changes affecting it represent a violation of EU core values.

judges 'attempt to generate agreement', and this is achieved 'through the medium of argumentative discourse' (Wohlrapp 2014: 384). This is the view of argument and evaluative language adopted in this book – a view reflected in the selection of constitutional cases (all revolving around conflicts of principles and values) as my basis for comparative case studies. But comparisons are also made using quantitative and empirical methods, drawing on large corpora from the two judicial institutions.

The book is organized into three parts. Part I consists of two chapters which provide explanation for key concepts and ideas, preparing the way for the ensuing discussion. Chapter 1 clarifies the concept of evaluation, explaining why it makes sense to apply it in the context of legal justification. It highlights the connections between evaluative language, judicial discourse and legal argumentation. Chapter 2 explains the difference between the linguistic and argumentative approaches to evaluation in legal justification to then focus on the concept of judicial justification – its definition, functions and audiences. After briefly comparing constitutional review in Poland and the United States, the chapter moves on to demonstrate how justification fits into the overall textual structure of legal decisions. Part II understands evaluation as evaluative language patterns which are used in justifications as persuasive devices. Using the corpus linguistics method, Chapter 3 focuses on adjective-centred patterns, formulated in English as *it v-link ADJ that* and *it v-link ADJ to-inf* and considers its Polish counterparts. Chapter 4 examines the *N that* pattern in English, mirrored by its Polish counterpart *N że/iż*. Part III marks the transition from a corpus-based to corpus-assisted method of analysis followed by detailed close readings of individual cases. Chapter 5 zooms in on the level of lexis denoting values and principles – such as *dignity, equality* or *fairness* – and which are shown to serve as argumentative premises (or legal *topoi*). Chapter 6 demonstrates how the use and role of evaluative language can be described more systematically by adopting the pragma-dialectical approach to legal justification, especially the concepts of the ideal model of critical discussion (IM) and of 'strategic manoeuvring'. Chapter 7 draws the different strands together to offer some conclusions.

Combining linguistics with legal argumentation theory, as I do here, presents a problem of audience. Who is the intended audience of the book? Linguists? Argumentation scholars? Rhetoricians? Lawyers? Professors or students? My ambition is to write a book that will interest all these potential audiences, under the assumption that how evaluation works in legal justification is a topic that will be of interest to all. Every effort was made to ensure that the concepts and theories are understandable to non-specialists yet without oversimplifying them. For readers seeking additional clarification, Chapters 3–6 include sections explaining the methodological procedures and the corpus data used.

This book was conceived and created over several years. Parts of it in their early versions were presented during numerous law and language conferences, especially those organized under the auspices of the International Language and Law Association (ILLA). A number of papers exploring the central theme of the book have also been published. Many thanks are due. I am grateful to colleagues reviewing my work, for their comments and suggestions and those attending these events, especially Łucja Biel, Ruth Breeze, Jan Engberg, Janet Giltrow, Anne Lise Kjaer, Davide Mazzi, Aleksandra Matulewska, Frances Olsen, Dieter Stein and Magdalena Szczyrbak.

I am particularly indebted to Gianluca Pontrandolfo with whom I carried out my early research on evaluation in judicial discourse for his ideas, inspiration and support.

I am grateful to Donato Mancini for his expert advice, helpful suggestions and meticulous copyediting. Last but not least, this book would not have been possible without the amazing and continued support of my family. I would like to thank my wife Ania for her unending support and encouragement.

Acknowledgments

Finally, my thanks go to the Polish National Science Centre (*Narodowe Centrum Nauki*) for supporting research presented in this book with Grant no. UMO-2018/31/B/HS2/03093.

Bibliography

Baumtrog, M. (2018). Reasoning and arguing, dialectically and dialogically, among individual and multiple participants. *Argumentation*, *32*(1), 77–98.

Brennan, Jr., William J. (1988). Reason, passion, and the "Progress of the Law". *Cardozo Law Review*, *10*(1–2), 3–24.

Dahlman, Ch., & Feteris, E. (Eds.). (2013). *Legal argumentation theory: Cross-disciplinary perspectives*. Springer.

Feteris, E.T. (2017). *Fundamentals of legal argumentation: A survey of theories on the justification of judicial decisions*. Springer.

Garlicki, L. (2007). Constitutional courts versus supreme courts. *International Journal of Constitutional Law*, *5*(1), 44–68.

Hinton, M. (2021). *Evaluating the language of argument*. Springer.

Kelemen, K. (2018). *Judicial dissent in European constitutional courts. A comparative and legal perspectives*. Routledge.

Krugman, R.L. (2002). Judicial personality: Rhetoric and emotion in Supreme Court opinions. *Washington & Lee Law. Review*, 59(1/6), 193–234.

Posner, R. (2008). *How judges think*. Harvard University Press.

Sadurski, W. (2019). *Poland's constitutional breakdown*, Oxford University Press.

Segal, J., & Spaeth, H. (2002). *The Supreme Court and the attitudinal model revisited*. Cambridge University Press.

Wohlrapp, H. (2014). *The concept of argument*. Springer.

Part I

Introduction

1 Evaluation

What is it, and why does it matter?

Evaluation: a definition

There are perhaps few phenomena in human communication as complex and multi-dimensional as evaluation. Understood broadly as 'the indication that something is good or bad' (Hunston 2004: 157), evaluation is universal and ubiquitous. Viewed as a behavioural phenomenon, evaluation is fundamental to the way we, as humans, operate in the world. Whether deciding on a holiday destination or considering a career move, we constantly carry out assessments as a prerequisite for making informed decisions. In fact, our perception and the subsequent (in)action are fundamentally decision-driven, and they involve the positive/negative dichotomy (Partington et al 2013). We decide to do or not to do something based on an earlier appraisal of potential benefit, risk or advantage. Even though, on its face, evaluation can be assigned a dualistic and essentialist sense and may seem deceptively easy to define in that way, it is, in fact, extremely complex when considered in its countless applications in discourse and communication. If values are reflected on and expressed through what may be termed as the evaluative function of language, then the expression of evaluation is closely linked with human emotions (Bednarek 2009). Emotions depicted through the affective use of language reflect not only the personalities of language users and their inner system of values but also socially and institutionally oriented principles of politeness and the discursive practices in which they occur. It is not surprising that evaluation has been approached and analyzed from many different disciplinary perspectives: from philosophical explorations of values, through cognitive investigations into emotion, to linguistic studies of evaluation, framed within a wide range of theories, such as appraisal (Martin & White 2005), stance (Conrad & Biber 2000) or evaluation (Thompson & Hunston 2000), and many more.[1] Indeed, there has been a growing interest in evaluation, in connection with interest in opinion and subjectivity, as part of what has been termed the 'affective turn' in humanities,

1 For an in-depth and historical overview of the phenomenon, see Alba-Juez and Thompson (2014).

DOI: 10.4324/9781003333302-2

sociology and political science (Clough & Halley 2007). As ~~my epigram from~~ Vološinov (1986) suggests, people have always constructed their worldview around systems of values. The expression of values is, indeed, a pervasive feature of language (Alba-Juez & Thompson 2014).

However, even within linguistics, there are different approaches to and perspectives on this phenomenon. A wide range of terminology is used in linguistic studies to refer to relevant domains of language use, including 'evaluation' (Hunston & Thompson 2000), 'appraisal' (Martin & White 2005), 'stance' (Conrad & Biber 2000) and 'stancetaking' (Englebretson 2007)[2]. As Hunston (2011) points out, the divergence in terminology can be traced back to different ways in which evaluation is conceptualized.

First, evaluation can be understood as *action* undertaken by an individual. The action may be purely private and unexpressed, or it may be performed in language. It is only when evaluation becomes verbalized that we can study it as linguists. Englebretson (2007) uses the term *stancetaking* to refer to situations when people actively engage in expressing evaluative stances.[3] As a concept originating in conversation analysis, as du Bois (2007) notes, the use of the term stancetaking implies a focus on the relationship between the speaker or writer and an external entity (an object evaluated), and simultaneously between themselves and their interactant(s). Evaluation, when understood as an expression of stance or stancetaking, implies something inherently interactive, reflecting individual or group values.

Second, evaluation can be viewed as a *set of meanings* which can be expressed using a wide variety of language resources. This understanding of evaluation is rooted in the systemic functional linguistics tradition. Martin and White (2005: 42) use the term *appraisal* to refer to a 'system of meanings' to which a speaker or writer has access and which that speaker/writer may use to 'approve and disapprove, enthuse and abhor, applaud and criticise, and [...] position their reader/listeners to do likewise'. As in the first case outlined above, this approach is clearly concerned with actions performed in discourse, in particular, the tripartite actions of expressing attitude, construing a subjective position and aligning with audience (Hunston 2011). Needless to say, the two ways of understanding evaluation outlined above call for a qualitative type of analysis which consists of a 'close reading' of a text considered in its entirety.

Third, evaluation can be conceptualized as the set of *words*, *phrases* and *language patterns* which express evaluative meaning. It is perhaps best to treat

2 Other related and overlapping terms include *connotation* (Lyons 1977), *attitude* (Halliday 1994), *sentiment* (Liu 2012), or *evidentiality* (Chafe & Nichols 1986).

3 It is worth noting that one of the ways to distinguish between evaluation and stance is that the latter is a broader concept including those cases when evaluation is not expressed, i.e., a pre-realization phase of the evaluation process. However, as soon as an individual 'decides to express a stance, whether though language or other semiotic means, we would be in the domain of evaluation' (Alba-Juez & Thompson 2014: 10).

these as overt markers of evaluation.[4] The research tradition used here is that of corpus linguistics, which takes the recurrence of linguistic items (words, phrases, grammatical categories or grammar patterns) as its object of study. In an excellent book on corpus approaches to evaluation, Hunston (2011) argues convincingly for treating the qualitative and quantitative traditions as complementary rather than as opposed or mutually exclusive. Hunston's is the approach adopted here. Despite using different terminology and methods, the qualitative and quantitative traditions share sufficient common ground that we can point towards some distinguishing characteristics:[5]

- Evaluative language represents meanings which tend to be associated with 'subjectivity' or 'attitude' rather than with 'objectivity' and 'factuality'.
- The positive–negative polar axis is given more prominence than the true–false axis. While evaluation is often perceived in terms of the good–bad dichotomy, it can also be examined across a number of other parameters or values. For example, propositions can be evaluated in terms of how important or how obvious they are or in terms of the degree of certainty or belief attached to them.
- Evaluative language fulfils many functions. Apart from expressing opinion, it performs roles in construing relationships in an interaction and in structuring discourse. The claim made here is that evaluative language is also central to the construction of an argument and the expression of a standpoint. Indicating an attitude towards an entity, process or proposition is important in socially significant speech acts such as persuasion and argumentation.
- Evaluation has many faces. The many ways in which evaluative meanings are expressed are notoriously difficult to pinpoint. Evaluation may be overt or covert. Overt (also referred to as 'explicit' or 'inscribed') evaluation uses recognizably evaluative lexis and/or constructions identified as evaluative, for example, *absurd*, *undesirable*, *it is important to*, *logically impeccable theory* and so on. Evaluative meanings can also be covert (or evoked), which means that evaluation may be implied rather than stated explicitly. In this case, the reader may be presented with evidence for an evaluation rather than the evaluation itself.
- Evaluative language has many distinct *phases*. The process of evaluation includes a 'pre-textual' or 'pre-realization' phase during which a decision is made regarding whether to perform the act of evaluation, what stance should be taken, and how the stance should be taken. In the pre-textual phase, evaluation can be regarded as a cognitive operation (Bednarek

4 Evaluation can, of course, be made manifest at other levels of linguistic description: the phonological, morphological, syntactic, etc. See Alba-Juez and Thompson for a more detailed discussion (2014: 9–14).

5 See Goźdź-Roszkowski and Hunston (2015)

2006), a yet-unexpressed stance which might or might not be manifested during the textual phase.

- Evaluative language is dependent on context, and it is cumulative. This means that taking items out of context is potentially an unreliable indicator of evaluative meaning, and linguistic signals of evaluation may be scattered across a stretch of text, and it may be necessary to study the entire text or at least a chunk of it to determine its evaluative function.

In an attempt to offer a comprehensive approach, combining both traditions, Hunston and Thompson famously define evaluation as

> the broad cover term for the expression of the speaker's or writer's attitude or stance towards, viewpoint on, or feelings about the entities or propositions that he or she is talking about. That attitude may relate to certainty or obligation or desirability or any of a number of other sets of values. When appropriate, we refer specifically to modality as a subcategory of evaluation.
>
> (2000: 5)

The designation 'evaluation' is, thus, used as a superordinate and maximally inclusive term to signal that there is a wide range of various parameters (or values) which can be included when analyzing evaluative language. Hunston and Thompson's definition gives leeway and discretion to the researcher to determine the scope and the number of parameters to take into account. The present book adopts Hunter and Thompson's definition of evaluation, above all, for practical reasons. Their definition offers the advantage of combining or choosing between two perspectives, depending on the object of enquiry. In some instances, it's most appropriate to consider the perspective of the user (the evaluator) and, in others, the perspective of the specific values that are 'ascribed to the entities and propositions which are evaluated' (Thompson & Hunston 2000: 5). The complementarity of these perspectives is underpinned by the distinction between 'stance' and 'evaluation'. 'Stance' is associated with evaluation as a social act, involving a complex web of interconnections between taking a stance and dialogicality – intersubjectivity (Du Bois 2007). More generally, stance refers to 'indications in the text that a human being, the writer, is communicating with another human being, the reader' (Hunston 2011: 51). 'Evaluation' focuses on evaluation *per se*, the ascription of a value to an entity as exercised in the text. The distinction is relevant to the present study of evaluation as considered both in terms of explicit lexico-grammatical patterns and implicit value-based lexis. Scrutiny of evaluative patterns reveals that an act of evaluation coincides with an act of stancetaking. This perspective enables the researcher to see how value is given to objects of interest, which, in the context of judicial justifications, are argumentative propositions. It also allows us to better see how legal actors are positioned with respect to these objects and one another. In addition, the lexico-grammatical patterns of evaluation as stance confirm the presence of what Bakhtin termed 'polyphony' (1984) and the inherent dialogicality of judicial discourse (Mazzi 2007). Referring to legal judgment as essentially argumentative, Bletsas correctly observes that argumentation derives from 'a *quaestio* at least in principle capable of arising a difference of opinion, a text laying out (at least) a *quaestio*, a decisional standpoint and its motivations, [which] is likely to host various voices' (2015: 80). The presence of these voices, with their legal standpoints and specific acts of stancetaking and evaluation, tends to be registered overtly through several discrete linguistic elements, including the language patterns described in Chapters 3 and 4 of the present book. The phenomenon of evaluation, viewed as a type of meaning that is context-sensitive and dependent on the argumentative realities of a specific judicial decision, is shown in Chapters 5 and 6. As this outline suggests, the study of evaluation calls for adopting a complementary and eclectic approach. Quantitative methods are used when studying lexico-grammatical patterns on the assumption that if a phenomenon is recurrent, it must be significant. On the other hand, the context-sensitive and multi-faceted nature of evaluation means that it must be interpreted based on a comprehensive understanding of the discourse in which it occurs. Furthermore, evaluation varies depending on the text type or text genre in which it is used. One of the primary concerns in this book is to study how the genre of judicial justification affects the use of evaluative language. The inclusion of a comparative perspective – comparison between justifications of decisions from the US Supreme Court (SCOTUS) and Poland's Constitutional Tribunal – is expected to shed light on the extent to which evaluation and evaluative strategies are both genre- and culture-specific.

Evaluative language in legal linguistics research on judicial argumentation

It is only recently that the evaluative function of language in legal discourse has begun to attract the attention of legal linguists. This upsurge of interest has taken place in the wake of a similar trend in the study of evaluation in linguistics more broadly.[6] The existing research into legal discourse has mirrored, to some extent, the proliferation of terms and concepts in linguistic studies. It would be difficult to do justice to the growing body of literature on the topic, especially given that, as we have seen, views on the phenomenon of evaluation diverge widely. I will, therefore, refer to studies that illustrate what I consider the most typical and representative ways of studying evaluation in the context of judicial argumentation.

There is a distinct trend towards the adoption of quantitative methods and the use of corpus data, cutting across different concepts such as *evaluation* (Mazzi 2010; Pontrandolfo & Goźdź-Roszkowski 2014), *stance*

6 See Alba-Juez and Thompson (2014) and Benamara et al. (2017).

(Hafner 2014), *attitude* (Finegan 2010), *stancetaking* (McKeown 2022), *appraisal* (Heffer 2007; Pérez 2022) and *evidentiality* (Szczyrbak 2022). In such studies, evaluation is explored in terms of pre-defined linguistic items associated with some aspect of evaluative meaning or stance. For example, Finegan (2010) examines judicial attitude by focusing on adverbial expressions of attitudinal stance and emphasis (e.g., *simply*, *certainly*). Adopting a quantitative approach enables Finegan to show that these expressions are much more frequent in a corpus of SCOTUS opinions than in a corpus of general English. Most studies go beyond simply locating and quantifying such forms, offering, in addition, some interpretation of their roles in discourse. McKeown (2022) investigates stancetaking by judicial opinion writers in SCOTUS's abortion jurisprudence. His study focuses on two kinds of stance evaluations: epistemic (im)probability and evidential (dis)belief. McKeown explores how these are marked in SCOTUS opinions with regard to two major jurisprudential issues: viability and state interests. A quantitative approach allows the researcher to make direct comparisons between large sets of data. McKeown's 2022 study compares the previously mentioned stance evaluations in majority opinions and dissent opinions. He is able to show that dissent writers display greater commitment to the propositions made in their opinions, using significantly more high certainty and high strength (dis)belief markers than majority opinion writers.

Another emerging feature of existing research into evaluative language in judicial discourse is its versatility in terms of combining different methods and theoretical perspectives. For example, Izes (2023) combines the framework of appraisal analysis (Martin & White 2005) with corpus linguistics methods to examine defamatory language and determine how the expression of stance differs between judicially determined statements of 'opinion' and 'fact' in defamation cases. This means that, apart from triangulating analytical methods, different scholars sometimes use concepts associated with evaluation almost interchangeably. Their specific choice of a term may depend on the emphasis they wish to place on a particular aspect of evaluation and how narrowly or broadly the scope of the analyses is defined.

Research into evaluative language in judicial discourse is predominantly monolingual and confined to English, but there is a growing body of research which attempts to account for the diverse uses of evaluative language in non-English legal cultures, institutions and languages (Pérez 2022; Pontrandolfo & Goźdź-Roszkowski 2014; Goźdź-Roszkowski & Pontrandolfo 2014, 2013; Goźdź-Roszkowski 2018). For example, Pérez (2022) uses the theoretical framework of the appraisal system (Martin & White 2005) to explore terms contained in the category of 'affect' in two corpora of British and Spanish judicial decisions related to the topic of immigration. The category of 'affect' includes linguistic items which appeal to or refer to emotion. Pérez's analysis of evaluative lexis, algorithmically extracted from British and Spanish national courts, has focused on differences and similarities in the way the phenomenon of immigration is projected in each corpus. In a series of publications (Pontrandolfo & Goźdź-Roszkowski 2014; Goźdź-Roszkowski & Pontrandolfo 2014, 2013) Pontrandolfo and Goźdź-Roszkowski investigate the extent to which grammar patterns in English, compared with equivalent patterns in Italian,[7] are an efficient diagnostic for retrieving instances of evaluative language in the opinions of SCOTUS and the Italian *Corte Suprema di Cassazione* and whether these patterns fulfil the same discourse functions. Goźdź-Roszkowski (2018) explores the phraseologies of *the fact that* and its Polish counterpart in SCOTUS opinions and judgments handed down by the Constitutional Tribunal of Poland, with a view to exploring the implications of their similarities and differences in terms of epistemology and argumentative strategies.

It is relatively rare that the linguistic study of evaluation is combined deliberately with a theory of argumentation. This may be a result of linguists' often loose understanding of argument and argumentation as theoretical and practical constructs, if not outright failure to engage with wider scholarly contexts. In the research outlined above, the analytical focus is on the micro-level of the linguistic utterance. In Goźdź-Roszkowski (2022), I argue for integrating the study of evaluative language into the argumentative reality of legal justification. Most linguistically oriented studies suffer from two limitations. First, they do not usually take into account the macro-context of the institutional environment in which judicial argumentation occurs, nor the impact of the generic conventions of legal judgment and opinion on language, in general, and evaluative language, in particular. Second, the linguistic account of legal justification may be fragmentary and inconclusive because such studies tend to focus on the micro-level of discrete language items. Given the open-ended nature of evaluative language, it does not seem feasible to compile an exhaustive inventory of evaluative language items, even in the relatively restricted context of legal justification. Judicial writers, especially in common law jurisdictions, will always find novel and sometimes idiosyncratic ways of voicing their opinions. Using quantitative methods of corpus linguistics can be relevant and useful because they help researchers to focus on frequent and typical ways of making assessments. However, Hunston points out that 'numbers themselves are useless without interpretation, and without the grounds for the interpretation being made clear' (2007: 28). Her reservation rings true, particularly for studies involving two different languages. Comparison of linguistic resources with regard to their evaluative function must be grounded in a thorough analysis of the surrounding discourse to see past superficial similarities between discrete and context-free language items. There are, of course, many other ways

7 Patterns such as, in English, *v-link + ADJ + that* and *v-link + ADJ + to-infinitive*, or, in Italian, equivalent patterns such as *copula + ADJ + che* and *copula + ADJ + verbo all'infinito*. It turns out that both English and Italian adjectives found in the patterns display striking similarities not only in terms of frequency of occurrence in the respective datasets but also with regard to the semantic property of being evaluative.

in which language and argumentation intersect. For example, Mazzi (2022) provides a discourse perspective on the use of causal argumentation in a corpus of the Supreme Court of Ireland's judgments on the issue of data protection. Mazzi's linguistic analysis of phraseology helps him identify judgments in which causal argumentation occurs as an instrument of reasoning.

Evaluative language, judicial discourse and legal argumentation

Our preoccupation here with judicial discourse as an area of language use that is particularly amenable to the study of evaluation is not surprising once we realize that this type of discourse is inherently evaluative. For example, the Constitutional Tribunal of Poland routinely assesses the admissibility of a constitutional complaint by examining the legal grounds on which it was filed. The judges evaluate whether the complaint is legitimate, and they usually evaluate the potential effects of their ruling. Determining whether a piece of legislation is constitutional or not amounts to an act of evaluation. Whatever decision the judge makes, it must be supported by justificatory arguments. Providing an assessment alone is never sufficient. Evaluation is, thus, invariably intertwined with justification. A substantial part of judicial opinions involves expressing agreement or disagreement with decisions given by lower courts, opinions expressed by counsel representing the parties and opinions arrived at by fellow judges from the same bench. Evaluation involves signalling different points of view and different legal standpoints.

Linguistic study of evaluative language in judicial discourse in many ways resembles the attitudinal model proposed in modern jurisprudence developed by Segal and Spaeth (1993, 2002). Segal and Spaeth's work dispels the myth that judicial decisions are objective, impartial and dispassionate. Their central concept is *attitude*, which, in their model, comprises a relatively enduring and interrelated set of beliefs about an object or situation. With the attitudinal model, it is possible to see judicial discourse, especially in the decision-making process, as a convergence of values, affect, linguistic expressions and judicial personality (Krugman Ray 2002). However, this research avenue is not explored in the present book. The focus here is on evaluative language, viewed as a patterned verbal and collective behaviour rather than as an instance of a judge's personal idiosyncrasies. Even when the analyses in this book provide examples of evaluative language from individual judges, the analytical focus is always on broader patterns of verbal, collective and institutional behaviour. My point of departure is the observation that argument and evaluation go hand in hand and that the two are often inseparable. To illustrate this point, we can consider a number of recent legal cases revolving around certain businesses' discriminatory refusal to provide services, cases litigated on the grounds of freedom of conscience, religion and speech (e.g., *Masterpiece Cakeshop Ltd v. Colorado Civil Rights Commission et al.* in the United States, or *Bull & Bull v. Hall & Preddy* in the United Kingdom, or *Case no. II KK 333/17 on the Refusal to Provide Services on the Grounds of Freedom of Conscience and*

Religion in Poland). Cases like these amount to a fundamental conflict of principles and values, and the arguments used in the justifications are based on value judgment. For example, SCOTUS Justice Anthony Kennedy drafted the majority opinion referring to the Colorado Civil Rights Commission's treatment of the case as having 'elements of a clear and impermissible hostility towards the sincere religious beliefs that motivated the Petitioner's (Masterpiece Cakeshop, Ltd. and Jack C. Phillips) objection'.[8] The negative evaluation of the Colorado Civil Rights Commission's treatment of the case underpinned the court's decision to reverse the Commission's ruling against Masterpiece Cakeshop (Goźdź-Roszkowski 2021). In a similar vein, the Polish Supreme Court's appraisal of the nature of the defendant's work and of his religious convictions greatly contributed to the final decision that religious beliefs cannot constitute a 'justified cause' for the failure to provide service to the client.[9] Evaluative items are not used merely to embellish the argumentation but are very often constitutive of the argument.

The analysis of evaluative language also helps to reveal rhetorical strategies adopted in judicial opinions to steer the discussion in a desirable direction – to promote a particular development of law. The study reported in Goźdź-Roszkowski (2021) shows how the rhetorical choices and the 'presentational devices' (Eemeren 2010) in the justification of the decision in *Masterpiece Cakeshop Ltd* includes value-laden language selected in order to elicit a conclusion, leaving the key question unresolved. The majority opinion frames the dispute as 'difficult' on several occasions, and this assessment signals the court's intention to limit the applicability of the final ruling. Evaluative language used in judicial decisions may also carry a referential function by denoting values themselves as sources of argument. Classical rhetoricians recognize in this practice the use of *topoi*. In Greek, *topoi* means 'places', a metaphor for places where arguments may be found and which serve as the identification and description of argumentative premises (Frost 2016). The evaluative nature of *topoi* was noticed in Perelman (1976), advocating the use of what he terms *loci* as starting points in law. In the context of legal argumentation, *topoi* are generally accepted legal values which judges choose for their persuasive power to better gain the acceptance of a legal audience.

In sum, evaluative language is an important tool used by an opinion writer to justify the decision and convince other judges, while it is also used to seek external approval. This may be particularly important in the case of decisions revolving around morally sensitive issues – cases which may lead to social

8 On 3 June 2018 SCOTUS ruled in favour of a Colorado baker who had refused to create a wedding cake for a gay couple.

9 On 14 June 2018 the Supreme Court in Poland upheld criminal charges against a print shop employee who refused to print banners for an LGBT business foundation because he did not want to 'promote' the gay rights movement (Case no. II KK 333/17 on the Refusal to Provide Services on the Grounds of Freedom of Conscience and Religion).

conflict outside the courtroom. Consider the widespread uproar caused by the recent SCOTUS decision in *Dobbs v. Jackson Women's Health Organization*, which put an end to the long-held compromise on abortion, enshrined in the landmark *Roe v. Wade*. In Poland, as soon as the ruling of the Constitutional Tribunal banning the termination of pregnancy in the event of a fatal foetal abnormality was announced on 22 October 2020, mass protests erupted across the country in defiance of the COVID-19-related restrictions on public gatherings. Court cases deciding morally sensitive issues, especially those concerned with expanding or limiting human rights, can receive intense media attention, evoking highly emotive responses from audiences within and outside the legal professions. Judges may feel compelled to incorporate rhetorical means into their reasoning to explain and justify their decision rather than merely interpreting legal norms in an abstract way. The justification must be crafted so as to make it generally acceptable. This is, of course, an enormously difficult task given that the audiences may range from fellow judges ('the bench') to lower court justices, litigants, the legal community, legislators and government officials to news outlets and the public at large.

Modern judicial opinion provides a unique opportunity to reach out to these audiences. Its importance is obvious in common law societies where it serves as a device for establishing precedents and, by extension, for setting forth the law. But it is just as important in civil law countries where it has several important functions, with the persuasive function being of prime importance (Królikowski 2015; Rzucidło 2020). In civil law countries, the justification is necessary to persuade all audiences that the disposition is rational and sound. It is becoming apparent that any act of evaluation should be seen as an indispensable part of, or an aspect of, persuasion and within the wider framework of legal rhetoric. Evaluation needs to be understood within a wider framework of attitudes, one reflecting the arguer's unique position in the controversy (dissenting, concurring or expressing the majority opinion), the particular standpoints adopted and the different audiences addressed. It is, therefore, instructive to see how evaluation, persuasion and justification are closely interlocked in the argumentative space of the opinion and how evaluative language contributes to the justificatory force of legal argument.

Bibliography

Alba-Juez, L., & Thompson, G. (2014). The many faces of evaluation. In G. Thompson & L. Alba-Juez (Eds.), *Evaluation in context* (pp. 3–23). John Benjamins.

Bakhtin, M. (1984). *Problems of Dostoevsky's poetik*. (C. Emerson, Trans.). University of Minnesota. (Original work written 1929)

Bednarek, M. (2009). Emotion talk and emotional talk: Cognitive and discursive perspectives. *Pragmatics and Cognition, 17*(1), 146–176.

Bednarek, M. (2006). Evaluation and cognition: Inscribing, evoking and provoking opinion. In H. Pishwa (ed.) *Language and Memory. Aspects of knowledge representation* (pp. 187-221). Mouton de Gruyter.

Benamara, F., Taboada, M., & Yannick, M. (2017). Evaluative language beyond bags of words: Linguistic insights and computational applications. *Computational Linguistics, 43*(1), 201–264. https://doi.org/10.1162/COLI_a_00278

Bletsas, M. (2015). The voices of justice: Argumentative polyphony and strategic manoeuvring in judgement motivations: An example from the Italian Constitutional Court. In F.H. van Eemeren and B. Garssen (Eds.), *Scrutinizing argumentation in practice* (pp. 79–97). John Benjamins.

Chafe, W., & J. Nichols (Eds.). (1986). *Evidentiality: The linguistic encoding of epistemology*. Ablex.

Clough, P.T., & Halley, J. (Eds.). (2007). *The affective turn: Theorizing the social.* Duke University Press.

Conrad, S., & Biber, D. (2000). Adverbial marking of stance in speech and writing. In G. Thompson & S. Hunston (Eds.), *Evaluation in text: Authorial stance and the construction of discourse* (pp. 56–73). Oxford University Press.

Du Bois, J.W. (2007). The stance triangle. In R. Englebretson (Ed.), *Stancetaking in discourse: Subjectivity, evaluation, interaction* (pp. 139–182). John Benjamins.

Englebretson, R. (Ed.). (2007). *Stancetaking in discourse: Subjectivity, evaluation, interaction.* John Benjamins.

Finegan, E. (2010). Corpus linguistics approaches to "legal language": Adverbial expression of attitude and emphasis in Supreme Court opinions. In M. Coulthard & A. Johnson (Eds.), *The Routledge handbook of forensic linguistics* (pp. 65–77). Routledge.

Frost, M. (2016). *Introduction to classical legal rhetoric.* Routledge.

Goźdź-Roszkowski, S. (2021). Hostility to religion or protection against discrimination? Evaluation and argument in a case of conflicting principles. In J. Giltrow, F. Olsen, & D. Mancini (Eds.), *Legal meanings: The making and use of meaning in legal reasoning* (pp. 57–76). De Gruyter Mouton.

Goźdź-Roszkowski, S. (2022). Evaluative language and strategic manoeuvring in the justification of judicial decisions: The case of teleological-evaluative argumentation. In S. Goźdź-Roszkowski & G. Pontrandolfo (Eds.), *Law, language and the courtroom: Legal linguistics and the discourse of judges* (pp. 98–111). Routledge.

Goźdź-Roszkowski, S., & Hunston, S. (2016). Corpora and beyond: Investigating evaluation in discourse: Introduction to the special issue on corpus approaches to evaluation. *Corpora, 11*(2), 131–141.

Goźdź-Roszkowski, S., & Pontrandolfo, G. (2013). Evaluative patterns in judicial discourse: A corpus-based phraseological perspective on American and Italian criminal judgments. *International Journal of Law, Language and Discourse, 3*(2), 9–69.

Hafner, C. (2014). Stance in a professional legal genre: The barrister's opinion. In R. Breeze, M. Gotti, & S. Guinda Carmen (Eds.), *Interpersonality in legal genres* (pp. 137–160). Peter Lang.

Halliday, M.A.K. (1994). *An introduction to functional grammar* (2nd ed.). Edward Arnold.

Heffer, C. (2007). Judgement in Court: Evaluating participants in courtroom discourse. In K. Kredens & S. Goźdź-Roszkowski (Eds.), *Language and the law: International outlooks* (pp. 145–179). Peter Lang.

Hunston, S. (2011). *Corpus approaches to evaluation: Phraseology and evaluative language*. Routledge.

Hunston, S. (2007). Using a corpus to investigate stance quantitatively and qualitatively. In R. Englebretson (Ed.), *Stancetaking in discourse: Subjectivity, evaluation, interaction* (pp. 27–48). Benjamins.

Hunston, S. (2004). Counting the uncountable: Problems of identifying evaluation in text and in a corpus. In A. Partington, J. Morley and L. Haarman (Eds.), *Corpora and Discourse* (pp. 157-188). Peter Lang.

Izes, A. (2023). Fact versus opinion in us defamation law: A corpus and appraisal analysis of speaker stance toward reputational harm. *International Journal for the Semiotics of Law, 36*, 1–32.

Królikowski, J. (2015). Uzasadnienia orzeczeń Trybunału Konstytucyjnego. In I. Rzucidło-Grochowska & M. Grochowski (Eds.), *Uzasadnienia decyzji stosowania prawa* (pp. 427–439). Wolters Kluwer.

Liu, B. (2012). *Sentiment analysis and opinion mining*. Morgan and Claypool.

Lyons, J. (1977). *Semantics*. Cambridge University Press.

Martin, J., & White, P. (2005). *The language of evaluation: Appraisal in English*. Palgrave.

Mazzi, D. (2007). "The rhetoric of judicial texts": The interplay of reported argumentation and the judge's argumentative voice. In: G. Garzone & S. Sarangi (Eds.), *Discourse, ideology and specialized communication* (pp. 379–399). Peter Lang.

Mazzi, D. (2010). "This argument fails for two reasons...": A linguistic analysis of judicial evaluation strategies in US Supreme Court judgements'. *International Journal for the Semiotics of Law, 23*(4), 373–385.

Mazzi, D. (2022). "Without proof of negligence or a causative connection": On causal argumentation in the discourse of the Supreme Court of Ireland's judgments on data protection. In S. Goźdź-Roszkowski & G. Pontrandolfo (Eds.), *Law, language and the courtroom: Legal linguistics and the discourse of judges* (pp. 112–125). Routledge.

McKeown, J. (2022). Stancetaking in the U.S. Supreme Court's abortion jurisprudence (1973-present): Epistemic (im)probability and evidential (dis)belief. *International Journal of Legal Discourse, 7*(2), 323–343. https://doi.org/10.1515/ijld-2022-2075

Partington, A., Duguid, A. & Taylor, Ch. (2013). *Patterns and meanings in discourse. Theory and practice in corpus-assisted discourse studies (CADS)*. John Benajmins.

Perelman, Ch. (1976). *Logique juridque: Nouvelle rhetorique*. Dalloz.

Pérez, M.J. (2022). A corpus-based comparative analysis of the evaluative lexicon found in judicial decisions on immigration. In S. Goźdź-Roszkowski & G. Pontrandolfo (Eds.), *Law, language and the courtroom: Legal linguistics and the discourse of judges* (pp. 126–143). Routledge.

Pontrandolfo, G., & Goźdź-Roszkowski, S. (2014). Exploring the local grammar of evaluation: The case of adjectival patterns in American and Italian judicial discourse. *Research in Language, 12*(1), 71–91. https://doi.org/10.2478/rela-2014-0014

Ray, L.K. (2002). Judicial personality: Rhetoric and emotion in Supreme Court opinions. *Washington and Lee Law Review, 59*(1/6), 193–234.

Rzucidło, I. (2020). *Uzasadnienie orzeczenia sądowego: Ujęcie teoretyczne a poglądy orzecznictwa*. Wolters Kluwer.

Sancho, G., Carmen, M., Gotti, R., & Breeze, R. (2014). Framing interpersonality in law contexts. In R. Breeze, G. Maurizio, & C. Sancho Guinda (Eds.), *Interpersonality in legal genres* (pp. 9–35). Peter Lang.

Segal, J.A., & Spaeth, H.J. (1993). *The Supreme Court and the attitudinal model.* Cambridge University Press.

Segal, J.A., & Spaeth, H.J. (2002). *The Supreme Court and the attitudinal model revisited.* Cambridge University Press.

Szczyrbak, M. (2022). Evidentiality in US Supreme Court opinions: Focus on passive structures with *say* and *tell.* In S. Goźdź-Roszkowski & G. Pontrandolfo (Eds.), *Law, language and the courtroom: Legal linguistics and the discourse of judges* (pp. 26–38). Routledge.

Thompson, G., & Hunston, S. (2000). Evaluation: An introduction. In S. Hunston & G. Thompson (Eds.), *Evaluation in text: Authorial stance and the construction of discourse* (pp. 1–27). Oxford University Press.

Van Eemeren, F.H. (2010). *Strategic maneuvering in argumentative discourse: Extending the Pragma-Dialectical Theory of argumentation.* John Benjamins.

Van Eemeren, F.H., & Henkemans, F.S. (2017). *Argumentation: Analysis and evaluation.* Routledge.

Vološinov, V.N. (1986). *Marxism and the Philosophy of Language* (L. Matejka & I.R. Titunik, Trans.) Harvard University Press. (Originally published 1929)

2 Evaluation, argumentation and the justification of judicial decisions

Evaluation in linguistics and argumentation studies: in search of common ground

In argumentation studies, the centrality of argument evaluation has been advocated as a possible 'direction and purpose' (Schiappa 2003: 51) for the discipline. The basic criterion against which argumentative discourse is evaluated is *soundness*. Van Eemeren and Henkemans, in *Argumentation: Analysis and Evaluation*, point out that an argument can be regarded as sound if it is acceptable and valid and if the argument scheme is 'appropriate and correctly used' (2017: 81). However, the standard of soundness may vary depending on the context in which argumentation occurs. Evaluation goes to the heart of legal argumentation theory because the question of which standards of legal soundness the argumentation should meet remains a perennial issue (see Feteris & Kloosterhuis 2013). Feteris (2017) links the acceptability of legal argumentation with the quality of its justification, pointing out that any legal decision 'must be justified adequately to make it acceptable to the parties involved as well as to other judges and the legal community as a whole' (xv). But the general goal of legal argumentation theory remains the development of methods for the analysis and evaluation of legal argumentation in judicial justifications.[1]

In contrast, the linguistic study of evaluation in judicial discourse is less concerned with assessing the quality of argumentation than it is with how judges make assessments in their argumentation. In other words, the scholar of argumentation is interested in the *what*, whereas the linguist is interested in the *how*. While the argumentation scholar will attempt to establish how arguments can be adequately analyzed and evaluated, the linguist's goal will be to identify linguistic resources marshalled by judges to make value judgments, express attitudes and take stances regarding arguments. As a simple example, let us consider the following dialogue:

1 See Feteris (2017) for an extensive and in-depth survey of theories on the justification of judicial decisions.

DOI: 10.4324/9781003333302-3

X: Mrs Borg is very reliable as an eyewitness.
Y: No, she is not. She has poor eyesight.[2]

An argumentation scholar will note that the argument of Actor Y is an *ad hominem*, i.e., an argument directed at a person rather than a proposition. Here, Y claims that Mrs Borg is not a reliable person. Y's argument is a counter-argument to X's proposition that Mrs Borg is reliable, which Y asserts is false. We could continue this analysis to schematize this exchange to indicate different premises and, perhaps, demonstrate how rashly erroneous *ad hominem* argument can be.[3] The linguist would demand to know more about the context of the exchange and may consider it from the perspective of genre theory as an instance of courtroom interaction. A linguist might then notice the use of value-laden lexis (*very reliable, poor eyesight*), the absence of stance markers (e.g., *I think*) and how Y's response could be viewed as an instance of conversational implicature (the negative assessment of the witness's eyesight implies, rather than explicates, her unreliability). If the linguist were working with politeness theory (see Brown & Levinson 1987), she may also note that Y's move is a potentially face-threatening act for the arguer.

What the two approaches share is their interest in reconstructing real-world argumentation in actual legal decisions. Kloosterhuis (2013) notes that arguments are not easily recognizable in the justification of a judicial decision because they are often not explicitly presented as such. Kloosterhuis points to a fundamental shift in the discipline, from reconstructing argumentation from a logical perspective to analyzing it from rhetorical and dialogical perspectives. Legal argumentation no longer needs be analyzed as an abstract product of a single language user (the judge), nor as a form of reasoning consisting of premises that lead to a conclusion. Rather than dwell on formal aspects of argumentation – questions such as: does the decision rest on a logically valid argument? – the rhetorical approach focuses on the content of arguments and context-dependent aspects of acceptability. From a rhetorical approach, a scholar is more likely to ask questions such as: is the argumentation effective for the audience to which it is addressed? Rooted in dialogical theories of legal argumentation (Aarnio 1987; Alexy 1989), the pragma-dialectical approach treats justification as a critical discussion 'in which a protagonist defends a standpoint against the anticipated or actual reactions of an antagonist' (Kloosterhuis 2013: 73). According to this approach, argumentation is reconstructed in terms of an exchange of arguments and counter-arguments analyzed in the context of actual judicial decisions (Feteris 2013, 2015). As an extension of pragma-dialectical theory, the concept of 'strategic manoeuvring' (van Eemeren 2010) was developed to account for the complexities of real-life argumentative practices. As arguers, legal actors want their argumentation to

2 Excerpted from Dahlman et al. (2013: 62).
3 Argumentation theorists use the term *ad hominem fallacies* (see Dahlman et al. 2013: 62).

be seen not only as reasonable but also as effective.[4] Van Eemeren's extension of pragma-dialectics, associated with rhetoric, comes closest to the linguistic approach. Strategic manoeuvring tackles the rhetorical component present in any justification by allowing for three major factors, which van Eemeren terms *topical potential* (viewpoint or perspective from which the arguer selects the argumentative move or moves), *audience demand* (also known as *audience orientation*) and *presentational devices.* Presentational devices pertain 'to the communicative means that are used in presenting the argumentative moves constituting a piece of strategic manoeuvring' (van Eemeren 2010: 118). They are directly relevant to linguistic descriptions of evaluative language that may act as *argumentative indicators* – words and expressions that may refer to argumentative moves such as putting forward a standpoint or argumentation (van Eemeren et al. 2007).

Apart from pragma-dialectics, the present study of evaluative language in argumentation is informed by the rhetorical (or topical) approach, espoused mainly in Perelman's 'new rhetoric' and, to a lesser extent, by Viehweg (1993). Both these representatives of the rhetorical approach emphasize the importance and role of values and legal principles (such as fairness, freedom, human dignity, etc.) as starting points, while they also stress the importance of argumentative techniques used by judges to convince a specific, concrete audience of the acceptability of a legal decision. Legal philosopher Chaïm Perelman was particularly concerned with values as represented in discourse, claiming (1969), centrally, that the orator's use of appropriate values determines the adherence of an audience. In Perelman's view, no value can be treated as universal. Rather, values need to be carefully selected to match the expectations of a specific audience. Viewed as a value, each *topos* can be pitted against another. Any audience can be characterized by the intensity of its adherence to one of the competing values, and this adherence is likely to influence the choices made by judges.

For his part, Viehweg (1993) proposed the understanding of rhetorical *topica* as a method for problem-solving in law. Soboleva (2020: 156) argues that the rhetorical perspective posits 'contemporary law as a system of arguments, drawn from different sources, rather than a closed system of legal rules'. The reliance on values and value hierarchies rather than legal rules can be best seen in cases in which judges have to resolve conflicts between competing rights and interests (e.g., animal welfare versus freedom of religion). In such cases, a judge's choice becomes a value choice. In deciding whether one right should be protected to the detriment of the other, judges construct a hierarchy of different values. As Perelman and Olbrechts-Tyteca insist, '[v]alue *hierarchies* are, no doubt, more important to the structure of an argument than the actual *values*' (1969: 81; my emphasis). The questions of value and axiology entered

4 As Breeze (2011) shows, reasonableness is one of the most prized professional values in the discipline of law.

linguistics via the structural and the transformational-generative traditions founded in the 1950s (Felices-Lago 2014). In the present book, the approach adopted is that the expression of value is a ubiquitous feature of language and one of enormous importance in legal justification due to the interrelatedness between value and argument. Chapter 5 shows how value-based lexis is utilized in the argumentation of two cases concerning a conflict between rights, namely the right to life versus the right to bodily integrity. What merits particular attention, from both argumentative and linguistic perspectives, is how judges account for their decisions in such hard cases. This book is an attempt to bring argumentative and linguistic perspectives closer together.

Justification of judicial decisions: a definition

Justification plays a central role in public, institutional discourse. There is a general expectation that decision-making in virtually any sector, private or public, will be supported with reasons. Indeed, this expectation is a pervasive feature of human communication. It would be difficult to imagine meaningful, productive interactions, be it in institutional or private contexts, in which the interactants provide no motives for their decisions and standpoints. Nowhere is the requirement for providing justifying arguments more conspicuous than in the legal sphere, especially in professional court practice. It is part of the universally accepted rule of law that legal decisions must be justified. As Feteris (2017) notes, there is a general expectation that presenting a legal thesis involves supporting it with arguments, whether in the context of a court case, a parliamentary bill or opinions advanced by legal scholars. In the context of judicial decision-making, legal justification is commonly understood simply as the reasons and rationale given by courts in rendering their decisions (see DiMatteo 2015; Gudowski 2015). In Polish jurisprudence, there have been some attempts at providing more accurate definitions of the concept of justification (Rzucidło 2020: 39–41). What these definitions share is the view that justification is primarily an argumentative activity. For example, Kotowski insists that 'in legal language, justification is treated as a presentation of a specific set of arguments to support a given thesis' (2015: 49; my translation). In what remains the fullest and most up-to-date definition of justification, Rzucidło proposes that

> justification of a court decision constitutes an act, having the form of a distinct language utterance, and supported with arguments (variously and to a varying degree), which is related to the outcome of cognitive operations. These operations aim to determine the way of understanding legal norms in the context of a specific case and its legal consequences.
> (2020: 40–41; my translation)

The perception of law and legal justification as an inherently argumentative action has been acknowledged and documented in elsewhere (MacCormick

2005; Alexy 1989, 2002), leading to the emergence of a variety of competing theories on the justification of judicial decisions.

For the purpose of this study, justification is understood in two ways. First, in the broadest terms, it refers to any ways of indicating reasons for adopting a particular stance. Viewed from this perspective, justification is a process which can be manifested in a variety of ways (e.g., verbal or non-verbal, body language or other semiotic means). Second, justification can be also perceived as a product or an outcome of that process. In the context of court practice, justification is a product either presented orally in a courtroom after announcing the decision,[5] or it is provided as a written document presenting arguments in support of the decision.[6] In the present study, we take up written justifications as our object of linguistic enquiry.

Given the pervasiveness of justification in law, it is crucial to consider justifications within the institutional contexts for which they are produced. Justifications, and their constitutive language, should be viewed as concrete textual products of the judicial decision-making process in a particular institutional setting. In the present analysis, the focus is on justifications provided for decisions made in the US Supreme Court and the Constitutional Tribunal of Poland. Justification is approached as a distinct but inseparable part of judicial opinion (judgment), and it is treated as being authored by the judge, as indicated in the text of the opinion. As such, the text of justification is usually characterized by a greater degree of idiosyncrasy than the other parts of the court decision. In the Polish legal context, justifications provided in support of the majority, or *per curiam* opinions, are not usually identified as written by a specific judge. Authors are identified only when there are separate opinions (*votum separatum*).[7] This means that argumentation is presented on behalf of the court, creating the artificial construct of a court persona associated with an idealized, ostensibly impersonal and emotionless, decision-making process. However, there are important differences in how authorship is marked in American versus Polish justifications. In the US system, all types of opinions

5 For example, the law for the Constitutional Tribunal allows for oral justification, which is communicated to the parties immediately after announcing the ruling. The oral justification is provided by the presiding judge (chief justice) or the rapporteur judge, and it focuses only on the major motives and argument that determined the disposition of a case. Full details are provided only in the written opinion so that this is the only means through which judges can lay out their arguments fully and at length (Królikowski 2015).

6 In addition, it is also possible to make a distinction between judicial justification and court justification. According to the distinction proposed by Rzucidło (2020), the latter is a broader category that allows for the realities of court practice, in which the judge does not need to be the sole author of justification. For example, justification can be drafted by a law clerk and only then edited by a judge. There is actually a considerable body of research and commentary on the impact of 'ghost-writing' on the quality of judicial opinion writing (see Rosenthal & Yoon 2010; Rzucidło 2020).

7 See Goźdź-Roszkowski (2020[a]) for a comparative analysis of how dissent is communicated in Constitutional Tribunal judgments and US Supreme Court opinions.

and justifications are explicitly marked for authorship, which provides for a greater individual variation in opinions than in the Polish system. Apart from dissenting, US judges can write concurring opinions. The more anonymous nature of Polish justifications in court (majority) opinions favours a more impersonal, uniform, even bland, style of judicial prose.[8]

Justification of judicial decisions: its functions and audiences

It appears to be generally accepted that the judge's 'opinion gives the rationale for the decision, the grounds accounting for it, an exposition of the reasons which justify it' (Levi 1971: 302). The core function of justification, irrespective of a given jurisdiction or even legal system, is to reveal the motives and the reasoning of those judges who have provided the disposition of a particular case in order to convince the legal community and the public that the disposition is correct. This apparently straightforward explanation becomes problematic when we realize that the range of functions associated with justification and their types can depend on many different factors. These can include factors such as the type of procedure (e.g., appellate), the type of audiences, the nature of a specific case and, of course, the nature of a particular judicial institution and so on. With respect to the Polish justice system, Rzucidło (2020: 111–128) lists numerous functions of judicial justification, including formal (courts are bound by law to provide a justification), descriptive (how the judges arrived at a particular outcome of a reasoning process), rationalizing (rationalize the outcome of the decision-making process), persuasive (to convince that the decision is correct), educational and cultural (promoting specific developments of law; propagating a certain vision of the state and law within the broad framework of a legal culture; appealing to the axiological and ideological dimensions of a particular legal culture with a view to ensuring the legitimacy of a decision) and controlling (enabling mechanisms of reviewing a given decision). These general functions appear to be relevant to the context of justifying decisions in the US judicial system. Romano and Curry note that judicial opinions 'do not exist merely to communicate the winner and loser of any given case' but that 'the language and the way the decision is communicated serves a multitude of purposes' (2020: 27).

In the context of the present analysis, the rationalizing and persuasive functions are most relevant. As Rzucidło (2020) rightly points out, the persuasive function should be distinguished from justification serving the function of referring to putatively objective criteria of rationality. In Rzucidło's view, the persuasive function is to use a variety of rhetorical devices to convince

8 In the Polish legal system, this feature does not necessarily apply to *voti separati*, which are often marked by a more personal style and even quite emotive responses to the majority opinion (see Goźdź-Roszkowski 2023; Boginskaya 2023).

the audiences of the validity of a particular decision[9] rather than doing so by demonstrating the reasoning behind the decision. The distinction between the rationalizing and persuasive functions has found expression in the logical and rhetorical approaches to legal justification discussed above (Feteris & Kloosterhuis 2013). As we have seen, justification is also persuasive because judges are expected to convince their audience that their decisions are acceptable in terms of the norms and standards provided for the application and interpretation of the law (Feteris 2017).[10] In both the logical and rhetorical approaches, however, arguments and argumentation are seen as playing a crucial role, one which combines elements of both rhetorical and rational persuasion. Along with rationalization, argument employs various rhetorical techniques (appeals to authority, emotions and values and uses stylistic means) to satisfy the intellect of the reader (Rzucidło 2020: 117).

Królikowski (2015: 429) specifies three main functions of legal justification crafted by judges in the context of adjudication by the Constitutional Tribunal. First and foremost, justifications by the Tribunal serve the persuasive function, convincing the reader that a particular decision was rational and correct. Combining the rationalizing and persuasive functions, Królikowski argues that justifications should be based on clear and logical argumentation, indicating all relevant premises and circumstances that the court took into account in the process of examining the constitutionality of a normative act. Unlike the ruling, which is universally binding, the justification is not universally binding, but it can provide an interpretation of the decision. In its own earlier decisions, the court has often pointed out that certain elements of a justification may constitute *ratio decidendi* closely bound up with the ruling, and the new justification, to some extent, may, indeed, complement the ruling. Second, justifying a judicial decision also serves an educational function because cases adjudicated by the Constitutional Tribunal usually attract considerable media attention and reach audiences outside of the legal professions. There is a general consensus that judicial decisions should be presented in a clear and accessible manner in order to raise the citizens' constitutional awareness. It is expected that a logical, clear line of argumentation in the written justification will help improve the quality of future applications filed to the court. Third, and perhaps most uniquely to this court, justifications perform a reporting (formal) function in the course of proceedings before the Constitutional Tribunal. The justification needs to present (in the section called *część historyczna* or 'historical' part) a variety of materials, including different stages in the proceedings, any relevant documents submitted by the parties, court orders and so on.

9 See Berger and Stanchi (2018) for a book-length treatment of how to apply rhetorical science and legal persuasion to construct legal arguments in US jurisdictions.

10 See Perelman (1969) and Aarnio (1987) for a discussion about the concept of judicial audience and its relation to acceptability,

Finally, judicial justification plays a crucial legitimizing role in ensuring that judicial decisions are not only complied with but are also widely accepted. The Court's broader legitimacy concerns (Schneider et al) are associated with the persuasive function, which aims to gain the approval of judicial audiences. The range of judicial audiences varies, depending on the particular judicial institution in question. Regarding apex courts, such as supreme courts and constitutional courts, justifications contained in judicial opinions must simultaneously appeal to several different audiences (Romano and Curry 2020): fellow judges (to win the majority of votes and ensure their colleagues do not oppose them), the litigants (and their lawyers) and the legal community (the decision usually serves as a benchmark for the law and a guide for other courts). There are also secondary audiences, including government officials, news outlets and the general public. When a legal decision addresses a constitutionally and socially important issue, it is the last two non-legal audiences that must be taken into account in justifications to ensure that the decision does not provoke public backlash. Legitimation may become a crucial issue if the credibility of a judicial institution has been undermined by its audiences. The erosion of public trust in the Constitutional Tribunal, as an independent judicial body, should be seen against a wider backdrop of Poland's ongoing rule of law crisis (Sadurski 2019).[11] In the US judicial system, the US Supreme Court operates as the most unaccountable court (Romano & Curry 2020), and the counter-majoritarian difficulty is often raised in the context of judicial review of legislation (Bickel 1962). However, recent research suggests that Supreme Court justices tend to be mindful of public opinion, even in cases when the public is unlikely to be aware of the court's activities (Casillas et al. 2011).

Constitutional review in the United States and Poland

It is often argued that constitutional courts should be examined separately from supreme courts. However, it is not uncommon to compare the case law and the mechanisms of European constitutional courts with supreme courts functioning in countries belonging to the common law tradition, especially the US Supreme Court (Kelemen 2018). What these courts have in common is the power of constitutional review. In continental Europe, the centralized model of constitutional review came into being following World War I.[12] In keeping with the model advocated by Kelsen (Vinx 2007), a specialized

11 See Goźdź-Roszkowski (2023) for the analysis of the justification of the controversial abortion ruling given by Poland's Constitutional Tribunal from the perspective of legal argumentation theory and incorporating certain elements of classical legal rhetoric including not only logical integrity (*logos*) and emotional content (*pathos*) but also *ethos* applied to the credibility of the adjudicating court.

12 https://www.venice.coe.int/SACJF/2006_02_Venice_Strasbourg/report_mazak.htm (last viewed 17 January 2023).

body was to be established outside of the regular judicial structure to review the constitutionality of legislative acts and provide a 'constitutional defence' against unconstitutional legislative actions. Like most European countries, Poland established its own constitutional court, the *Trybunał Konstytucyjny*, or 'Constitutional Tribunal', in 1982. The Tribunal is uniquely empowered to set aside legislation that does not comply with the Polish constitution. According to Garlicki (2007: 57), the Polish system of judicial review relies on three basic procedures: abstract review, legal questions referred by ordinary or administrative judges deciding individual cases and constitutional complaints that are filed with the Constitutional Tribunal after appellate procedures have been exhausted. Poland's court system is a complex four-level hierarchy: regional, district, appellate and the highest court. The Constitutional Tribunal, stands apart from this hierarchy, resolving disputes related to the constitutionality of actions undertaken by public institutions. Central to the adjudication of the Constitutional Tribunal is *skarga konstytucyjna*, or 'constitutional complaint', which enables any individual whose constitutional rights or freedoms have been infringed to petition the court.

The role of the US Supreme Court is complex because it acts as the highest appellate court and the final arbiter of the law. The Supreme Court also exercises the power of judicial and constitutional review with the power to invalidate legislation or executive actions which have been found to be in conflict with the US Constitution. Parties not satisfied with the decisions of lower courts can petition the US Supreme Court to hear their case as the final court of appeal. The primary means to petition the court for review is to ask it to grant a *writ of certiorari*.[13] In practice, the court is under no obligation to hear these cases, and it usually only does so if the case could have national significance. That is, the Supreme Court normally only hears cases that might harmonize conflicting decisions in the federal circuit courts and could have precedential value.

Relevant to the analyses presented in this book, the Constitutional Tribunal exercises 'abstract review', which means that the question of constitutionality does not arise from actual litigation. The court 'compares two normative texts and assesses their compatibility without regard to their concrete application' (Kelemen 2018: 14).[14] In contrast, in the US model of constitutional review, the focus is on resolving a specific issue, with the constitutional conformity

13 The term *writ of certiorari* refers to a request made by the Supreme Court through its order issued to a lower court to send up the record of the case for review. More detailed information about the procedures can be found at the US Supreme Court website https://www.uscourts.gov/about-federal-courts/educational-resources/about-educational-outreach/activity-resources/supreme-1 (last viewed 20 April 2021).

14 The European model also allows for 'concrete review' initiated by an ordinary judge and leading to a concrete controversy. However, even this type of case is treated in an abstract and formal way disregarding the specifics of a particular case (Sweet 2003; see also Koszowski 2019, p. 220).

of a given legislative act often treated as largely incidental. As we shall see, especially in Chapter 6, the nature of judicial review might be the main factor shaping the different styles of argumentation in European constitutional courts and common law supreme courts.

Justification as text genre

As textual objects, legal justifications necessarily must vary in form. The legal system, jurisdiction and type of court all exert some influence over the textual and discursive conventions in which justifications are eventually drafted. It is useful to consider these differences from the perspective of genre, a view which prioritizes conventions (both linguistic and professional) as central to any type of generic description. Genre provides for a broader perspective on justification as an integral part of judicial opinion while, at the same time, recognizing its separateness (Goźdź-Roszkowski 2020[b]). Law, as a social construct, responds to specific situational requirements. Law has consequently evolved specific discourse patterns over the course of its long tradition. Conceptualized in different ways, the socio-cultural construct of genre can help us describe legal texts and instruments because it takes into consideration not only formal linguistic features or conventional structures but also the communicative purposes of a situation – purposes recognizable to members of the professional community (Bhatia 2004, 2017). One preferred method of analyzing the internal organization of a legal genre is known as *move analysis*. The aim of move analysis, which amounts essentially to qualitative analysis, is to 'identify the rhetorical moves of a text, or the parts of a text that carry out distinct rhetorical functions' (Tardy & Swales 2014: 168). A *move* is, thus, a structural segment that has a specific communicative function and purpose. Moves are described in terms of their perceived rhetorical form rather than in terms of linguistic regularities. That is, moves are not described in terms of recurrent lexico-grammatical patterns. However, there is now consensus that move analysis should be also approached in pragmatic terms to allow for the conventionalized nature of many genres, especially institutional and specialized genres. Conventional forms are useful in 'mark[ing] out aspects of their rhetorical organization' (Groom & Grieve 2019: 208). In the case of well-established and relatively fixed genres, there is usually considerable overlap between the textual organization of a document and its rhetorical move structure.

Table 2.1 shows the major organizational format of a judgment (Constitutional Tribunal) and judicial opinion (US Supreme Court)[15] from each court to show how justifications fit in within their overall structure.

15 It should be noted that in the US Supreme Court the term 'opinion' is used in two senses. First, it denotes 'the statement by a judge or court of the decision reached in regard to a cause tried or argued before them, expounding the law as applied to the case and detailing the reasons upon which the judgment is based' (Black 1990: 1092). Second, it can be used to refer

Table 2.1 The textual structure of the Constitutional Tribunal of Poland's judgments (based on the searchable electronic collection of the court's decision (*Internetowa Baza Orzeczeń*)[a] and US Supreme Court opinions (based on Opinions of the Court as published officially in the United States Reports).[b]

The structure of Polish judgment		*The structure of US opinion*
1.	Headnote (Pl. *komparycja*)	Headnote (syllabus)
2.		Procedural history
3.	Ruling (Pl. *tenor*)	Holding
4.		Summary of argumentation
5.	Justification	Justification (Opinion of the Court)
Part 1	Historical part	I
Part 2	'At the trial'	II
Part 3	Justification proper (merits)	III
6.	Separate opinions	Dissenting, concurring opinions

[a] https://ipo.trybunal.gov.pl/ipo/Szukaj?cid=1 (20.04.2023).
[b] https://www.supremecourt.gov/opinions/USReports.aspx (20.05.2023).

The two formats tend to overlap, revealing some basic similarities in how Polish judgments and US opinions are organized. Both include sections which identify the court, the names of the parties and the date of the opinion. Both recount what decisions were taken by lower courts, and both announce the final ruling (termed the *holding* in US judicial discourse). However, even this basic information is arranged differently. In US opinions, the syllabus (headnote), which is prepared by the Reporter of Decisions, constitutes no part of the opinion of the court. It briefly describes the legal issue at stake in a case and how it was dealt with before it reached the Supreme Court. After providing the holding, the arguments put forward by the litigants are summarized. A standard judgment of the Polish court opens with a *komparycja*, or 'headnote', which specifies items such as the type of case and its number, the names of judges on the bench (adjudication panel) and the date when the decision is given. The following part, known in Polish as the *tenor*, which corresponds to the ruling or holding in common law jurisdictions, contains the disposition of a case. The *tenor* is invariably signalled by means of the performative verbs *orzeka i postanawia* 'the court adjudicates and decrees' and is followed with the justification of a court's decision. The Polish judgment does not contain a summary (which makes is somewhat less reader-friendly than its US counterpart), and the procedural history of a case is included in a part referred to as *uzasadnienie* or 'justification'. On the face of it, the textual space earmarked

to an expression of the reasons why a certain decision (the judgment) was reached in a case. In this second sense, there are different types of opinion (majority opinion, plurality opinion, dissenting opinion). This means that the term 'opinion' can refer to several types of writing by the judges (cf. www.supremecourt.gov/opinions/opinions.aspx last viewed 14 April 2023).

for justification appears to differ between the two courts. Justifications of the Constitutional Tribunal's judgments invariably consist of three parts marked with Roman numerals.[16] First, there is a section called the *część historyczna* or 'historical part' because it refers to all the documents deemed relevant to the case and which have been filed at different stages of the proceedings. Basically, in the *część historyczna*, the nature of the petition or complaint is presented in conjunction with its justification and the legal grounds on which it was filed. Moreover, the *część historyczna* also provides the details of a charge or complaint and the arguments advanced by parties to the proceedings. If the case concerns the non-compliance of a statutory act with the constitution, this 'historical' part of the justification furnishes broader context for the legal issue which led to the filing of a complaint or petition. In linguistic terms, the *część historyczna* uses 'reporting' and 'descriptive' language because its main function is to describe the history of the case and then, set against the background provided, describe the current legal situation. The second part called *na rozprawie* or 'at the trial' reports all material circumstances which occurred between the first hearing held before the Constitutional Tribunal and the final verdict. Recognizing that the designation 'at the trial' is somewhat confusing, the name of this section is usually placed in inverted commas. It is only the third part, referred to as *uzasadnienie prawne* ('legal justification' rather than 'justification'), that contains the court's reasoning and argumentation and can be regarded as justification *sensu stricto*. The first two parts combined seem to correspond to what is known as 'procedural history' in common law jurisdictions and which is placed in the syllabus of a US Supreme Court opinion. In contrast, justification embodied in a US opinion, whether the majority or separate (dissenting or concurring), does not contain any explicit marking of fixed internal organization. However, this does not mean that there are no regularities in how justifications are organized rhetorically. For one, the opinion of the court tends to open with the presentation of a legal issue and the questions submitted to the court for its consideration. At this point, the opinion may signal the difference of opinion between the litigants, and it outlines in very broad terms the argumentation advanced by the parties to a case. The next parts of the justification are marked with Roman numerals (I, II, III), and each part is usually further subdivided using capital letters (A, B). Part I usually recounts facts of the case constituting the historical dimension of a case. Part II may describe and interpret any law, e.g., the federal law, relevant to the case. Part III analyzes argumentation advanced by the parties, and it comes closest to Part 3 (justification proper) found in the Constitutional Tribunal judgments. It should be noted, however, that a US Supreme Court opinion may contain more than three parts and that their organization exhibits much more flexibility and variability than a Polish opinion, which is always organized

16 See Goźdź-Roszkowski 2020[b] for a discussion on how the justification is organized in terms of organizational structure and the rhetorical structure.

into the tripartite hierarchical structure. Nevertheless, as this brief description shows, justifications crafted in the two judicial contexts show marked similarities both in formal and discursive terms. The distinction between the historical and the legal elements is found in both Polish and US justifications, demonstrating that justification performs different functions. Consequently, the language of justification should also be expected to range from the reportative and descriptive to the argumentative and persuasive.

The method of move analysis introduced at the outset of this section can complement the analysis of the organizational format found in a legal document by providing a more precise description of its rhetorical structure as realized by means of recurrent functional segments of text. Goźdź-Roszkowski (2020)[b] lists rhetorical moves identified in the corpus of Constitutional Tribunal justifications (e.g., specifying the object of constitutional review and constitutional issue, evaluating the admissibility of application and so on). Chapter 6 shows how the different rhetorically oriented parts of justifications can be mapped onto different stages of the pragma-dialectical ideal model of a critical discussion (IM) to see how evaluative language contributes to the realization of the argumentative moves found in the different stages of the justification.

Bibliography

Aarnio, A. (1987). *The rational as reasonable: A treatise of legal justification*. Reidel.

Alexy, R. (1989). *A theory of legal argumentation: The theory of rational discourse as theory of legal justification*. Clarendon.

Alexy, R. (2002). *A theory of constitutional rights* (J. Rivers, Trans.). Oxford University Press. (Originally published 1985).

Baum, L. (2006). *Judges and their audiences: A perspective of judicial behavior*. Princeton University Press.

Baumtrog, M. (2018). Reasoning and arguing, dialectically and dialogically, among individual and multiple participants. *Argumentation, 32*(1), 77–98.

Berger, L., & Stanchi, K. (2018). *Legal persuasion: A rhetorical approach to the science*. Routledge.

Bhatia, V.K. (2017). *Critical genre analysis: Investigating interdiscursive performance in professional practice*. Routledge.

Bhatia, V.K. (2004). *Worlds of written discourse: A genre-based view*. Continuum.

Bickel, A. (1962). *The least dangerous branch*. Bobbs-Merrill.

Black, H.C. (1990). *Black's Law Dictionary*. West Publishing CO.

Boginskaya, O. (2023). Dissenting with conviction: Boosting in challenging the majority opinion. *International Journal of Legal Discourse, 7*(2), 257–279. https://doi.org/10.1515/ijld-2022-2073

Breeze, R. (2011). Disciplinary values in legal discourse: A corpus-study. *Iberica, 21*, 93–116.

Brennan, Jr., William J. (1988). Reason, Passion, and the "Progress of the Law". *Cardozo Law Review, 10*(1–2), 3–24.

Brown, P., & Levinson, S.C. (1987). *Politeness: Some universals in language use*. Cambridge University Press. (Originally published 1978)

Cardozo, B. (2012). *The nature of the judicial process.* Dover Publications. (Originally published 1921)

Casillas, C.J., Enns, P.K., & Wohlfarth, P.C. (2011). How public opinion constrains the US Supreme Court. *American Journal of Political Science, 55*(1), 74–88.

Clough, P.T., & Halley, J. (2007). *The affective turn: Theorizing the social.* Duke University Press.

Condello, A. (2020). *New rhetorics for contemporary legal discourse.* Edinburgh University Press. https://doi.org/10.1515/9781474450584

Dahlman, Ch., Reidhav, D., & Wahlberg, L. (2013). Fallacies in *Ad Hominem* arguments. In Ch. Dahlman & E. Feteris (Eds.), *Legal argumentation theory: Cross-disciplinary perspectives* (pp. 57–70). Springer.

DiMatteo, L. (2015). Legal justification in Anglo-American common law. In Rzucidło-Grochowska Iwona and Mateusz Grochowski (Eds.) *Uzasadnienia decyzji stosowania prawa [Justification in judicial decision-making process]*, (pp. 512–524. Wolters Kluwer

Felices-Lago, A. (2014). The emergence of axiology as a key parameter in modern linguistics: A review of significant contributions from 1950s to the 1980s. In G. Thompson & L. Alba-Juez (Eds.), *Evaluation in context* (pp. 27–45). John Benjamins.

Feteris, E.T. (2013). Strategic manoeuvring with the argumentative role of legal principles in the case of the "unworthy spouse". In Ch. Dahlman & E. Feteris (Eds.), *Legal argumentation theory: Cross-disciplinary perspectives* (pp. 85–101). Springer.

Feteris, E.T. (2015). A pragma-dialectic approach of legal argumentation: The role of pragmatic argumentation in the justification of judicial decisions. In F. van Eemeren & B. Garssen (Eds.), *Scrutinizing argumentation in practice* (pp. 99–119). John Benjamins.

Feteris, E.T. (2017). *Fundamentals of legal argumentation: A survey of theories on the justification of judicial decisions.* Springer.

Feteris, E.T., & Kloosterhuis, H. (2013). Law and argumentation theory: Theoretical approaches to legal justification. SSRN: https://ssrn.com/abstract=2283092 or http://dx.doi.org/10.2139/ssrn.2283092

Garlicki, L. (2007). Constitutional courts versus supreme courts. *International Journal of Constitutional Law, 5*(1), 44–68.

Goźdź-Roszkowski, S. (2020a). Communicating dissent in judicial opinions: A comparative, genre-based analysis. *International Journal for the Semiotics of Law, 33*(2), 381–401. https://doi.org/10.1007/s11196-020-09711-y

Goźdź-Roszkowski, S. (2020b). Move analysis of legal justifications in Constitutional Tribunal judgments in Poland: What they share and what they do not. *International Journal for the Semiotics of Law, 33*(3), 581–600. https://doi.org/10.1007/s11196-020-09700-1

Goźdź-Roszkowski, S. (2023). Argumentation, rhetoric and legal justification: The case of Poland's Constitutional Tribunal ruling on abortion. In J. Engberg (Ed.), *Between text, meaning and legal languages: Linguistic approaches to legal interpretation.* De Gruyter.

Groom, N., & Grieve, J. (2019). The evolution of a legal genre: Rhetorical moves in British patent specifications, 1711 to 1860. In T. Fanego & P. Rodriguez-Puente (Eds.), *Corpus-based research on variation in English legal discourse* (pp. 201–234). John Benjamins.

Kelemen, K. (2018). *Judicial dissent in European constitutional courts: A comparative and legal perspective*. Routledge.
Kloosterhuis, H. (2013). The rule of law and the ideal of a critical discussion. In Ch. Dahlman & E. Feteris (Eds.), *Legal argumentation theory: Cross-disciplinary perspectives* (pp. 71–83). Springer.
Koszowski, M. (2019). *Anglosaska doktryna precedensu: Porównanie z kontynentalną praktyką orzeczniczą* [The Anglo-Saxon doctrine of precedent: A comparison with the civil law judicial practice]. Wydawnictwo CM.
Kotowski, A. (2015). Teoretycznoprawna analiza pojęcia uzasadniania. In I. Rzucidło-Grochowska & M. Grochowski (Eds.), *Uzasadnienia decyzji stosowania prawa* (pp. 43–86). Wolters Kluwer.
Królikowski, J. (2015). Uzasadnienia orzeczeń Trybunału Konstytucyjnego [Justifications of Constitutional Tribunal Decisions]. In I. Rzucidło-Grochowska & M. Grochowski (Eds.), *Uzasadnienia decyzji stosowania prawa* [Justification in judicial decision-making process] (pp. 427–439). Warsaw.
Levy, B.H., & Levy, B.F. (1971). On justification of judicial decisions: Some American contributions. *Logique et analyse, 14*(53/54), 301–312.
MacCormick, N. (2005). *Rhetoric and the rule of law: A theory of legal reasoning*. Oxford University Press.
Perelman, Ch., & Olbrechts-Tyteca, L. (1969). *The new rhetoric: A treatise on argumentation*. University of Notre Dame Press.
Romano, M., & Curry, T. (2020). *Creating the law: State Supreme Court opinions and the effect of audiences*. Routledge.
Rosenthal, J.S., & Yoon, A. (2010). Judicial ghostwriting: Authorship on the US Supreme Court. *Cornell Law Review, 96*(6), 1307–1343. SSRN: https://ssrn.com/abstract=1668735 or http://dx.doi.org/10.2139/ssrn.1668735
Rzucidło, I. (2020). *Uzasadnienie orzeczenia sądowego: Ujęcie teoretyczne a poglądy orzecznictwa*. Wolters Kluwer.
Sadurski, W. (2019). *Poland's constitutional breakdown*. Oxford University Press.
Schiappa, E. (2003). *Defining reality: Definitions and the politics of meaning*. Southern Illinois University Press.
Schneider, S., Nullmeier, F., & Hurrelmann, A. (2007). Exploring the communicative dimension of legitimacy: Text analytical approaches. In A. Hurrelmann, S. Schneider, & J. Steffek (Eds.), *Legitimacy in an age of global politics* (pp. 126–155). Palgrave Macmillan.
Soboleva, A. (2020). Law as a system of *topoi*: Sources of arguments v. sources of law. In A. Condello (Ed.), *New Rhetoric for Contemporary Legal Discourse* (pp. 156–170). Edinburgh University Press.
Sweet, A. (2003). Why Europe rejected American judicial review - And why it may not matter. *Michigan Law Review, 101*(8), 2744–2780.
Tardy, C.M., & Swales, J. (2014). Genre analysis. In K.P. Schneider & A. Barron (Eds.), *Pragmatics in discourse* (pp. 165–187). De Gruyter.
Van Eemeren, F.H. (2010). *Strategic maneuvering in argumentative discourse: Extending the pragma-dialectical theory of argumentation*. John Benjamins.
Van Eemeren, F.H., & Henkemans, A.F. (2017). *Argumentation: Analysis and evaluation*. Routledge.
Van Eemeren, F.H., Houtlosser, P., & Henkemans, A.F.S. (Eds.). (2007). The identification of argumentative indicators. In *Argumentative indicators in discourse* (pp. 137–191). Springer. https://doi.org/10.1007/978-1-4020-6244-5_1

Viehweg, T. (1993). *Topics in law: A contribution to basic research in law*. Peter Lang. (Originally published 1953)

Vinx, L. (2007). *Hans Kelsen's pure theory of law: Legality and legitimacy*. Oxford University Press.

Part II

Evaluative language patterns as a persuasive device

It can be extremely difficult to pinpoint the exact ways in which evaluative meanings are expressed. One reason for this is that the linguistic expression of evaluation can be realized in a multitude of ways. Writers and speakers have a potentially unlimited range of language resources they can exploit. However, algorithmic analysis of large language corpora has shown that it is possible to use grammatical patterning in language to identify and quantify evaluative meanings (see Bednarek 2008; Hunston 2011, 2007) because evaluations are frequently expressed by means of a restricted number of patterns. The concept of language or grammar pattern comes from the linguistics subdiscipline of pattern grammar, initially developed by Francis et al. (1996, 1998). Pattern grammar is an empirically driven, corpus-based grammar of the English language using aggregated corpus data to describe the lexico-syntactic environments of individual lexical items. Hunston and Francis define these 'grammar patterns' as 'a phraseology frequently associated with (a sense of) a word, particularly in terms of the prepositions, groups, and clauses that follow the word' (2000: 3), including 'all the words and structures which are regularly associated with the word and which contribute to its meaning' (ibid.: 37). In other words, 'pattern', here, indicates the recurrent behaviour of a lexical item expressed as a sequence of elements. Approached from this perspective, 'evaluative meaning does not occur in discrete items but can be identified across whole phrases, or units of meaning, and [...] it is cumulative' (Hunston 2007: 39). Semantically, the phraseological whole is much more than the sum of its parts. Evaluative choices in language are not reducible to ad hoc selection of value-laden lexis. Instead, expressing evaluation should be viewed in terms of predictable lexico-grammar patterns, a level of language description in which lexis, or vocabulary, and grammar, or syntax, combine into one. Pattern grammar analysis starts with a hypothesis about certain possible patterns and tests this hypothesis against corpus evidence. In the present book, my hypothesis concerns the persuasive role of predefined language patterns in the argumentative discourse of legal justification. Corpus linguistics methods – such as focusing on a search item and observing its immediate environments, generating keyword-in-context analysis or concordance lines, calculating relative

DOI: 10.4324/9781003333302-4

frequency of terms and patterns, annotating such categories as a word class and so on – are combined with close readings of legal texts. However, it should be stressed that the research documented in Part II is not meant to be a comprehensive study of evaluative language in American and Polish judicial opinions. Rather, the quantitative part of the analyses helps reveal regularities in the judges' discursive practices which might otherwise go unnoticed. Evaluation is an extremely context-sensitive phenomenon which can be studied meaningfully only by close attention to detail. Hence, the quantitative findings here are treated as a starting point for the ensuing textual explorations.

In the context of judicial opinions, evaluation is, thus, investigated here in terms of what has been identified as common and preferred forms of encoding opinion not as idiosyncratic or ad hoc language choices made by individual writers. Importantly, evaluative patterns are seen primarily as persuasive devices deployed with a view to critically assess arguments advanced by various legal actors and toward convincing others that the decisions made were the correct ones. The cross-language approach adopted here enables a researcher to explore the relationship between recurring patterns and evaluative meaning in two different legal languages and judicial contexts. In particular, it is possible to examine the extent to which specific language resources – in this case in English and Polish – overlap, fulfilling discourse functions that are functionally equivalent across the two languages. A cross-language, comparative perspective can provide strong evidence as to whether the use of evaluative patterns is specific to the context in which the patterning occurs. The evaluative patterns investigated in this part of the book are, naturally, found in other genres and registers of English and Polish. However, the analyses presented in the next two chapters suggest that their use is particularly salient in legal contexts and that there are good reasons to assume they are used in unique ways in legal justification.

Chapter 3 focuses on adjective-centred patterns, formulated as *it v-link ADJ that* and *it v-link ADJ to-inf* and its Polish counterparts (e.g., *ADV v-link, aby*, *ADV v-link* or *ADV*, the last two followed by verbs in the infinitive form). Chapter 4 examines the *N that* pattern, mirrored by its Polish counterpart *N że/iż*. I have selected these patterns because they are among the most frequently occurring and, therefore, most relevant in legal justifications, both in US and Polish justifications. In Chapter 3, classes of words that share a particular pattern/meaning association are referred to as 'meaning groups'. Three major meaning groups are expressed– difficulty, desirability and importance – using the *it v-link ADJ to-inf* pattern to assess processes and their agents. The semantic value of validity is expressed by means of the *it v-link ADJ that* pattern to evaluate propositions. My analysis of the Polish data has revealed that the two patterns *it v-link ADJ that* and *it v-link ADJ to-inf* correspond to a much wider range of Polish syntagmatic patterns that are used to signal the same major functional concerns. Chapter 4 problematizes the notion of evaluation by demonstrating that it can be used to reify propositions by assigning them an epistemic status. Given that evaluation occurs in a discourse type that uses rationality as a means of persuasion, indicating and evaluating the status of propositions contributes to the construction and construal of argument in legal justification.

Bibliography

Bednarek, M. (2008). *Emotion talk across corpora*. Palgrave.

Francis, G., Manning, E., & Hunston, S. (1996). *Collins COBUILD grammar patterns 1: Verbs*. HarperCollins.

Francis, G., Manning, E., & Hunston, S. (1998). *Collins COBUILD grammar patterns 2: Nouns and adjectives*. HarperCollins.

Hunston, S. (2007). Using a corpus to investigate stance quantitatively and qualitatively. In J. Englebretson (Ed.), *Stancetaking in discourse* (pp. 27–48). John Benjamins Publishing.

Hunston, S. (2011). *Corpus approaches to evaluation. Phraseology and evaluative language*. Routledge.

Hunston, S., & Francis, G. (2000). *Pattern grammar: A corpus-driven approach to the lexical grammar of English*. John Benjamins Publishing.

3 Evaluating processes and propositions

Introduction

The patterns selected for analysis in this chapter are referred to as 'introductory it' patterns and, as the name suggests, these are phraseological units in which the dummy subject pronoun *it* is followed by a linking verb such as *be, become* or *seem*; an adjective or noun group and a finite or non-finite *that* clause, to-clause, wh-clause, or an -ing clause. My analysis will focus on patterns with *that* clause and *to-clause* complementation because previous research has established these as particularly salient in judicial discourse (Pontrandolfo & Goźdź-Roszkowski 2014). Indeed, introductory *it* patterns formulated as *it v-link ADJ that* and *it v-link ADJ to-inf* are among the most common options available for writers intending to express evaluation across different genres and disciplines (Groom 2005). What makes this pattern so effective and productive is that virtually all the adjectives used are evaluative (Hunston & Sinclair 2000). Consider the following passage, taken from a dissenting opinion (emphasis added)[1]:

> For the reasons set forth in Justice Scalia's dissent, **it is clear that** this Court lacks jurisdiction to entertain petitioner's claims, see ante, at 1–11. The Court having concluded otherwise, **it is appropriate to** respond to the Court's resolution of the merits of petitioner's claims because its opinion openly flouts our well-established duty to respect the Executive's judgment in matters of military operations and foreign affairs. The Court's evident belief that it is qualified to pass on the '[m] ilitary necessity,' ante, at 48, of the Commander in Chief's decision to employ a particular form of force against our enemies is so antithetical

1 Bolds are used in the example texts throughout the chapter to indicate the occurrence of specific phraseologies within the analysed grammar patterns. Italics are used to draw the reader's attention to particular evaluative or/and argumentative lexical items.

DOI: 10.4324/9781003333302-5

> to our constitutional structure that it simply cannot go unanswered. I respectfully dissent.
>
> (Justice Clarence Thomas dissenting in *Hamdan* v. *Rumsfeld*)

This opening paragraph of Justice Thomas's dissenting opinion contains two illustrative examples of how this pattern can be effectively used in legal justification. First, the phrase *it is clear that* frames a claim made by the writer. The claim is strengthened by a reference to another dissenting opinion, enabling Justice Thomas to align his stance with that of Justice Scalia in his dissent. The other phrase *it is appropriate to* does not simply evaluate a proposition but proposes a course of action that should be followed. In fact, it signals an argumentative move in which the court's argument is going to be rebutted. The phrase conveys a sense of necessity which is enhanced by the evaluative expression *that it simply cannot go unanswered*. It is worth noting the presence of other value-laden lexis, namely *openly flouts* and *antithetical to our constitutional structure*, which function to negatively appraise the court's argumentation and to justify the reason for the dissent.

In this chapter, I argue that introductory *it* patterns offer a valuable rhetorical device which serves the purpose of ascribing value to particular argumentative propositions and to processes or actions that need to be undertaken but in which the presence of *it* as a grammatical subject can help obfuscate the evaluator and thereby diminish the impression of subjectivity and the sense of involvement inherent in any act of evaluation. This use can be of particular importance in the case of negative, potentially face-threatening evaluations in which a more softening, 'toning down' effect may be needed. In addition, expressing evaluation using this pattern often entails identifying dialogic and intersubjective dimensions of stance related to the evaluators' actions. Acts of evaluation often resonate both formally and functionally with evaluations and stances taken in other opinions of the same case (whether majority, concurring or dissenting) or even in prior opinions. Analyzing the patterned use of evaluative language exemplified by these patterns offers a useful point of entry into the argumentative and persuasive discourse of legal justification. It is further argued that this genre selects and prioritizes certain phraseological patterns in order to serve specific communicative and institutional goals and, in so doing, prioritizes different rhetorical strategies.

The purpose of this chapter is to verify the above claims by focusing on a single group of phraseological patterns identified in legal justifications of two apex courts adjudicating in two different legal cultures and in different languages. The analyses, and their results presented in the subsequent sections, draw their theoretical framework from pattern grammar and large-scale corpus linguistics research. These two traditions have independently discovered that words which share aspects of the same meaning will also be couched in the same grammatical patterns (Groom 2005). For example, returning to the sample text from Justice Thomas's dissent, the phrase *it is clear that* assesses the validity of a proposition, while the expression *it is appropriate to* assesses whether an action is suitable and whether it should be undertaken. According to pattern grammar, other adjectives with a meaning associated with the notion of 'validity' will also be found in the *it v-link ADJ that* pattern, and adjectives with a meaning related to the notion of 'appropriacy' will follow the pattern *it v-link ADJ to-inf.* The importance of a pattern can be illustrated by comparing the following two examples.

> (1) 'I see no justification for striking down the entire commission structure simply because **it is possible that** petitioner's trial might involve the use of some procedure that is improper' (*Hamdan* v. *Rumsfeld*).

> (2) Furthermore, just as the clause 'if that right has been newly recognized by the Supreme Court' describes the date indicated in the phrase 'the date on which the right asserted was initially recognized,' **it is possible to** read the subordinate clause 'if that right has been [...] made retroactively applicable to cases on collateral review' as amplifying the description of the date in the provision's main clause, rather than adding an additional qualifier.
>
> (*Dodd v. United States*)

As can be seen, (1) assesses the validity or likelihood of a proposition, while (2) assesses whether an action is relatively easy or difficult to accomplish. These two examples underscore the important point that the difference in meaning does not need to be inherent in the word *possible* itself but, rather, the meaning can reside in the phraseological unit which consists of 'it plus link verb, plus the adjective possible, plus a that-clause/to-infinitive clause'.[2] The phraseological whole is semantically much more than the sum of its parts. Further, we can note how the adjectives in these patterns form a number of meaning groups much more specialized than the general category of evaluation. Each adjective, indeed, performs a specific function in the discourse of legal justification. In other words, once words that share both pattern and some semantic similarity are grouped together (Hunston 2011), functional roles can be mapped onto patterns. After describing the data and methods used, the remainder of this chapter is devoted to presentation of this phenomenon.

The quantitative stage of the analyses was carried out using Sketch Engine as a tool to explore two sets of data: a corpus of US Supreme Court opinions (1,270,049 words in 108 documents) and a corpus of opinions from Poland's *Trybunał Konstytucyjny,* the Constitutional Tribunal of Poland (1,234,162 words in 102 documents). All frequency data provided in this chapter will

2 Following the notation conventions of Francis et al. (1998), the patterns are represented as 'it v-link ADJ that' and 'it v-link ADJ to-inf'.

be presented as normalized figures calculated per million words. The data were algorithmically annotated for parts of speech. Drawing on the theoretical framework of pattern grammar (Hunston & Francis 2000; Su & Hunston 2019), the analyses first focused on identifying adjective complementation patterns in opinions of the US Supreme Court. The Corpus Query Language function (part of Sketch Engine) was adopted for querying the annotated data. For example, the following query was used to retrieve instances of the *it v-link ADJ to-inf* pattern:

[word="it"][lemma="be"][tag="J.*"][word="to"].

Each sequence of words was then coded according to a classification system based on taxonomies provided by Francis et al. (1998) and by Groom (2005). The correct coding for each attested sequence was determined by analyzing its context (the relevant concordance lines) in order to ensure a high degree of accuracy. The analysis revealed the relevance of four major semantic values in legal justification: DIFFICULTY, DESIRABILITY, IMPORTANCE, and VALIDITY. In terms of frequency, the pattern with the *to-inf* clause is significantly more frequent than the one with a *that*-clause (112.26 versus 79.31 occurrences per million words, respectively). In addition, the former has turned out to be more semantically varied, covering as many as three major meaning groups: DIFFICULTY, DESIRABILITY and IMPORTANCE. In contrast, it is only VALIDITY that is expressed by means of the *it v-link ADJ that* pattern. The analysis of the Polish data has shown the two patterns *it v-link ADJ that* and *it v-link ADJ to-inf* correspond to a set of Polish syntagmatic patterns used to express the same major semantic values (cf. Grabowski & Groom 2021).

What follows is a detailed presentation and discussion of how these patterns are actually used in legal justifications. This approach was made possible by pairing the quantitative study with context-sensitive, corpus-assisted discourse analysis (Partington et al. 2013) used to examine the language input in the context of the institutional environment in which the argumentative discourse occurs. Finally, a note on terminology used in this chapter: while the term 'pattern' is used to refer to abstract representations such as *it v-link ADJ to-inf*, the term 'sequence' will refer to attested lexical combinations that are describable by the 'pattern' (e.g., *it is clear that this Court lacks jurisdiction*).

The phraseologies of DIFFICULTY

It is striking that judges, in various ways, seem to prefer to draw on the notion of DIFFICULTY using a limited but frequently recurring range of expressions, as shown in Table 3.1.[3]

3 The figures provided are normalized frequencies (per one million words).

Table 3.1 Textual realizations of the grammar pattern *it v-link adj to-inf* in English texts and the Polish comparable patterns: discoursal function of DIFFICULTY

Sequences in English	*Sequences in Polish*	*Generalized patterns in Polish*
it is difficult to (35)	trudno jest (16)	adv v-link (v-inf)
it is hard to (19)	trudno (120)	adv (v-inf)
it would be difficult to (2)	trudno byłoby (13)	adv byłoby
it is easy (4)		

Closer analysis, however, reveals that this apparently limited phraseology actually provides a wide and flexible range of evaluative possibilities. It tends to co-occur with a number of mental verbs (*believe*, *conclude*, *discern*, *imagine*, *see*, *understand*) that are used to convey negative assessments of specific claims and arguments.[4]

> (3) Regardless, **it is difficult to understand** why the presence or absence of price and output regulations could make a critical First Amendment difference. The Court says that collective fruit advertising (unlike mushroom advertising) was the 'logical concomitant' of the more comprehensive 'economic' regulatory 'scheme.' But it does not explain how that could be so.
>
> (Justice Stephen Breyer dissenting in *United States and Department of Agriculture, Petitioners v. United Foods, Inc.*)

> (4) Under the facts of this case, **it is difficult to imagine** that a jury could find Sorrell negligent in a manner that contributed to his injury, but only indirectly. Norfolk urged in this Court, belatedly and unsuccessfully, that the charge on negligence was erroneous and should have been revised to conform to the charge in fact delivered on contributory negligence. That argument cannot be reconciled with our precedent.
>
> (Unanimous decision in *Norfolk Southern Railway Co. v. Sorrell*)

The extended contexts (co-texts) in which the sequences are found reveal that the evaluated propositions are often named explicitly as *argument*, as in Example (4), or that the propositional content is attributed to specific legal actors. In Example (3), the evaluated content is attributed to the majority opinion. The indication of specific evaluation targets depends on the type of opinion and the need to align or disalign the evaluator's position with those of

4 Emphasis has been added in the examples for ease of reference.

other actors. In other words, making assessments leads, inevitably, to a concern with intersubjectivity, as Du Bois (2007) has noted. Understood as a relation between the subjectivities of participating actors, this draws our attention to the more interpersonal aspects of evaluation. The meaning group DIFFICULTY is used to signal (dis)alignment rather than (dis)agreement. While the latter term should be reserved for utterances which display alignment in a transparent way, for example, via a first-person pronoun in syntactic subject role (*I/ we agree*), the former is more implicit, calibrating the relationship between the stances differently. The co-texts of the sequences in (3) and (4) contain other evaluative words which are not neutral descriptions of external reality but which imply value judgments concerning some referent. In (4), these are two adverbs, *belatedly* and *unsuccessfully*, and one adjective, *erroneous*. In excerpt (3), the evaluation is semantically less straightforward and syntactically more varied: *But it does not explain*, because it is not further explained in the majority opinion, implies negative assessment. Evaluation can be attributed, i.e., assigned to other voices, or averred, i.e., affirmed by the author as her/his own (Tadros 1993; Partington et al. 2013). The expression *logical concomitant* in (3) is attributed *verbatim* to the court, and the use of the adjective *erroneous* is attributed in (4) (to the petitioner), albeit indirectly. However, *belatedly* and *successfully* are an evaluation averred by the judge drafting the majority opinion, directed at the petitioner's role in the court process.

An even more restricted pattern can be observed in the use of phraseologies in which the sequence *it is difficult/hard to see* is followed by clauses introduced with *how*:

> (5) 'As the question has been thoroughly briefed before our Court, **it is difficult to see how** the lower court would resolve it, if we could not' (Justice Anthony Kennedy, dissenting in *Tom L. Carey, Warden, Petitioner v. Tony Eugene Saffold*).

> (6) 'Nothing about AEDPA suggests that Congress wanted to inject this degree of unpredictability into the 1-year statute of limitations, and **it is hard to see how** federal courts are to approach this state-law inquiry'.

The assessment is based on a reference to a standard, which in (5), is related to the court's own conduct. It is substantiated by foregrounding, in the subordinate clause, the fact that the question had already been scrutinized by the judges. It is an 'argument from authority' (Walton 1997) because the dissenting judge invokes the authority of the court to cast a doubt on whether another attempt to address the question, this time taken by a lower court, is at all viable. 'Argument from authority', also known as 'argument from position to know' (Walton 2002), usually relies on an external authority for its credibility. Uncharacteristically, in this case, the opinion invokes the authority of the court. However, two things seem to be characteristic. First, the negative assessment is constructed around the notion of DIFFICULTY. The judges present themselves as struggling to be appropriately fair and reasonable. Second, the assessment is hardly ever provided as a bare assertion but, rather, tends to be prefaced by providing some grounds for the decision. Providing grounds could involve referring to some relevant circumstance – for example, an earlier stage in the court proceedings, as shown in (5) – or by referring to an interpretation of the legislator's intention, as seen in (6). But this phraseology, when co-occurring with the modals ***could have*** or ***would have,*** is also used to offer praise:

> (7) '**It is difficult to see** how Thompson's counsel **could have been clearer** in telling the Court of Appeals that it was wrong' (*Connick v. Thompson*).

> (8) '**It is hard to imagine** what a more thorough consideration of the Arlington Heights factors in these cases **would have looked like**'.

The phraseologies with DIFFICULTY are rhetorically useful, providing an opportunity for the writers to construct an appropriate judicial persona. Here, judges tend to project themselves as making every effort to be appropriately critical, objective and rational. This is true even in cases in which they clearly identify themselves as evaluators. For example:

> (9) 'Given these observations, **it is difficult for me to discern** what principle besides doctrinaire formalism actually motivates today's decision' (Justice Sandra Day O'Connor, dissenting in *Blakely v. Washington*).

In addition, this pattern serves usefully as an 'evaluation pointer' in that it never represents an isolated instance of evaluation but is grounded in co-texts. The co-texts provide justification and elaborate on the assessment, itself replete with evaluative items as we saw in (3) and (4).

Furthermore, the act of evaluation invariably involves subjectivity and positioning. Both are present in judicial justification to a varying extent. A clear illustration can be found in (10):

> (10) **It is difficult to say**, as the plurality does, that §2a(c) 'continues to apply,' ante, at 18, and also to say, as the plurality does, that §2a(c) applies only if 'the election is so imminent that no entity competent to complete redistricting pursuant to … the mandate of §2c […] is able to do so without disrupting the election process.' Ante, at 19. Unless and until Congress expressly repeals §2a(c), I would hold that federal courts are required to order some form of at-large elections '[u]ntil a State is redistricted in the manner provided by the law thereof after any apportionment.'
>
> (Justice O'Connor concurring in part and dissenting in part in *Branch v. Smith*)

In this excerpt, the subjective dimension is registered overtly through the personal pronoun *I*. Example (10) shows how the dissenting/concurring judge carefully demarcates the position of the plurality from her own position on the applicability of the legislative provision. This example shows how some utterances can combine two functions: evaluating a proposition and positioning the writer as an evaluator and stance-subject.

There is something unique about the rhetorical use of DIFFICULTY, as manifested in the adjectival patterns found in the argumentative discourse of legal justification. Judges assign the value DIFFICULTY to the expression of (un)alignment with the propositional content contained in various arguments they consider. The opinions of the Constitutional Tribunal of Poland are no exception. As can be seen in Table 3.1, the sense of DIFFICULTY is conveyed grammatically by means of sequences centred around the adverb *trudno* ('hard') followed by a bare infinitive clause. The most frequent co-occurring verbal collocates are *uznać* ('recognize') and *przyjąć* ('accept'), which, together, correspond to the English sense of 'acceptance', and *wskazać* ('indicate'), *zgodzić się* ('agree') and *znaleźć* ('find'). While quantitively frequent, the Polish phrases are used more narrowly than their English counterparts. Their almost sole function is to signal non-acceptance of an argument. For example, (11) shows how the court first undermines the petitioner's argumentation by pointing to the absence of any justification for the claims made, which makes it difficult to assess their merit.

> (11) W odniesieniu do wskazanej argumentacji należy stwierdzić, że choć skarżąca zarzuca niezgodność zakwestionowanych przepisów z art. 20 w związku z art. 32 Konstytucji, to nie przedstawia odpowiedniego uzasadnienia zarzutu naruszenia art. 20 Konstytucji. Ponadto, **trudno** jednoznacznie ocenić, czy *argumentacja* zawarta w skardze konstytucyjnej dotyczy naruszenia wolności działalności gospodarczej, czy też wolności wykonywania zawodu. W tym zakresie, w ocenie Trybunału Konstytucyjnego, skarżąca również nie spełniła wymogu uzasadnienia zarzutów powołanych w skardze.(SK 10/08)[5]
>
> [Regarding the argumentation in question, it should be pointed out that though the petitioner challenges the constitutionality of the provisions in connection with Art. 32 of the Constitution, she fails to specify grounds for the alleged violation of Art. 20 of the Constitution. Moreover, **it is difficult** to assess unambiguously whether the argumentation contained in the application refers to the violation of economic freedom or the freedom of profession. In this respect, the petitioner also

5 Judicial decisions heard by the Constitutional Tribunal are usually identified by reference to their case numbers (Pol. sygnatura). The decisions are available in the publicly available online database (https://ipo.trybunal.gov.pl/ipo/Szukaj?cid=1 last seen 10 October, 2023).

failed to satisfy the requirement of providing sufficient grounds for the complaint.][6]

Here, the relevance of the argumentation is questioned, as the court finds it difficult to determine what the argumentation even concerns. Just as we noticed in the expression of DIFFICULTY in US Supreme Court opinions, the act of evaluation is invariably combined with a counter-argument explaining why the negative assessment was made. In effect, the court's view is that the argumentation does not stand up to scrutiny because the claims made by the petitioner are groundless.

The next example, taken from a separate opinion, further illustrates this evaluative practice. In (12), the judge engages with the merits of an argument by reiterating its content and signalling that he is not prepared to accept it. The reason for the rejection can be found in the following sentence (starting with *This means that*...), which points to the negative consequences of the tribunal's decision. Made by the dissenting judge, the following can be considered, as per MacCormick (1978), a consequentialist argument:

(12) **Trudno jest** przyjąć argument o konieczności dokończenia procedur spraw rozpoczętych w sytuacji, w której Trybunał orzeka o niekonstytucyjności regulacji dotyczących własności. Oznacza to, że mimo stwierdzenia niekonstytucyjności odpowiednich przepisów prawnych, w okresie odroczenia kontynuowany będzie proces przekształceń własnościowych, a więc kontynuowany będzie proces przekształceń własnościowych kosztem jednego z podmiotów procesu przekształceń. (Justice Wyrzykowski's separate opinion in case no. P 16/08).

[**It is difficult to accept** an argument on the necessity of finalizing proceedings of cases when the Constitutional Tribunal rules on the unconstitutionality of provisions related to ownership. This means that despite the ruling, during the period of deferral, the ownership transformation process will be continued to the detriment of one of the entities of the process.]

As can be seen, Polish judges also tend to project their personae as critical but objective, reasonable and rational. However, the justification provided in Example (13) uses language that is overtly negative, especially in the passage referring to how the tribunal used the principles of social justice and social solidarity.

6 The translations are provided by the author. They are as close as possible to the source texts to foreground the evaluative element contained in a pattern.

(13) Po piąte, **trudno jest zrozumieć**, jak można doszukiwać się uzasadnienia zaskarżonych przepisów w zasadach sprawiedliwości i solidarności społecznej. **Trybunał potraktował te zasady instrumentalnie**, wręcz w rozumieniu potocznym, w oderwaniu od ich konstytucyjnego zakotwiczenia oraz innych norm, zasad i wartości konstytucyjnych. (Justice Maria Gintowt-Jankowicz's separate opinion in case no. K 9/12).

[**It is difficult to understand** how it is possible to justify the challenged provisions by referring to the principles of social justice and solidarity. The Tribunal used these principles in a manipulative way, in their everyday sense, detached from their constitutional context and the context of other constitutional norms, principles and values.]

The scrutiny of patterns expressing difficulty in Polish and American justifications shows that this evaluative meaning is first and foremost used to signal non-acceptance of argumentation. Both American and Polish judges tend to adopt it so that they can avoid more direct, explicitly negative and potentially face-threatening evaluation.[7] The functional scope of these patterns is markedly broader in American opinions, in which they are also used to offer praise.

The phraseologies of DESIRABILITY

Another clearly distinct meaning group can be distinguished based on sequences used to foreground what writers view as desirable or undesirable under specific circumstances. As can be seen in Table 3.2, this semantic category can be quite broad and certain, more specific values can be found. The sequences below are used to signal what the writers see as appropriate, proper or reasonable.

It is instructive to compare the use of the phrase *it is appropriate* to in (14) and (15). In the former, taken from a dissenting opinion, the dissenting judge signals a need to take an individual stance separate from the majority opinion. It is a rhetorical move intended to create a sense of necessity, or even a sense of duty, to rebut an argument that the judge regards as erroneous. The justification for voicing a separate opinion can be found in its strongly worded evaluation (*because its opinion openly flouts our well-established duty* [...] *so antithetical to our constitutional structure*), and it precedes the formulaic performative expression routinely used to indicate a dissenting opinion (*I respectfully dissent*).

7 As defined by Brown and Levinson, positive face is 'the want of every member that his wants be desirable to at least some others' (1987 (1978): 62). A face-threatening act may occur when the speaker or writer does not respect their interlocutor's feelings and their needs.

Table 3.2 Textual realizations of the grammar pattern *it v-link adj to-inf* in English texts and the Polish comparable patterns: discoursal function of DESIRABILITY

Sequences in English	*Corresponding sequences in Polish*	*Generalized patterns in Polish*
it is appropriate to (17) it is inappropriate to (3) it would be inappropriate to (3.66)	uprawnione jest (6) nieuprawnione jest (5)	adj v-link NN
it is proper to (5) it is improper to (3)	dopuszczalne jest (43) niedopuszczalne jest (33)	adj v-link NN
it is reasonable to (4) it is unreasonable to (4) it would be unreasonable (2) It would be illogical to (4)	jest / wydaje się racjonalne (10) jest logiczne (4) zbędne jest (7)	v-link adj
it would be inadmissible/ unrealistic/ ridiculous/ a paradox / nonsense, etc. to (10)	jest / byłoby nie do przyjęcia /trafne/ paradoksem, etc. (12)	adj v-link v-link adj byłoby adj NN
it is wrong to (2) it is better to (1)	prawidłowe jest (5) nie jest poprawne (4)	adj v-link neg v-link adj

(14) The Court having concluded otherwise, **it is appropriate to respond** to the Court's resolution of the merits of petitioner's claims because its opinion *openly flouts* our *well-established duty to respect* the Executive's judgment in matters of military operations and foreign affairs. The Court's evident belief that it is qualified to pass on the '[m] ilitary necessity,' ante, at 48, of the Commander in Chief's decision to employ a particular form of force against our enemies is *so antithetical to our constitutional structure* that it simply cannot go unanswered. I respectfully dissent. ...[...] Accordingly, *it is important to take* measure of the respective roles the Constitution assigns to the three branches of our Government in the conduct of war.

(Justice Thomas dissenting in *Hamdan* v. *Rumsfeld*)

The counter-argument can be found in the ensuing text, which is introduced by the judge using an IMPORTANCE phrase (*it is important to take measure*). In contrast, (15) shows how the phrase *it is appropriate to* is primarily used to communicate a course of action, a procedure that the evaluator thinks should be followed. The institutional context for this expression is important here. The expression of the court's stance (*we believe, we conclude*) is followed with procedural language, announcing the court's decision through a series of performative expressions (*we reverse, we remand*).

(15) Given the uncertainties, *we believe* **it is appropriate to remand** this case so that the Veterans' Court can decide whether re-consideration is necessary. *We conclude* that the Federal Circuit's harmless-error framework is inconsistent with the statutory requirement that the Veterans Court take 'due account of the rule of prejudicial error.' 38 U. S. C. §7261(b)(2). *We reverse* the Federal Circuit's judgment in Sanders' case, and we vacate its judgment in Simmons' case. *We remand* both cases for further proceedings consistent with this opinion. It is so ordered.

(Opinion of the court in *Shinseki v. Sanders*)

While the use of *we believe* in (15) is syntactically (and semantically) superfluous in the first sentence, the presence of *we* is mandatory in the next in order to properly announce the court's decision. The personal pronouns are not used merely to refer to a stance-taker. The court, here, adopts a distinctly institutional voice in its opinion. Note that stance expressions such as *we believe* (or *we think*) are usually used in discourse to signal that the writers (or speakers) have taken account of the possible existence of alternative viewpoints. In the analytical framework of appraisal theory (Martin & White 2005), these expressions belong to the category of expansion (which itself belongs to the larger category of engagement) because they are used to indicate that the writer's opinion is one among many possible viewpoints. One possible explanation for using the seemingly redundant stance expression *we believe* in (15) is that it reflects and recognizes the presence of the uncertainties mentioned at the beginning of the sentence. At the same time, this sentence marks the end of the argumentative discourse, as the rest of the opinion adopts strictly procedural language.

As we see, the sense of appropriacy can be conveyed for argumentative purposes in order to signal a need for another argumentative move. But it can also be used to indicate a desirable or allowable procedural move. The same duality of function is found in Polish justifications. For example, in (16), the judge provides his argument on constitutional interpretation premised on the ontological metaphor of the constitution as one living organism.

(16) 'Konstytucja tworzy pewną całość. **Niedopuszczalne jest** takie *przemieszanie celów*, środków i wartości konstytucyjnych, gdzie *każda z nich żyje własnym życiem*, albo *wyrasta bez należytego aksjologicznego uzasadnienia* ponad inne'.(Justice Marian Zdyba's separate opinion in case no. K 28/01).

['The constitution forms a self-contained whole. **It is inadmissible** to mix constitutional goals, measures and values, where each of these has a life of its own, or one grows above the other without a proper axiological justification'.]

The argument is constructed negatively by insisting on how constitutional interpretation must *not* be made, while it points to the importance of the values of coherence and consistency in constitutional reasoning (Feteris 2017). These values are apparently lacking in the evaluated argumentation which, the judge argues, fails to demonstrate that it is coherent and consistent with various legal principles prevailing in the constitutional axiological framework. However, in most cases, the question of appropriacy is invoked in Polish justifications to signal a procedural move, and the focus is on what is or is not permitted under the relevant law.

In a number of cases, the phraseologies of DESIRABILITY are used in US Supreme Court opinions to assess arguments by drawing attention to their negative consequences. The sequences with *would* followed by an adjective and/or a noun function to evaluate propositions by indicating how a particular legal decision could cause an undesirable state of affairs or could lead to an undesirable effect. This is illustrated in two instances in (17).

> (17) As for the fact that this Court granted certiorari in Artuz eight days after the Eleventh Circuit denied petitioner a COA (certificate of appealability), **it would be unrealistic** to fault petitioner for failing to capitalize on this fortuity. In my experience, even lower courts and counselled litigants are often not aware of our grants of certiorari on issues that may be relevant to their current business. **It would be particularly inappropriate to impose** such a strict expectation on a pro se prisoner, particularly in the absence of any indication of when, given his circumstances in prison, he could have reasonably been expected to learn of our grant in Artuz.
>
> (Justice John Paul Stevens dissenting in *Gonzalez v. Crosby*)

This form of argumentation bears traces of consequentialist reasoning, in which an argument takes into account the positive or negative consequences of a given legal decision as a reason to support or reject it (Carbonell 2013). In MacCormick's view (1978), consequentialist argument concerns the impact of a universal rule behind a decision rather than the specific consequences of a decision affecting the parties in a case. Indeed, in (17) the dissenting judge refers to the notion of appropriacy in order to focus on the negative evaluation of the majority decision rather than on suggesting rival interpretations and offering alternative solutions.

The next example comes from a case that relied to a large extent on linguistic argument and plain language meaning. At issue was whether a non-citizen released from criminal custody becomes exempt from mandatory detention under 8 U.S.C. § 1226(c) if, after the non-citizen is released from criminal custody, the Department of Homeland Security does not immediately take the non-citizen into immigration custody. This example demonstrates how indicating undesirability can lead to the identification of a special type of consequentialist argument: *argumentum ad absurdum*.[8]

> (18) The 'when ... released' clause could not possibly describe aliens in that sense; it plays no role in identifying for the Secretary which aliens she must immediately arrest. If it did, the directive in §1226(c)(1) **would be nonsense. It would be ridiculous** to read paragraph (1) as saying: 'The Secretary must arrest, upon their release from jail, a particular subset of criminal aliens. Which ones? Only those who are arrested upon their release from jail.' Since it is the Secretary's action that determines who is arrested upon release, 'being arrested upon release' cannot be one of her criteria in figuring out whom to arrest. So it cannot 'describe' – it cannot give the Secretary an 'identifying featur[e]' of – the relevant class of aliens. On any other reading of paragraph (1), the command that paragraph (1) gives the Secretary **would be downright incoherent**.
>
> (Opinion of the Court in *Nielsen* v. *Preap*)

In (18), the negative consequences of statutory interpretation are foregrounded as an argument for rejecting a particular reading of a statutory text. Also known as 'pragmatic argument', it enables one to evaluate an act or event in light of purported favourable or unfavourable consequences (cf. Perelman & Olbrechts Tyteca 1969: 266). The absurdity indicated in a critical assessment of an argument could be of an analytical nature and could be determined based on the mutual relationship between words and their syntactic arrangement. But it could also be construed as derived from the conclusion that a particular interpretation of a legal text is inadmissible if it results in creating a state of affairs that would be impossible to implement. That is exactly the situation illustrated in (18). The judge uses as many as three distinctly negative terms (*nonsense, ridiculous, downright incoherent*) to reject a particular interpretation of a legislative provision. This example is also noteworthy for the role of DESIRABILITY sequences in expressing the strength of the evaluation. Martin and White (2005) propose the concepts of intensity and density/saturation to interpret 'more evaluatively' in terms of both intensity (how strongly evaluative) and density/saturation (how extensively evaluative). As can be seen in (18), the sheer quantity of instances in which DESIRABILITY sequences are used (density), coupled with the intensity of the evaluation markers (*nonsense, ridiculous, downright incoherent*), contribute to the strength of the evaluation.

8 After Bustamante (2013), I use the term in its less strict sense as an argument about the desirability or undesirability of a certain proposition. It should be noted that Bustamante demonstrates how the *reductio ad absurdum* is "a special case of pragmatic argumentation whose strength is noticeably higher in comparison with the general forms of pragmatic argumentation" (2013: 21–22).

In addition, an *argumentum ad absurdum* usually relies on some perceived contradiction, such as a contradiction between norms or a contradiction between the consequences of norms. Example (19) illustrates this:

> (19) **It would be an odd state of affairs** for a foreign state's inhabitants to enjoy more protections in federal courts than the foreign state itself, particularly given that the foreign state's immunity from suit is at stake. The natural reading of §1608(a)(3) avoids that oddity.
>
> *(Republic of Sudan vs. Harrison et al.)*

Note how in (19) the sense of the undesirability of a particular consequence is followed by offering an alternative way of interpreting the relevant legislative provisions. In this way, the generalized pattern *it would +noun/adj* could have some application in algorithmically assisted detection of text segments that are likely to contain consequentialist arguments, including the *argumentum ad absurdum.*[9] Negative, undesirable consequences of legal decisions are also conveyed in Polish justifications using phraseologies beginning with *byłoby* ('it would be').

> (20) '**Byłoby paradoksem**, aby ten właśnie przepis, uznany za niekonstytucyjny w niniejszym postępowaniu i w granicach wynikających z zakresu skargi, był traktowany jako wyznacznik skutków niniejszego orzeczenia'.
>
> (SK 5/03)
>
> ['**It would be paradoxical** to treat this provision, which has been considered as unconstitutional in the course of these proceedings, as a benchmark for determining the effect of this ruling'.]

The occurrence of intensely negative adjectives observed in (18) is relatively rare, especially in majority or plurality opinions, but it suggests that judicial opinions are, indeed, replete with lexical items which communicate evaluation directly and explicitly. Many such expressions are positioned along a varying good–bad continuum, and they can, of course, be found in several discrete and co-occurring linguistic elements, illustrating how evaluative meaning is achieved by the cumulative interplay of items. An interesting instance of such interplay can be found in a discursive phenomenon known as 'evaluative embedding'. Evaluative embedding occurs 'where evaluation of one type is

9 Clearly, there are other linguistic cues capable of indicating the presence of *argumentum ad absurdum*. For example, lexical searches focusing on the consequences of a given legal effect could start by concordancing items such as *result, effect, consequences*, etc. Other relevant searches could include the adjective *absurd*. A concordance search for the word *absurd* carried out in the corpus using Sketch Engine has retrieved 33 hits, showing that the most frequent phrases are to *produce absurd results, absurd limitation, unjust or absurd consequences.*

found embedded within that of another' (Partington et al. 2013: 48). Let us consider the following example taken from a concurring opinion prepared by Justice Kennedy:

> (21) 'In this case, the Court is ***correct*** to find that the plain language of the statute is ***ambiguous***. **It is proper**, therefore, to invoke Chevron's rule of deference. The opinion of the Court, however, ***inverts*** Chevron's ***logical*** progression' (*Zuni Public School District No. 89, et al., Petitioners v. Department of Education et al.*).

The overall appraisal in the first sentence is positive, despite the occurrence of two items with opposite polarity: *correct* and *ambiguous*. The evaluation predicate (*is correct*) prevails because of its syntactic position. This is followed by an utterance which expresses the concurring judge's view of what a desirable course of action should be, i.e., referring to Chevron's rule of deference,[10] initiated through the phrase *it is proper*. But the following sentence indexes the writer's negative assessment of the majority opinion, and it brings a reversed instance of embedded evaluation. Positive evaluation is inherent in how the word *logical* imparts a positive appraisal of the doctrine and affects the neutral reading of *invert* (turning down something logical is viewed as negative). The evaluative relations for individual clauses, along with the two sentences in (21), could be annotated as follows (in which round brackets indicate favourable evaluation and square brackets unfavourable):

> ((the Court is correct to find that) [the plain language of the statute is ambiguous]).
>
> ((It is proper, therefore, to invoke) Chevron's rule of deference).
>
> [The opinion of the Court, however, inverts Chevron's (logical progression)].

But the overall appraisal of the opinion of the court is negative, demonstrating that evaluation is always more than the context-free connotations of linguistic items. The sentences analyzed in (21) are framed by their context of use: they are found in a concurring opinion in which the judge disagrees with a specific argument even though he ultimately approves of the court's ruling. Towards the end of his very brief opinion, Justice Kennedy indicates what he deems to be a desirable solution when he adds: 'It is our obligation to set a good example; and so, in my view, ***it would have been preferable***, and more faithful to Chevron, to arrange the opinion differently' (No. 05-1508, p.2).

10 Also known as the Chevron doctrine, it compels federal courts to defer to a federal agency's interpretation of an ambiguous or unclear statute that Congress has delegated to the agency to administer https://www.law.cornell.edu/wex/chevron_deference (viewed 23.11.2022)

As can be seen in Table 3.2, the basic *good/bad* evaluative polarity is relatively unpreferred, consisting, as it does, of low-frequency lexical items found only once or twice in the corpus (*it is better to, it is wrong to, it unwise to*).[11] The same observation applies to intense, negative evaluation illustrated in (22). The example in (22) is rare and seems confined to idiosyncratic lexical choices made by individual judges in their separate (dissenting or concurring) opinions. The reluctance to use these types of evaluative statements can be partly attributed to the risks inherent in using face-threatening overt expressions of negative evaluation.

> (22) '**It is nonsensical to continue** to apply §3742(f)'s provisions governing the "Decision and Disposition" of appeals, which clearly track those now-excised standards' (Justice Antonin Scalia, concurring in part and concurring in the judgment in *Rita v. United States*).

In the Polish opinions, this type of straightforward evaluation tends to be toned down with certain mitigating grammatical forms such as *wydaje się* ('it seems') and *byłoby* ('it would be'):

> (23) **Nie wydaje się więc trafne** przytaczanie *argumentacji*, która godzi w istotę funkcji sprawowanych przez druga izbę. Na marginesie można jedynie dodać, że taka *argumentacja* pomija fakt, że konsens wypracowany na etapie prac sejmowych może być zburzony także i w wypadku poprawek wąsko rozumianych, w ramach zakreślonych restryktywną wykładnią art. 121 ust. 2 Konstytucji i wyznaczonych ścisłym pojęciem ustawy przyjętej przez Sejm.
>
> (Justice Marek Safjan's separate opinion in case no. K 14/02).
>
> [**It does not seem correct** to put forward arguments which undermine the very nature of the function performed by the house [of the Parliament]]. Incidentally, it could be only added that *this argument ignores the fact that* ...]

In this excerpt, the choice of argument is the object of evaluation. What is, in fact, a very negative assessment of an argument, one found to be at odds with the fundamental property of the legislative body, is softened. Consider the next sentence, which explains why the argument is not correct but frames the explanation as if it is something mentioned almost in passing. Of course, this does not mean that overt expressions of highly negative evaluation (positive

11 What we refer to as 'basic evaluative polarity' are adjectives which tend to be used to express more strongly positive or negative evaluations. Paradis (1997) provides a scale for classifying adjectives according to the degree to which they express evaluation. On that continuum, these are either scalar or extreme adjectives.

evaluation is virtually non-existent) is not conveyed by other language means. As we will see in greater detail in Chapter 4, the more productive and frequent patterns used in Polish opinions to express strong negative evaluation are centred around nominal forms (*nn*, *nn v-link* and '*nn v-link* (, *że*)'). The advantage for writers using these patterns is that they foreground evaluative adjectives by placing them in sentence-initial positions[12]:

(24) '**Oczywiście zupełnie błędne jest twierdzenie, że** nakaz samooskarżenia się wynikający z ustawy lustracyjnej może być traktowany tak samo jak obowiązek prawny złożenia deklaracji podatkowej'

(Justice Bohdan Zdziennicki's separate opinion in case no. K 44/02).

['Clearly, completely wrong is the assertion that (...)']

In (24), the negative evaluation is made even more emphatic by qualifying the adjective *błędne* ('wrong') with two adverbs: *oczywiście* ('clearly') and *zupełnie* ('completely').

(25) 'Dlatego **złudne jest wyobrażenie, że** tworząc wykaz nazw, służących określeniu dóbr, którymi powszechnie się posługujemy, można dokonać istotnych zmian w świecie realnym'

(K 32/99).

['Therefore, **misleading is the notion that** compiling a list of names to define goods we commonly use will lead to important changes in the real world'.]

Among all evaluative concerns, invoking reasonableness seems to be the most desirable and most readily associated with judicial argumentation. Reasonableness is a standard used almost universally to assess the merits of judicial reasoning. Drawing on the quality of reasonableness, as a tacit assertion of legitimacy, is in keeping with the commonly accepted equation between reasonableness and the soundness of an argument (cf. Feteris 2017). Phraseologies centred around reasonableness in US opinions typically feature mental processes in the *to* infinitive clauses: *assume, conclude, consider, expect* and *interpret*. Example (26) illustrates a fairly typical use of 'reasonable' to indicate logical, deductive inferencing. The judge presents a logical conclusion based on the short narrative account of a sequence of events.

12 The Polish excerpts have been rendered literally into English in order to highlight their grammatical structure and the sentence position of the evaluative adjectives. They are equivalent to the English pattern and can be rephrased as 'It is completely wrong to assert that, it would be irrational to claim that'. Only relevant parts have been translated.

(26) In this case, however, Brown and Drayton were seemingly pinned-in by the officers and the customary course of events was stopped flat. The bus was going nowhere, and with one officer in the driver's seat, **it was reasonable to** suppose no passenger would tend to his own business until the officers were ready to let him.

(Justice Breyer, dissenting opinion in *United States v. Drayton*)

There is an additional rhetorical advantage to using expressions such as *it is/was/would be reasonable to*. Apart from focusing on evaluating propositions (rather than other interactants), it helps construct a positive aura around the figure of the judge-as-writer and arguer by exploiting the fact that, in this pattern, the adjective evaluates a to-infinitive clause and, thus, by implication, evaluates the performer of the action indexed by the to-infinitive verb itself. As we see in (27), in the linguistic context of 'reasonable', the expression contributes to conferring an appropriate 'judicial persona' on the voice of the author, which adds persuasive force to the conclusion.

(27) The inference that respondents and the dissent would draw from the silence is, in any event, implausible, as §1326(b) is silent not only with respect to cost-benefit analysis but with respect to all potentially relevant factors. If silence here implies prohibition, then the EPA could not consider any factors in implementing §1326(b) – an obvious logical impossibility. **It is eminently reasonable to** conclude that §1326(b)'s silence is meant to convey *nothing more than* a refusal to tie the agency's hands as to whether cost-benefit analysis should be used, and if so to what degree.

(*Entergy Corp. v. Riverkeeper, Inc.*.)

It is worth noting the co-occurrence of *inference* as a useful anaphoric device to refer to the respondents' argument and the use of certain explicitly negative lexical items: *implausible* and *an obvious logical impossibility*.

Overt appeals to reasonableness can be also found in Polish opinions. Just as in the case of American justifications, the appeal to rationality and logic co-occurs with other evaluative markers. This is particularly evident in (29). In the first sentence of (29), the rejection of an interpretation, phrased quite emphatically (*neither correct nor logical*), is supported in the next sentence with a factual proposition flagged by the dissenting judge as obvious and undeniable (*It is indisputable that*). The consistently negative evaluation prepares the reader to view the final sentence of (29) in a negative light, even though there is nothing inherently negative in the phrase *fundamental economic knowledge*.

(28) **Jest natomiast racjonalne** , aby – na podstawie zgromadzonych ekspertyz oraz Konstytucji – ustawodawca samodzielnie rozstrzygał,

> tworząc definicję prac w szczególnych warunkach i o szczególnym charakterze, które z obiektywnych kryteriów medycznych zastosować i jak bardzo rygorystycznie kwalifikować poszczególne rodzaje prac, biorąc pod uwagę wybrane kryteria medyczne
>
> (K27/09).
>
> [**It is reasonable** [for the legislator] to resolve independently, based on the collected expert opinions and the Constitution, and creating a definition of work in special conditions, which of the medical criteria should be applied and how rigorously different types of work should be classified, depending on the selected medical criteria.]

Worth pointing out at this point is the fact that Polish judges often refer to the concept of the 'rational legislator' as an assumption on which they base their interpretations.

> (29) W mojej ocenie, **nie jest poprawne ani logiczne** nazywanie takiego uregulowania waloryzacją. **Bezsporne jest**, że świadczenia pieniężne o różnej wysokości tracą na wartości proporcjonalnie do swojej wysokości, a zatem ich deprecjacji nie można wyrazić równą (jedną) kwotą pieniężną. Jest to elementarna wiedza ekonomiczna.
>
> (Justice Maria Gintowt-Jankowicz's separate opinion in case no. K 9/12.
>
> [In my view, **it is neither correct nor logical** to refer to such regulation as valorization. **It is indisputable** that financial benefits of varying amount tend to lose their value in proportion to the amount. As a result, their depreciation cannot be expressed through one equal sum of money. This is fundamental economic knowledge.]

An even more complex interplay between the evaluative language and argument can be found in Example (30), sampled from a dissenting opinion in *Herrera v. Wyoming*. Wedged between two occurrences of ***argument***, which correspond to two different arguments addressed in Justice Samuel Alito's dissent, the expression *it is reasonable to* is used to provide clarification and justification for the negative evaluation of the first argument. The argument is rebutted because it was based on an apparently false and misguided assumption about the way in which judges reach their decisions. Worth noting again is how evaluative consistency is achieved by meeting primed expectations, a phenomenon termed by Partington et al. (2013) as 'evaluative harmony'. The positive evaluation below, framed as *careful judicial reasoning*, is readily associated with reasonableness.

(30) This argument is based on an unjustified assessment of the way in which courts do their work. Even when a court bases its decision on multiple grounds, **it is reasonable to expect** that such a finding is the product of careful judicial reasoning. The other argument cited for the Second Restatement's rule is that the losing party may decline to appeal if one of the two bases for a judgment is strong and the other is weak. §27, Comment i, at 259. There are reasons to be skeptical of this argument as well.

(Justice Alito dissenting in *Herrera v. Wyoming*)

In addition, the expression *it is reasonable to* has a cohesive function linking it with the evaluation of the other argument: *There are reasons to be sceptical.* The reader has been forewarned by the evaluation of the first argument that the evaluation of the other will not be affirmative.

As a final, rather surprising example, consider an instance of invoking reasonableness to index the writer's affective stance. The example is found in the *Memorandum* written by Justice Scalia to address a potential conflict of interest, in which he provided his reasons for not recusing himself from a case involving the Sierra Club and US Vice President Dick Cheney. An excerpt from the *Memorandum* was even published in the *New York Times*, where it received considerable media attention.[13]

(31) 'If **it is reasonable to think** that a Supreme Court Justice can be bought so cheap, the Nation is in deeper trouble than I had imagined' (Justice Scalia in *Richard B. Cheney, Vice President of The United States, et al. v. United States District Court for the District of Columbia et al.*).

This example, marked very clearly for subjectivity, as registered through the personal pronoun *I*, is an instance of how the REASONABLE phraseology can be used to achieve a rhetorical goal, based on appeal to *pathos* rather than *logos*, or emotions rather than reason. It relies on the dramatic effect of juxtaposing two polarized evaluative items. *It is reasonable to think*, evoking the association of reason, reasonableness and logic, is set against the lexical items imbued with affective, negatively charged value, *can be bought cheaply* and *deeper trouble*.

The phraseologies of IMPORTANCE

Appraising propositions as important and/or necessary is another key meaning group fundamental in justifications both from the US Supreme Court and from the Constitutional Tribunal of Poland.

13 https://www.nytimes.com/2004/03/19/us/excerpt-from-scalia-s-statement.html (viewed 24 November 2022).

The sequences built around IMPORTANCE are often placed at clearly designated textual points. Their discursive function is to highlight a point that the judge is making in her reasoning and to introduce a supporting argument. In particular, signals of IMPORTANCE are used to indicate an argumentative move. Example (32) comes from a case in which the US Supreme Court affirmed a previous decision that the Commonwealth of Kentucky's lethal injection protocol does not violate the Eighth Amendment's ban on cruel and unusual punishment. The opinion rebuts an argument that the State's lethal injection protocol, based on the administration of four drugs[14] to carry out death sentences, amounts to a violation of the Eighth Amendment ban. The supporting counter-argument is based on an expert opinion:

> (32) '*At the outset*, **it is important to reemphasize** that a proper dose of thiopental obviates the concern that a prisoner will not be sufficiently sedated. All the experts who testified at trial agreed on this point' (*Baze v. Rees*).

In the next example, (33), Justice Kennedy signals IMPORTANCE in the penultimate section of the court's opinion, clarifying the court's stance regarding the challenged enactment of the Child Online Protection Act (COPA), 47 U.S. C. §231. The American Civil Liberties Union (ACLU), along with online publishers concerned with protecting the freedom of speech, filed suit for a preliminary injunction against COPA's enforcement. The act was found to be unconstitutionally 'overbroad' and likely to violate the First Amendment by restricting too much protected speech and was also found to use a method that is not the last restrictive one available.

> (33) '*On a final point*, **it is important to note** that this opinion does not hold that Congress is incapable of enacting any regulation of the Internet designed to prevent minors from gaining access to harmful materials' (*Ashcroft v. American Civil Liberties Union*).

The IMPORTANCE sequences are indicative of a discourse which often aims both to explain a legal choice and to persuade the reader. Examples (34) and (35) show that the judge as an arguer is not only concerned with the negative evaluation of the argument but also with explaining how and why she/he arrived at the negative evaluation. The explanatory discourse, however, is not used in a justificatory way (as is often the case) but is utilized strategically to introduce their own argument.

> (34) 'Even though the majority does not endorse that argument, I think **it is important to explain** why it lacks merit, before considering the

14 https://www.oyez.org/cases/2007/07-5439 (last viewed 23.11.2022)

argument the majority does accept' (Justice Stevens dissenting in *Boy Scouts of America and Monmouth Council, et al., Petitioners v. James Dale*).

(35) The statute might be susceptible of some limiting construction here, but again the Court of Appeals did not address itself to this question. The answer affects the breadth of the Act and hence the significance of any variation in community standards. Likewise, **it is essential to answer** the vexing question of what it means to evaluate Internet material 'as a whole,' 47 U. S. C. §§231(e)(6)(A), (C), when everything on the Web is connected to everything else.

(*Ashcroft v. American Civil Liberties Union*)

In (34) the stance expression *I think* can be interpreted as opening dialogic space for potential counter-arguments. It is yet another illustration of how subjectivity and positioning can go hand in hand. This is surprising, given that the *it v-link adj to-inf* is usually selected to obfuscate subjectivity. By offering to provide an explanation of why the argument lacks merit, the dissenting judge seems to tacitly align with the majority's position. In principle, it is possible to imagine that the argument accepted by the majority could then be considered without paying attention to rejected one. But the explanation establishes a cohesive link between the evaluation of the two arguments, and it is rhetorically important. It prepares the grounds for dealing with the argument that the majority opinion accepts while it, simultaneously, primes the reader to expect that the writer, as a dissenter, does not accept the argument. In a similar way, in Example (35), the explanation of 'what it means to evaluate Internet material "as a whole"' is provided as grounds for the majority opinion that the Child Online Protection Act (COPA) was unconstitutionally 'overbroad' – that is, that it could apply to too much protected material.

Finally, Example (36) illustrates how the sequence is used to advocate for a particular course of action. This is similar to what we documented with respect to the *it is appropriate/proper* sequences found in the DESIRABILITY meaning group. Here, by contrast, IMPORTANCE seems prevalent. Sequences with the words *important* and *necessary* use a range of communication verbs (*explain*, *reemphasize*) and mentation verbs (*explore*, *note*). The effect of using the phraseologies of NECESSITY is to signal urgency and imply inevitability. Even though he is known for his agonized ambivalence (Krugman 2002), Justice Kennedy's stance in this dissent is very firm. Apart from the opening sentence (*The Court's decision commits us to a new and, in my view, unwise course*), the dissent opinion does not use any personal stance-markers. Kennedy's strategy is to establish impersonality of stance, and his use of the phraseologies of NECESSITY contributes to this effect.

(36) These precise terms have not been used in the Court's adequacy jurisprudence before, and **it is necessary to explore** their implications.

The *argument* is not that Missouri has no interest in enforcing compliance with the Rule in general, but rather that it had no interest in enforcing full compliance in this particular case.

(Justice Kennedy dissenting in *Lee v. Kemna*)

As shown in Table 3.3, Polish judges convey the sense of IMPORTANCE by relying on sequences including the adjectives *ważny* ('important') and *istotne* ('essential') with positional variation due to free word order, e.g., *ważne jest, że* (literally 'important is that'):

(37) '**Ważne** w takim stanie rzeczy **jest ustalenie**, czy w analizowanym przypadku istnieje możliwość interpretacji i zastosowania zakwestionowanych przepisów w zgodzie z Konstytucją'.

(P 29/09)

['Under these circumstances, **it is important to determine** whether it is possible to interpret and apply the challenged provisions in accordance with the Constitution'.]

(38) 'Poza tym **istotne jest** uwzględnienie skutków wyroku Trybunału'.

(K 39/07)

['In addition, **it is essential** to allow for the effect of the Tribunal's ruling'.]

The value of IMPORTANCE is ascribed to processes of interpretation that occur in the court's own reasoning, playing a role similar to what we observed in the US Supreme Court justifications. The sequences are utilized to signal an argumentative move: what the judge needs to do next to support or defend their position.

Table 3.3 Textual realizations of the grammar pattern *it v-link adj to-inf* in English texts and the Polish comparable patterns: discoursal function of IMPORTANCE

Sequences in English	*Corresponding sequences in Polish*	*Generalized patterns in Polish*
it is important to (15)	ważne jest, aby (3)	adj v-link, *aby*
	ważne jest umożliwienie	adj v-link NN
	ważne jest, że (16)	adj v-link, *że*
it is essential to (2)	istotne jest (22)	adj v-link
It is necessary to (19)	konieczne jest (97)	adj v-link
	niezbędne jest (22)	
it is crucial to (1)	kluczowe znaczenie ma (17)	adj nn v

When we consider equivalent sequences centred around NECESSITY in opinions prepared by Polish judges, we find analogous concerns. Two phrases are used most often: *konieczne jest* ('it is necessary') and *niezbędne jest* ('is necessary'). It is worth noting the link between IMPORTANCE and NECESSITY in Example (39). The NECESSITY phrase signals an argumentative move which derives from the relative importance of the preceding argument. In other words, the argument is so important that it is necessary to elaborate on it in order to justify the prohibition mentioned in the opening clause.

(39) W przypadku zakazu łączenia mandatu z funkcjami sprawowanymi w organach samorządu terytorialnego pojawia się inny, niezwykle doniosły **argument**. Chodzi mianowicie o personalny aspekt zasady podziału władz, która stanowi jeden z fundamentów demokratycznego państwa. [...] W ocenie Trybunału **konieczne jest określenie** pozycji organów władzy samorządowej na tle wskazanego trójpodziału.

(K 7/99)

['In case of a ban on combining a mandate with functions performed in local government bodies, there is another exceptionally significant **argument**.[...] In the Tribunal's view, **it is necessary to** specify the position of local government bodies against the background of the tripartite division'.]

(40) W tym kontekście **niezbędne jest** przypomnienie *stanowiska* Trybunału Konstytucyjnego w kwestii dopuszczalności modyfikacji przez Rzecznika Praw Obywatelskich wzorców konstytucyjnych wskazanych w skardze. W dotychczasowym orzecznictwie Trybunału Konstytucyjnego przeważył *pogląd, że* 'pozycja Rzecznika Praw Obywatelskich w postępowaniu w trybie skargi konstytucyjnej, jako fakultatywnego uczestnika tego postępowania, nie daje podstaw do dokonywania zmiany granic zaskarżenia.'

(SK 34/08)

['In this context, **it is indispensable** to refer to the *position* of the Constitutional Tribunal taken with respect to the admissibility of modifying by the Ombudsman constitutional standards indicated in the constitutional application. The prevalent *view* in the existing Tribunals' case law is that "the status of the Ombudsman in the proceedings does not offer grounds to make any changes to the scope of a complaint"'.]

In (40), the NECESSITY phrase also signals an argumentative move which introduces an argument of consistency. That is, it introduces the argument that a proposed legal solution must be consistent with the existing body of legal rules found in the tribunal's case law.

The phraseologies of VALIDITY

As can be seen in Table 3.4, meanings associated with VALIDITY are expressed almost entirely using the *it v-link ADJ that* pattern. This observation is broadly in line with findings documented for other registers of English.[15]

The sense of VALIDITY in US Supreme Court justifications is expressed using several sequences, some of which are very frequent, especially *it is/was clear that* or *it is undisputed that*. The corresponding Polish phrases include *oczywiste jest, że* ('it is obvious that') and *bezsporne jest, że* ('it is indisputable that'). One way of looking at these phrases is to view them as prime vehicles for providing validity assessment based on *prima facie* evidence and as appealing to notions of obviousness.

> (41) 'In each place, **it is clear that** the statute refers to a specific legal document; in none is the word used as a substitute for the ordinary collateral review process'.
>
> TOM L. CAREY, WARDEN, PETITIONER v. TONY EUGENE SAFFOLD

It is possible to generalize that the sequences *it is clear/evident/plain/undisputed that* frame a claim made by the writer. On closer examination, it emerges that there are regularities of use that go beyond both the lexical combination and the pattern. First, the claim preceded by *it is clear that* frequently follows

Table 3.4 Textual realizations of the grammar pattern *it v-link adj that* in English texts and comparable patterns in Polish: discoursal function of VALIDITY

Sequences in English	*Corresponding sequences in Polish*	*Generalized patterns in Polish*
it is/was clear that (40) it seems clear that (2) it is/was evident that (7) it is plain that (2)	oczywiste jest, że (23) 'obvious is that'	adj v-link
it is possible that (3.66)	możliwe jest, że (46)	adj v-link
it is undisputed that (15) it is uncontested that (2)	bezsporne jest, że (11)	adj v-link

15 Biber et al. (1999) show how the frequencies of these meaning groups are not evenly distributed across the two patterns. In particular, the *it v-link ADJ that* pattern is principally associated with VALIDITY (Biber et al., 1999: 675), while *it v-link adj to-inf* is more closely associated with IMPORTANCE, DIFFICULTY and DESIRABILITY (ibid. 721).

an indication of some evidential statement which provides a logical basis for the claim.

> *When the statute is read as a whole, it is clear that* [...] *Applying that principle here, it is clear that courts should not create* [...] *Given the nature of such details, it is clear that* [...] *Under these circumstances, it is evident that...*

Second, the claim is often presented as contrasting with the previous proposition – the contrast signalled by *however*, *but* or *by contrast.*

'Under such an analysis, however, it is clear that, Similarly, petitioners argue for better trained personnel. But it is clear that [...] *Here, by contrast, it is undisputed that...'*

The claim is then usually followed with some clarification providing justification for making the claim (underlined).

> (42) Here, by contrast, **it is undisputed that** the Court of Appeals did not mention the government speech theory now put forward for our consideration. The Government's failure to raise its *argument* in the Court of Appeals deprived respondent of the ability to address significant matters that might have been difficult points for the Government.
>
> (Opinion of the Court in *United States v. United Foods, Inc.*)

These observations can be further generalized and interpreted as representing two distinct semantic sequences:

> Evidential basis + *it is clear/undisputed* + claim.
> Argumentative proposition + *it is clear/ undisputed* + claim + clarification.

The concept of 'semantic sequence', introduced in Hunston (2008), refers to the co-occurrence of not only wordforms or lemmas but also of grammatical forms and 'broadly-defined elements of meaning' (Hunston 2011: 7). Hunston's approach to the study of textual recurrence enables us to locate regularities in meaning and function in which, apart from the core element (i.e., the sequence *it is clear*), the wording of other meaning elements (e.g., evidential basis) may be different.[16]

Similar regularities, going beyond the level of a grammar pattern, are found in Polish justifications. The phrase *oczywiste jest, że* ('it is obvious that') is invariably preceded by indicating an evidential statement, a source of information or a logical basis for the claim. Some other Polish examples to consider:

> *na tle tej regulacji* ('against the background of this provision').

16 See Goźdź-Roszkowski (2018) for a study of semantic sequences in judicial discourse.

w świetle powyższego ('in light of the above').
w tym kontekście ('in this context').
zatem ('therefore').
więc ('so').

However, the second semantic sequence is rarely used by Polish judges in justifications, as they prefer to use it to support their line of argumentation rather than as a counter-claim:

(43) **Oczywiste jest , że** zarówno stwierdzenie niekonstytucyjności kwestionowanego przepisu ze względu na jego treść, jak i ze względu na tryb uchwalenia, prowadzi do tego samego skutku, tzn. eliminacji danego przepisu (lub całej ustawy) z porządku prawnego.(K 39/07)
['**It is obvious that** regarding the provision as unconstitutional both due to its content as well as the way in which it was enacted, will lead to the same effect, i.e., the removal of the provision (or the entire statute) from the legal order'.]

Two further points can be made about the presence of these phraseologies of VALIDITY. First, it should be borne in mind that there is pressure on judges to speak decisively. As Lawrence Solan notes, no matter how much a judge might anguish over a decision, they are likely to focus on their own reasons and 'brush aside the arguments to the contrary' (1993: 2). The analysis of the Polish opinions shows that judges are just as concerned as US judges with the requirement to adopt a decisive voice. The phraseologies of obviousness are useful for accomplishing this goal, even if their actual use varies in terms of amplification or intensity, depending on how committed the judge is and how unequivocal and categorical their voice is projected to be.

Second, appealing to notions of self-evidence and obviousness runs the risk of having the argument assessed as *ipse dixit*, undermining its persuasive force. Consider the following example taken from the opinion of the court in *Church of the Lukumi Babalu Aye v. City of Hialeah*:

(44) 'According to the city, it is "self-evident" that killing animals for food is "important"; the eradication of insects and pests is "obviously justified"; and the euthanasia of excess animals "makes sense"'.
(Id., at 22)

These *ipse dixits* do not explain why religion alone must bear the burden of the ordinances when many of these secular killings fall within the city's interest in preventing the cruel treatment of animals.

The observed semantic co-occurrence between the evidential basis and the *it is clear* sequences could be attributed to the writers' desire that the claims are not projected as bare, unfounded assertions.

Summary and conclusions

The focus of this chapter has been on adjectival patterns as the most obvious and most overt linguistic means of signalling evaluative concerns. The patterns identified offer a useful way of uncovering some of the mechanisms used to evaluate judicial reasoning and interpretation. They function as argumentation pointers because they co-occur with argumentative propositions and can be indicative of argumentative moves. My analysis has found that the English pattern *it v-link adj to-inf* corresponds with a range of Polish syntagmatic patterns, depending on the adjectives used. For example, when using adjectives that convey the sense of DIFFICULTY, the pattern corresponds with one set of patterns in Polish: *adv v-link (v-inf), adv (v-inf), adv byłoby.* By contrast, there is a one-to-one correspondence between the *it v-link adj that* pattern in English and the generalized pattern *adj v-link* in Polish. In both legal contexts, these patterns are used to signal VALIDITY.

Overall, four major semantic values have been found relevant in the justifications of decisions by both the US Supreme Court and the Constitutional Tribunal of Poland: DIFFICULTY, DESIRABILITY, IMPORTANCE, and VALIDITY. It should be noted that my findings have shown that the use of such recurrent phraseologies is, first and foremost, rhetorically motivated. The phraseologies of DIFFICULTY are generally preferred because they enable the judges to signal non-acceptance of argumentation in a less face-threatening manner. Their use confers an appropriate judicial persona on the voice of the writer who comes across as making every effort to be appropriately fair, objective and reasonable.

Some phraseologies perform more than one function. The sense of appropriateness subsumed under the more general category of DESIRABILITY is expressed for argumentative purposes in order to signal a need for another argumentative move. But it can also be used to indicate a desirable or allowable procedural move. The same duality of function is found in Polish justifications. The sequences centred around the sense of appropriacy are particularly favoured in separate opinions because the dissenting or concurring judge can signal that they need to take a separate and individual stance to the majority opinion. Other phraseologies associated with DESIRABILITY are used to assess arguments by pointing to their negative consequences, and they are potentially capable of identifying consequentialist reasoning and specific forms of argumentation, such as *argumentum ad absurdum.* Unsurprisingly, judges refer to reasonableness as something that is highly desirable. The appeal to rationality in Polish justifications tends to be combined with evaluative markers indicating whether an argument is also considered logical, consistent and coherent. In US justifications, sequences such as *it is logical to* contribute to constructing a positive aura around the figure of the judge-as-writer and arguer because the adjective evaluates a *to-infinitive* clause and, thus, implicitly evaluates the performer of the action indexed by the *to-infinitive* verb itself. The use of DESIRABILITY sequences may also vary in terms of intensity and density of evaluation. US Supreme Court justifications are more likely than their Polish counterparts to intensify evaluations by a number of mechanisms, including the addition of an item such as a modifying adverb (*downright incoherent*), using a more intense lexical item (*nonsense, ridiculous* as opposed to *wrong, unacceptable*) or by repetition (*would be nonsense, It would be ridiculous*).

Conveying a sense of the importance of making a claim is a universal concern in virtually any type of argumentative writing, but in legal justifications, there is a close connection between IMPORTANCE and NECESSITY. The recurrent sequence *it is necessary to* and its Polish counterpart *konieczne jest* ('it is necessary') and *niezbędne jest* ('is necessary') are used to signal argumentative moves which are premised on the importance of preceding arguments. They are evidence of how argumentative and justificatory concerns interlock to produce persuasive discourse.

Finally, VALIDITY assessments represent the most direct means of persuading the reader. Claims are framed to foreground the obviousness of certain propositions, but they tend to be accompanied by an evidential and/or logical basis also provided. In this case, it is useful to understand textual recurrence as a series of meaning elements spread across discrete words and phrases, a phenomenon termed by Hunston (2008) as 'semantic sequence'. Semantic sequences reflect the consistency of function manifested through diverse language forms. In US Supreme Court justifications, the relatively fixed sequence *it is clear/undisputed* is often preceded by argumentative propositions and followed by clarification – a function not detected in the Polish texts.

In sum, the use of these patterns is evidence of constant movement between arguments (*logoi*) and counter-arguments (*counter-logoi*). Exploiting the patterns to project a positive aura of objectivity and fairness corresponds to *ethos* as persuasion through personality and stance. As we have seen, judges frequently resort to intensely negative and value-laden lexical items, a use of language that amounts to persuasion through the arousal of emotion (*pathos*). While the idea of arousing emotion might not seem intuitively acceptable for the expression of judicial opinion, it is worth bearing in mind that it was Justice William J. Brennan who challenged the idea that judges should confine their writing to only the impersonal tones of the detached and dispassionate professional (Brennan 1988; see also Krugman 2002). In sum, if rhetoric is understood as the art of persuasive discourse, and if we accept that it is, in Aristotelian terms, 'the faculty of discovering the possible means of persuasion in reference to any subject whatever' (Aristotle, Art of Rhetoric), then the grammar and semantic patterns presented in this chapter represent rhetorical devices *par excellence*.

Bibliography

Aristotle. (1926). *Art of Rhetoric.* (J.H. Freese, Trans). Cambridge and London: Clarendon Press.

Biber, D. Johansson, S., Leech, G., Conrad, S., Finegan, E. (1999). Longman Grammar of Spoken and Written English. Longman.

Brennan, Jr., William J. (1988). Reason, Passion, and the "Progress of the Law". *Cardozo Law Review, 10*(1–2), 3–24.

Brown, P., & Levinson, S.C. (1987). *Politeness: Some universals in language use.* Cambridge University Press. (Originally published 1978)

Bustamante, T. (2013). On the *argumentation ad absurdum* in statutory interpretation: Its uses and normative significance. In Ch. Dahlman & E. Feteris (Eds.), *Legal argumentation theory: Cross-disciplinary perspectives* (pp. 21–43). Springer.

Carbonell, F. (2013). Reasoning by consequences: applying different argumentation structures to the analysis of consequentialist reasoning in judicial decisions. In Ch. Dahlman and E. Feteris (Eds.), Legal Argumentation Theory: Cross-Disciplinary Perspectives (1-19). Springer.perle

Du Bois, J.W. (2007). The stance triangle. In R. Englebretson (Ed.), *Stancetaking in discourse: Subjectivity, evaluation interaction.* John Benjamins Publishing.

Feteris, E.T. (2017). *Fundamentals of legal argumentation: A survey of theories on the justification of judicial decisions.* Springer.

Francis, G., Manning, E., & Hunston, S. (1998). *Collins COBUILD grammar patterns 2: Nouns and adjectives.* HarperCollins.

Goźdź-Roszkowski, S. (2018). Between corpus-based and corpus-driven approaches to textual recurrence: Exploring semantic sequences in judicial discourse. In Kopaczyk J. and Tyrkkö (Eds.) *Applications of Pattern-driven methods in Corpus-Linguistics* (131-158). John Benjamins Publishing Company.

Grabowski, Ł., & Groom, N. (2021). Grammar patterns as an exploratory tool for studying formulaicity in English-to-Polish translation: A corpus-based study. In A. Trklja & Ł. Grabowski (Eds.), *Formulaic language: Theories and methods* (pp. 171–190). Language Science Press.

Groom, N. (2005). Pattern and meaning across genres and disciplines: An exploratory study. *A Journal of English for Academic Purposes, 4*, 257–277.

Hunston, S. (2008). Starting with small words: Patterns, lexis and semantic sequences. *International Journal of Corpus Linguistics, 13*(3), 271–295.

Hunston, S. (2011). *Corpus approaches to evaluation: Phraseology and evaluative language.* Routledge.

Hunston, S., & Sinclair, J. (2000). A local grammar of evaluation. In S. Hunston & G. Thompson (Eds.), *Evaluation in text: Authorial stance and the construction of discourse* (pp. 74–101). Oxford University Press.

Krugman, R.L. (2002). Judicial personality: Rhetoric and emotion in Supreme Court opinions. *Washington & Lee Law. Review, 59*(1/6), 193–234.

MacCormick, N. (1978). *Legal reasoning and legal theory.* Oxford University Press.

Martin, J., & White, P. (2005). *The language of evaluation: Appraisal in English.* Palgrave.

Paradis, C. (1997). *Degree of modifiers in spoken British English.* Lund University Press.

Partington, A., Duguid, A., & Taylor, Ch. (2013). *Patterns and meanings in discourse. Theory and practice in corpus-assisted discourse studies (CADS).* John Benjamins Publishing.

Perelman, Ch. & Olbrechts-Tyteca, L. (1969). *The new rhetoric: A treatise on argumentation.* University of Notre Dame Press.

Pontrandolfo, G., & Goźdź-Roszkowski, S. (2014). Exploring the local of grammar of evaluation: The case of adjectival patterns in American and Italian judicial discourse. *Research in Language, 12*(1), 71–91.

Solan, L. (1993). *The language of judges.* University of Chicago Press.

Su, H., & Hunston, S. (2019). Language patterns and attitude revisited adjective patterns, attitude and appraisal. *Functions of language, 26*(3), 343–371.

Tadros, A. (1993). The pragmatics of text averral and attribution in academic texts. In M. Hoey (Ed.), *Data, description, discourse* (pp. 98–114). HarperCollins.

Walton, D. (1997). *Appeal to expert opinion: Arguments from authority.* Penn State University Press.

Walton, D. (2002). *Legal argumentation and evidence.* Penn State University Press.

4 Evaluating status and sites of contention

Introduction: assigning and appraising epistemic status

In the previous chapter we saw how grammar patterns can provide a useful point of entry into the construction of persuasive argumentation. The analysis has shown how linguistic choices can steer the reader towards certain argumentative moves imbued with evaluative propositions. The main objects of evaluation were themselves processes (and their agents) and argumentative propositions. Appraising argumentative propositions remains my primary focus in the present chapter but, here, are approached from the perspective of their epistemic status. With this shift of emphasis, I follow Hunston's claim that 'one of the functions of evaluation is to reify texts and propositions by assigning them an epistemic status and [t]he status so assigned aligns a text or a proposition to a construed world' (2011: 26). My focus is on propositions rather than texts, and the first important point to make is that the alignments, between text or proposition and construed world, are not predetermined. Rather, they are rooted in the subjective assessment and the individual choices made by the writer. Examples of how the alignments of argumentative propositions are accomplished include their labelling as *arguments*, *suggestions*, *notions* or *facts*. To appreciate the importance of assigning status, consider the following example sampled from a US Supreme Court opinion (emphasis added):

'Justice Thomas' *suggestion* that <u>our conclusion precludes the Government from bringing to justice those who conspire to commit acts of terrorism</u> is therefore *wide of the mark*'.

In this single sentence, taken from an opinion of the court in *Hamdan v. Rumsfeld*, the argumentative proposition made by Justice Thomas in his dissent is evaluated twice. The first evaluation is made by means of the expression *wide of the mark*, which simply means 'inaccurate'. The second, less overt evaluation is found in the use of the word *suggestion*, which encapsulates the propositional content in the *that*-clause (underlined in the example). The proposition *our conclusion precludes the Government from bringing to justice those who conspire to commit acts of terrorism* is labelled by the judge as 'suggestion'. The evaluation occurs in a text that is concerned with using projected rationality as a rhetorical means of persuasion. Assigning a relatively

DOI: 10.4324/9781003333302-6

low epistemic value to the propositional content of the utterance diminishes its argumentative force because if an utterance is labelled as merely a *suggestion*, it is not amenable to verification. It should then be viewed as potentially less trustworthy. In another example from *Hamdan vs. Rumsfeld*, a dissenting Justice Thomas labels a statement from the plurality's opinion as *suggestion*. The entire sentence containing this term reveals a complex interplay of different legal voices and a close relationship between status and attribution:

> Moreover, the Attorney General's conclusions specifically refute the plurality's unsupported *suggestion* that I have blurred the line between "those categories of 'offender' who may be tried by military commission … with the 'offenses' that may be so tried"
>
> (Justice Thomas dissenting in *Hamdan vs. Rumsfeld*).

The example above shows that status may be dialogic, and it may become more complex when different points of view are construed. Justice Thomas has a voice even in the statement attributed to the attorney general. What, therefore, matters is attribution itself, which can be instrumental in modifying the status of a proposition (Hunston 2011). As shown in Sinclair (1987), all propositions are either averred (construed as produced by the writer) or attributed (construed as produced by someone else). Attribution can be persuasive because it can contribute to a sense of the reliability of a proposition by attributing it to an authoritative and influential source. The sense of veracity and confirmation of a statement can also be strengthened if the attributing mechanism functions to reaffirm author commitment. The act of evaluation involves indicating who is responsible for a particular claim. Suggestions (and, incidentally, conclusions) are invariably attributed to specific interactants. What appears to be important is that these utterances are always framed by their context of use. That is, they are framed by the requirements of a particular argumentative and persuasive discourse.

Interestingly, in both examples, *suggestions* are assessed negatively and co-occur with *conclusions* as another 'discourse' object referring to propositions made by the author of the texts. The intensity of evaluation may vary depending on whether the suggestion is qualified predicatively (*suggestion is* […] *wide of the mark*), as in the first example, or attributively, as in the second (*unsupported suggestion*). Given the already weak epistemic status of *suggestion*, its evaluation as *unsupported* heightens a sense of the unreliability of the argument made in the plurality opinion. In addition, while in the first example, *conclusions* are defended, in the second example, *conclusions* are invoked to add fuel to the negative evaluation and to rebut the plurality's argument.

This chapter is, then, concerned with describing how indicating and evaluating the status of propositions contributes to the construction and construal of argument in legal justification. Drawing on yet another instance of a very frequent phraseological pattern, I demonstrate how the linguistic choices made regarding even a single lexical item can lead to the creation of sites of contention.

The linguistic resources to evaluate status

While all propositions in texts are evaluated in terms of how they align with the world, status may be marked or unmarked (Hunston 2011). In (1), taken from the facts of the case in *Dobbs v. Jackson Women's Health Organization,*[1] the default interpretation is that this proposition is directly aligned with the world, so it is presented without modification.

> (1) In 2018, Mississippi passed a law called the "Gestational Age Act," which prohibits all abortions, with few exceptions, after 15 weeks' gestational age.
>
> (*Dobbs v. Jackson Women's Health Organization*)

The reader is expected to accept the statement as a factual and, therefore, accurate representation of when the legislation was passed and a fair representation of what the legislation stands for. However, in (2), the proposition (underlined) is modified by the modal verb *may*, which alters the represented alignment. The consequences of the court decision for women seeking an abortion is represented as 'what might be' rather than as 'what is':

> (2) After this decision, <u>some States</u> *may* <u>block women from traveling out of State to obtain abortions, or even from receiving abortion medications from out of State</u>.
>
> (Justice Elena Kagan's dissent in *Dobbs v. Jackson Women's Health Organization*)

In (3), the evaluation of status is less straightforward. The status of the proposition is evaluated using lexis marked for subjectivity: the argument made in defence of Roe is labelled as a *circular assertion*. But it is worth nothing that the main clause of this sentence is preceded by an expression suggesting that the subsequent statement has gained general approval. The proposition in question is underlined below:

> (3) *As has been often noted*, *Roe*'s defense of the line boiled down to the *circular assertion that* <u>the State's interest is compelling only when an unborn child can live outside the womb, because that is when the unborn child can live outside the womb</u>.
>
> (Chief Justice John Roberts, concurring in the judgment in *Dobbs v. Jackson Women's Health Organization*)

1 https://www.oyez.org/cases/2021/19-1392 (last viewed 21 March 2023).

The examples provided above hint at a wide range of ways in which the assignment of status can be coded linguistically. Apart from modal auxiliaries (*may*, *might*, *could*), some typical resources used to modify status include verbs, nouns and adjectives governing that-clauses (*it has been suggested that, the belief that, it is possible that*). Verbs, nouns and adjectives are also found modifying status in other grammatical patterns (*as was suggested*, *this possibility*, *the probable cause*), along with adverbs and adverbials such as *apparently, probably*, *in fact*, and the evidentials, which here are various forms of attribution or identification of the source of a proposition (*according to the Government/the Secretary/Congress, there is a general consensus that, as has often been noted*). The distribution of such resources is related to many factors, one of which is the genre of text in which they are found. Some of them are rarely used in legal justifications. For example, evidentials, such as *as is well known*, or certain verbal constructions (*it has been suggested that*) are unpreferred in judicial writing for reasons linked to the epistemological underpinnings of the discipline and the genre of legal justification. In legal justification, a judge is expected to write decisively and to rely on a received corpus of law and neutral principles rather than resort to common knowledge (Solan 1993). The presence of nouns such as *suggestion*, as illustrated above, is motivated by argumentative concerns; these modifiers are used to label and to epistemically downgrade other interactants' propositions but never the judge's own.

Earlier research has shown the relevance of the *N that* pattern to legal justifications in English (Goźdź-Roszkowski & Pontrandolfo 2013; Goźdź-Roszkowski 2018) from a comparative perspective. The pattern is mirrored by its Polish counterpart *N że/iż*, enabling us to make direct comparisons beyond the English language and to ascertain the degree to which status-indicating strategies might indeed be unique to judicial expression. However, there is yet another valid reason for giving prominence to nouns occurring in this pattern. If status can be intrinsically linked with polar evaluations of 'good' versus 'bad', then we can see that the status-indicating nouns in legal justifications express negative assessments in a vast majority of cases. In the context of legal justification, arguments are the usual objects of such assessments. In the remainder of this chapter, I demonstrate how the frequent use of nouns in the *N that* pattern amounts to the construction of what I call 'sites of contention'. That is to say, they construct points in the discourse of justification in which judges signal their opinion, (dis)agreement and the acceptance or rejection of other interactants' arguments.

The *N that* pattern is a linguistic resource in which nouns are followed by a *that*-clause. It can be viewed as a subcategory of a larger grammatical structure in which a head noun takes a nominal complement, either in the form of a *that*-clause, a *to*-infinitive, or an *of*-prepositional clause. Head nouns found in the noun complement construction have attracted considerable attention in the literature, especially in the literature on academic discourse (Coxhead 2000; Charles 2007; Gardner & Davies 2013), albeit under different labels. These nouns have been explored as general nouns (Halliday & Hasan 1976), anaphoric nouns (Francis 1986), carrier nouns (Ivanič 1991), shell nouns (Schmid 2000) or signalling nouns (Flowerdew & Forest 2015). What these diverse studies have in common is their focus on the discourse organizing functions of these nouns and how they contribute to cohesion in discourse. However, the stance-taking and rhetorical potential of the noun complement structure has only more recently been noticed. As Jiang and Hyland (2015) demonstrate, this structure is among the linguistic resources extensively employed by writers from a range of different academic disciplines to signal their orientations with respect to a claim or a finding. Jiang, Hyland and others, list the noun complement construction as one of the linguistic features that overtly communicates authorial stance. The noun complement construction is used to express a writer's 'personal feelings, attitudes, value judgments or assessments' (Biber et al. 1999: 966). Research adopting the term *N that* pattern (Hunston 2011; Goźdź-Roszkowski 2019) provides confirming evidence that nouns in this pattern indicate the epistemic status of the proposition contained in the *that*-clause and that such clauses are central to disciplinary epistemology. This chapter capitalizes on and extends previous studies of this pattern in judicial discourse. I investigate the pattern's use as the primary status indicator, with wide-ranging applications in argumentative discourse and in the persuasive discourse of legal justification. The chapter discusses how the assignment of status to a proposition is an exercise in subjective and evaluative judgment by the judicial writer and how both US and Polish justifications show a remarkable regularity in their use of this single discourse element. The overarching aim of the chapter is to construct a picture of common epistemological and rhetorical practices in legal justifications.

Data and method

The Sketch Engine software was used to explore two corpora annotated for parts of speech: a corpus of US Supreme Court opinions (1,270,049 words in 108 documents) and a corpus of opinions from the Constitutional Tribunal of Poland (1,234,162 words in 102 documents). A quantitative method was applied to both the US and Polish data to carry out a targeted search for the sequence Noun + *that* and its Polish counterpart, in which a noun is followed by *że* or *iż* (the complementizer *that* in English corresponds to two variants in Polish: *że* and *iż*). The search was limited to nouns that occur at least five times per 1,000,000 words. Additionally, in an attempt to reduce bias resulting from judges' idiosyncratic writing styles, it was decided that each noun had to be found in at least five different opinions. The next stage involved scrutinizing concordance lines centred around the selected nouns in order to identify their collocational patterns. The co-occurrence patterns, thus, obtained were interpreted in functional terms. Sentence examples in Polish were glossed in English. The translations are literal/direct, covering only relevant passages in which a particular phrase is found.

Status-indicating nouns: an overview

'Suggestion' is clearly not the only epistemic label that can be assigned to evaluate propositions. Table 4.1 lists the most frequent nouns found in the *N that* pattern in the corpus of US Supreme Court opinions and in the academic section of the Corpus of Contemporary American English.[2] In a vast majority of cases, these nouns are markedly more frequent in judicial opinions than in scholarly discourse. Their occurrence constitutes further evidence of the specificity of legal opinion writing in contrast with other academic genres. The high frequency of these particular nouns also points to one of the hallmark features of legal argumentation. The occurrences of some of these nouns in legal argumentation is not surprising. For example, we would expect a high occurrence of the word *fact* in legal writing, to aver a more direct alignment between a proposition and the construed world. After all, facts play a crucial role in determining the content of the law, something that is particularly true of empirical, descriptive facts which provide knowledge about human conduct in various circumstances (Greenberg 2004).[3] In a similar way, it is not surprising to see that propositions are reified into the objects of which legal argumentation (and perhaps other types of argumentation) is typically comprised: ***arguments, conclusions, contentions, presumptions*** and so on. The presence of ***belief, notion*** or ***idea*** may seem less obvious, and these words are, indeed, found more frequently in academic discourse.

Another point worth making concerns the relative evaluative weight of these nouns. Most appear evaluatively neutral, at least at first sight, especially when considered out of context. The only exception is the noun ***allegation,*** which carries an overtly unfavourable association with some illicit activity. The

Table 4.1 Frequencies (per 1 milion words) of nouns in *N that* pattern in US Supreme Court (SC) and Corpus of Contemporary American (COCA) English (academic register)

No.	*Noun*	*SC*	*COCA*	*No.*	*Noun*	*SC*	*COCA*
1.	*fact*	276	144.3	10.	*suggestion*	41.0	6.5
2.	*argument*	141	11.5	11.	*assertion*	36.7	6.5
3.	*conclusion*	123	12.4	12.	*belief*	27.7	30.2
4.	*claim*	90.3	27.8	13.	*notion*	27.0	24.2
5.	*view*	76	19.3	14.	*presumption*	23.2	1.7
6.	*proposition*	60.0	3.8	15.	*premise*	19.5	5.4
7.	*possibility*	45.0	19.5	16.	*idea*	15.0	35.2
8.	*assumption*	43	20.5	17.	*impression*	13.5	7.4
9.	*contention*	41.2	5.6	18.	*allegation*	12.0	.45

2 https://www.english-corpora.org/coca/

3 See Goźdź-Roszkowski (2018) for a comparative study of fact and its phraseologies in American and Polish judicial discourse.

nouns also vary in terms of their genre or register specificity. Some, such as *argument, assertion, contention, premise, presumption* or *proposition*, are readily associated with argumentative and persuasive discourse. Readers are primed by these words to expect evaluative polarities resulting from the expression of (dis)agreement or (dis)alignment with their propositional contents in a line of argumentation. In other words, although their evaluative weight is not intrinsic, these nouns are likely to attract evaluative prosody. Their evaluative intensity also differs at the fundamental level of the indication of status. For example, when a dissenting judge labels a proposition as *belief* or *notion*, they effectively evaluate it by assigning it a non-factual status.

Turning to the Polish data, Table 4.2 shows that, overall, the nouns are relatively less frequently used in this pattern. While Polish justifications are concerned with *facts*, they label propositions as *argument* rather sparingly. But the occurrence of other nouns such as *view, assumption, proposition* and *contention*, all point towards argumentative concerns.

Status-indicating nouns and their roles in legal argumentation

But how are these nouns actually used in legal justifications? What roles do they perform in legal reasoning apart from averring or attributing evaluation? Do they vary depending on whether they occur in American or Polish justifications? These questions are addressed in this section.

One obvious role these words play is bound up with evaluating propositions. It has now become apparent that evaluation is a broad semantic category, which is expressed at two levels. First, and perhaps most typically,

Table 4.2 Frequencies (per 1 million words) of nouns in *N that* pattern in the corpus of Constitutional Tribunal decisions (CT)

No.	*Noun*	*CT*	*No.*	*Noun*	*CT*
1.	*fakt* 'fact'	156	8.	*konkluzja* 'conclusion'	28
2.	*pogląd* 'view'	130	9.	*przypuszczenie* 'conjecture'	7.3
3.	*założenie* 'assumption'	71	10.	*domniemanie* 'presumption'	6.2
4.	*teza* 'proposition'	65.4	11.	*wrażenie* 'impression'	5
5.	*twierdzenie* 'contention'	51	12.	*spostrzeżenie* 'observation'	4
6.	*przekonanie* 'belief'	48	13.	*oczekiwanie* 'expectation'	3
7.	*argument* 'argument'	30	14.	*sugestia* 'suggestion'	3

judicial writers can express their attitudes by indicating an assessment of the value of an epistemic object, as in the following two examples (the epistemic object and the corresponding evaluative marker are indicated in bold).

> (4) In any event, **the notion that** a parolee legitimately expects only so much privacy as a prisoner is **utterly without foundation**.
>
> (*Donald Curtis Samson, Petitioner v. California*)

> (5) The dissent's **suggestion that** capital defendants are especially liable to suffer from the lack of 100% perfection in our criminal justice system is **implausible**.
>
> (*Kansas vs. Marsh*)

These examples show some of the most common, almost prototypical ways in which propositions are evaluated in legal justifications. Examples from the Polish data corroborate this observation.[4]

> (6) **Twierdzenie , że** kwestionowane przepisy naruszyły równowagę dóbr prawem chronionych, a tym samym istotę wolności i praw obywatelskich **nie znajduje oparcia w przepisach konstytucji**.
>
> (SK 21/99)
>
> [The contention that (...) does not find support in constitutional provisions.]

> (7) **Błędne jest** także **przekonanie wnioskodawców, że** art. 32 ust. 1 Konstytucji nakazuje jednakowe traktowanie wszystkich osób podlegających lustracji.
>
> (K 11/02)
>
> [Incorrect is the applicants' belief that (...)]

These examples demonstrate that this type of evaluation occurs at two levels. First, it can be seen in the choice of status noun. A proposition is labelled as a *notion* or *belief* and not, for example, as an *argument* or a *claim*. The choice of status noun may, of course, be motivated by the role and textual position of a proposition in a stretch of discourse, i.e., propositions found in the final part of an opinion or other document are more likely to be viewed as *conclusions*. But, in many cases, status-indication is an exercise in judicial subjectivity. It

4 The translations of these examples include only the relevant parts (the epistemic objects and the evaluative markers).

is difficult to account for the specific choice of *notion* or *suggestion* in (4) and (5) without considering the judge's act of evaluation as a rhetorically motivated strategic action. The other level of evaluation resides in the qualification of a particular noun (*utterly without foundation*, *implausible*, *does not find support in the constitutional provisions*, *incorrect*), and it can be expressed by means of structurally diverse lexical items.[5] These two types of evaluation are closely linked and interrelated, together providing a useful rhetorical device. Combining the choice of a status noun with its evaluation increases its evaluative intensity and increases the persuasive force of the utterance in which it is used. The nouns in the *N that* pattern act as 'evaluation pointers'. The selection of nouns enables the writer to ascribe a positive or negative value to a proposition, indicating not only the object but also its authors (*the dissent's suggestion*, *the applicant's belief*), identifying their distinct points of view and their different roles in the legal proceedings.

This brings us to the second subcategory of evaluation: the expression of agreement or disagreement, and, in the latter case, signalling rejection. In many cases, evaluation and agreement are interrelated. The acceptance or rejection of a proposition is most often rooted in a favourable or unfavourable assessment of its merit. This type of evaluation amounts to stancetaking (Du Bois 2007). Judges assume the role of a stance-taker who evaluates an object, positioning themselves by adopting a standpoint in alignment with another interactant:

> (8) Moreover, we do not **agree with Justice Kennedy's suggestion that** it is necessary for the Court of Appeals to revisit this question upon remand.
>
> (Justice Stevens, dissenting in *John Ashcroft, Attorney General vs. American Civil Liberties Union et al.*)

Evaluation, positioning and alignment are three distinct acts, but in such cases, all three are integrated through the dialogic stance act. In this type of evaluation, we find a polyphony of institutional voices permeating the legal justifications. As Mazzi notes, 'the concept of polyphony [...] is inherent in the genre of judgments, because the argumentative discourse that constitutes their backbone may indeed be interpreted in terms of a dialogue, where different voices are interwoven' (2007: 395). In the context of the Polish judgments, there is an additional institutional requirement that the views of all involved

5 Still, it is possible to detect certain lexical and semantic regularities occurring within the evaluation of status nouns. For example, the Polish word *twierdzenie* ('contention') is usually qualified as *nieuzasadnione* ('unjustified'). In other examples, propositions tend to be assessed as baseless.

parties and interactants are represented in the *historyczna część* or 'historical part' of the justification:

> (9) Ustosunkowując się w pierwszej kolejności do zarzutów skierowanych wobec art. 2 ust. 1 pkt 2 i 3 oraz art. 2 ust. 2 ustawy o zaliczaniu, **Prokurator Generalny nie zgodził się z twierdzeniem wnioskodawców, że** przywołane przepisy naruszają art. 2, art. 21, art. 31 ust. 3, art. 32, art. 52 ust. 1 i art. 64 ust. 1 i 2 Konstytucji.
>
> (K 2/04)
>
> [The **Attorney General** did not agree with the applicants' **contention that** (...)]

Finally, in the US Supreme Court justifications, a strong co-occurrence can be observed between the act of rejection and the rejecting agent who invariably stands for a collective body – a court, rather than an individual judge: *this court, however, rejected Justice Brennan's argument that*; *the court of appeals rejected the commissioner's arguments that*; *finally, the court rejects the commissioner's suggestion that*. These examples highlight a discursive practice whereby US judges, in majority or plurality opinions, adopt a definitive and unequivocal voice by means of some straightforward device used to simply brush aside arguments they do not accept.

Another distinct role performed by status nouns is the indication that certain propositions are the cause of something else. That is, that certain propositions provide a basis or foundation for other arguments. In (10), the source of argumentation comes from 'assertion'. The effect of treating the proposition as an 'assertion' is that it is presented as an arbitrary outcome of the Court's subjective judgment, rather than the result of rigorous legal reasoning.

> (10) The Court's **argument** is instead based on its **assertion that** the categorical remedy the Secretary has chosen is too harsh.
>
> (*Justice O'Connor dissenting in Tracy Ragsdale, et al. vs. Wolverine World Wide, Inc.*

The word *assumption*, and its Polish equivalent *założenie*, further illustrate this point. *Assumption* is, in fact, a particularly good example of an evaluative status noun. In almost half the instances, it occurs in the phrase frame *on + ADJ + assumption*, as attested by the following phrases: *on an assumption that*, *on the unfounded assumption that*. If one also adds the phrase *under the assumption* (e.g., *the Court laboured under the mistaken assumption that*) it is easy to see that 'assumption' is phraseologically coded to signal causal relations. Indeed, assumptions are often, thus, construed as foundations for arguments, conclusions, statements or interpretations: *the court's resolution of that ambiguity is based on the assumption that* or *the majority's reading of CAFRA for a contrary proposition is premised on the assumption that.* In addition, *assumption* may be used in any number of other contexts such as in the justification for a decision (*I join the opinion of the court on the assumption that it does not foreclose a reading of*) or as a basis for interpreting legislation (*the California death penalty statute in effect in 1982 quite plainly rested on the assumption that*). When we turn to consider the co-texts of the Polish equivalent phrase *założenie, że* ('assumption that'), we see that marking propositions as *assumption* serves essentially the same purpose in both languages. There are 66 occurrences of this phrase in the corpus of Constitutional Tribunal judgments. *Assumptions* are referred to as bases or causes for other propositions in over half of the cases, as illustrated by the following example.

> (11) Zarzuty sądu pytającego są obecnie bezprzedmiotowe, gdyż jego **argumentacja** została oparta na **założeniu, że** niedopuszczalna jest sytuacja, w której ustawodawca pozbawił pewną grupę osób maksymalnie ukształtowanej ekspektatywy.
>
> (P 31/10)
>
> [The charges put forward by the Court are now irrelevant because its **argumentation** is based on the **assumption that**]

Note that the marking of causal relations is often combined with overt evaluative signals directed at the epistemic object. In a third of the cases (in the US data) in which assumptions are used as basis for a proposition, they are preceded by negatively charged adjectives. The two examples provided below are very similar with respect to the lexical choices made (the *assumptions* are assessed as erroneous) and in terms of the gravity of the evaluation.

> (12) Justice Stevens' contrary conclusion is predicated **on the** *erroneous* **assumption that** the ordinance proscribes large amounts of constitutionally protected and/or innocent conduct.
>
> (*City of Chicago, petitioner v. Jesus Morales et al.*)

> (13) Tak sformułowany zarzut **opiera się jednak na błędnym założeniu, że** obie grupy ubiegających się o zwolnienie z kosztów sądowych powinny mieć zagwarantowane prawo do dwukrotnego rozpatrzenia ich wniosków przez niezależne i niezawisłe sądy.
>
> (P 54/07)
>
> ['As it stands, the complaint **is based on the erroneous assumption that**'.]

In (12), the conclusion of the entire opinion is challenged in a dissenting opinion, and the fact that Justice Stevens is singled out as the author of the opinion adds to the intensity of the evaluation. This also shows that, unlike in science writing, in which *conclusions* are generally construed as 'the goal or consequence of an enquiry' (Hunston 2011: 98), in legal justification, they are the target of negative evaluation, and they may need to be defended and justified.

In some cases, a status noun can be used to indicate that a conclusion is a result rather than a cause. As we see in Figure 4.1, conclusions are most frequently framed as results of other epistemic objects. In these cases, positive evaluation supports those conclusions: *Justice Holmes's impeccable theory yields the clear conclusion that.* What appears to be quite characteristic of Polish judicial writing is the use of *assumption* as a basis for marking logical relations between two propositions, in particular by highlighting that a given proposition is the consequence or result of an assumption. This use is realized in recurrent phrases such as *wyjść z założenia* ('make an assumption') *punkt wyjścia* ('point of departure').

(14) Punktem wyjścia dla tych orzeczeń było **założenie, że**

(P 61/08)

[The point of departure for these rulings was the **assumption that**]

(15) Trybunał **wyszedł z założenia**, wyrażanego w dotychczasowym orzecznictwie, że sposób określenia obowiązku w art. 84 Konstytucji został powierzony ustawodawcy zwykłemu.

(K 21/14)

[The Tribunal **started from the assumption** reflected in the existing caselaw that]

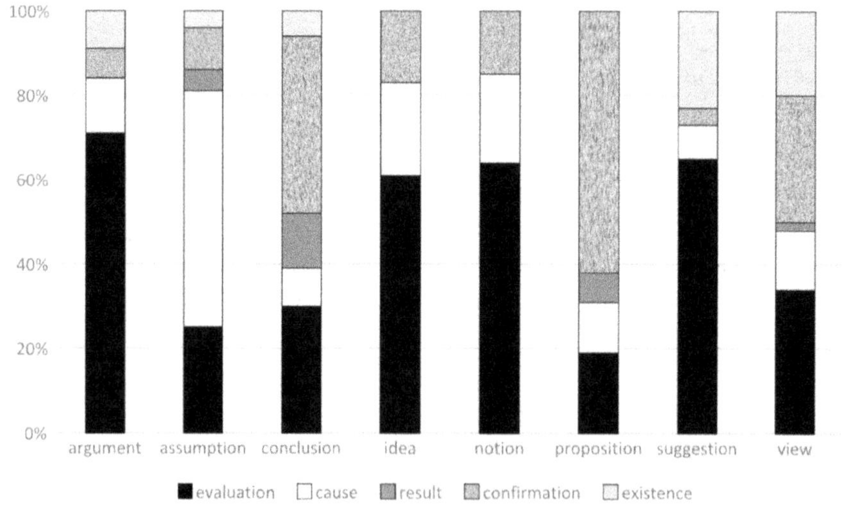

Figure 4.1 Breakdown of discourse functions across status nouns in the US Supreme Court (based on Goźdź-Roszkowski 2018).

But, as already indicated, conclusions in legal justification can be thrown into doubt and openly challenged, and the process of reaching a conclusion can be problematic, as illustrated in (16).

> (16) I agree with the majority's analysis, but not with its *conclusion*. That is to say, I agree that, classically speaking, the difference between a traditional sentencing factor and an element of a greater offense often comes down to a legislative choice about which label to affix. *But I cannot jump* from there to **the conclusion that** the Sixth Amendment always requires identical treatment of the two scenarios. *That jump is fraught with consequences* that threaten the fairness of our traditional criminal justice system; *it distorts* historical sentencing or criminal trial practices; and *it upsets* settled law on which legislatures have relied in designing punishment systems.
>
> (Justice Breyer dissenting in *Blakely vs. Washington*)

In Justice Breyer's argument here, it is the conclusion that comes under attack, as he expresses his negative standpoint on the majority's proposition. The scope of the standpoint is clearly marked out – that is, the judge makes clear that he disagrees with the conclusion but not the analysis. Given that the standpoint is negative, it should be then defended. The justification is conveyed through a metaphor (*I cannot jump*), which is then grammaticalized through nominalization (*that jump*). In fact, the noun *jump* also has the status-indicating function of reifying the elusive process of reaching the conclusion into something that the reader can relate to. (That is, most people have had at some point in their lives experienced difficulty making a leap literally or figuratively, when making a decision.) The word *jump* itself triggers negative connotations of risk and difficulty, and the negative evaluation is also accumulated by describing its consequences (*fraught with consequences that threaten the fairness*, *it distorts*, *it upsets*).

The previous section helps account for the presence of yet another important discourse role performed by status nouns in legal justifications: confirmation. The noun 'confirmation' refers to the many cases in which status objects themselves need to be recognized as valid and need support. Figure 4.1 shows that the words *conclusions, propositions* and *views* are co-selected for this discourse role. We have already seen why conclusions may need to be confirmed. There is a universal requirement that judicial opinions must provide a clear and unequivocal outcome of the legal reasoning, and the conclusions must be framed as such. More generally, it appears that the discourse of legal justification often amounts to a commentary on a previous event or decision, and then provides confirmation of the decision-making process attested by the judge writing the opinion. According to Aarnio's (1987) rules for rationality of discussions, every proposition must be justified on demand. In the discourse of justification, the label 'proposition' seems to be reserved for those propositions that need to be confirmed, as in (17) or disconfirmed, as in (18).

(17) They both contain statements *supporting* **the proposition that** in determining how to calculate income that qualifies for a tax benefit, the expenses to be deducted from gross income are those expenses that are “directly related” to the income.

The confirmation can derive from factual statements contained in reports prepared by the tax-writing committees of the House and the Senate, as in (17), or the support may be traced to the standpoint adopted in a contradictory opinion, as in (18).

(18) *Even the dissenters in the Court of Appeals did not disagree with* **the proposition that** Penn Central forecloses the conclusion that there was a regulatory taking effected by the Washington IOLTA program. In their view, *however*, the *proper focus* was on the second step, the transfer of interest from the IOLTA account to the Foundation.

(Justice Stevens delivered the opinion of the Court in *Allen D. Brown and Greg Hayes, Petitioners v. Legal Foundation of Washington et al.*)

But the support may be illusory, cited only to draw attention to an aspect that the author regards as appropriate to strengthen their own line of argumentation. In (19), where a proposition is disconfirmed, we notice a positive evaluation of evidence embedded within the overall negative evaluation, whereby it is assigned an anecdotal status.

(19) The only objective evidence cited in the dissenting opinion for **the proposition that** COPA ‘will restrict a substantial amount of protected speech that would not be considered harmful to minors in many communities’ are various anecdotes compiled in an amici brief.

(Justice Stevens, dissenting in *John Ashcroft, Attorney General, Petitioner vs. American Civil Liberties Union et al.*

In other words, the linguistic label ‘proposition’ is used for statements that purport to be true but which arguably lack evidence of their truthfulness.

Finally, status nouns are used to signal standpoints adopted by interactants in the course of an exchange of arguments. Most illustrative examples of this role come from the use of *views* and its Polish counterpart *pogląd*. In most cases, standpoints are attributed rather than averred, but, as we see in (21), they are also found in separate opinions wherein judges are expected to justify their dissent and, in case of concurrence, indicate the specific area of divergence (*I agree with, I write separately, however*). This way of presenting standpoints is found in the early stages of argumentation, where it functions to signal the difference of opinion (cf. Goźdź-Roszkowski 2020[a]).

(20) *Judge Sloviter* wrote separately to express her view that Mills v. Maryland, 486 U. S. 367 (1988), established a new rule that qualified for neither Teague v. Lane, 489 U. S. 288 (1989), exception. 316 F. 3d 228, 253-254 (CA3 2003) (opinion concurring in judgment)
(21) I agree with the Court that *Glickman* v. *Wileman Brothers & Elliott*, Inc., 521 U.S. 457 (1997), is not controlling. *I write separately*, however, to reiterate **my views that** 'paying money for the purposes of advertising involves speech,' and that 'compelling speech raises a First Amendment issue just as much as restricting speech.'

(Justice Thomas concurring in *United States and Department of Agriculture, Petitioners v. United Foods, Inc.*)

It is worth pointing out that the propositions in (21) labelled as 'views' are citations from Justice Thomas's earlier dissenting opinion, and that they are held as valid and relevant in the present argument. Indicating standpoints adopted by other interactants is routine practice in Polish justifications of the Constitutional Tribunal, as may be surmised from the following examples.

(22) Marszałek Sejmu *wyraził* jednak **pogląd, że** obecnie obowiązujący w Polsce model środków zaskarżenia przyjęty w wykonaniu Rozporządzenia nr 44/2001 jest zgodny z Konstytucją.

(SK 45/09)

[However, the Speaker expressed the view that (…)].

(23) Wnioskodawca *wyraził* **pogląd, że** zaskarżony przepis godzi także w zasadę nullum delictum sine lege certa.

(K 11/10)

[The petitioner expressed **the view that** (…)].

In (22) and (23), the phrase *pogląd, że* ('view that') is used to report on how the interactants' are positioned with respect to a given legal issue. In terms of the textual structure of legal justification, this reporting use is commonly found in either the historical part of justification or the part 'at the trial'. Recall that this part of the justification serves to present the arguments of the parties to the proceedings, and it precedes the legal justification proper (see Chapter 2; see also Goźdź-Roszkowski 2020[b]). The uneven distribution of certain lexical items across different sections of a text can be partly explained by reference to the concept of 'local textual functions' (Mahlberg 2009). Their characteristic feature is that the functions are restricted to a specific set of lexical items, a specific text and even a specific part of a text.

The analyses provided in this section have shown that nouns occurring in *N that* pattern have a range of important discourse roles, summarized in Table 4.3.

Table 4.3 The *N that* pattern and its discourse functions in the US Supreme Court

Evaluation

- assessing the value of the epistemic object:
  unremarkable, and completely unrelated proposition that
  the Court's absolutist view that
  wildly implausible conclusion that
  The commentary's assumption that … is beyond reproach

- agreeing or disagreeing with a proposition:
  refute the plurality's unsupported suggestion that
  We agree with the Government's suggestion that
  Even the dissenters in the Court of Appeals did not disagree with the proposition that

- rejecting a proposition
  Court of Appeals for the First Circuit rejected the District Court's conclusion that
  We unanimously upheld the statute and rejected the Ninth Circuit's view that
  Petitioners' suggestion that … is also rejected, we have firmly rejected the notion that

Marking cause – result relations

relied on Cominco's suggestion that
the contention is premised on the notion that
in response to the majority's suggestion that
the consequence of the proposition that
While my view that … informs my belief that
lead inexorably to the conclusion that
Nothing in our opinion commits the Court to the view that
relying on Holbrook for the proposition that
Justice Holmes's logically impeccable theory yields the clear conclusion that,

Confirmation

- consistency
  These cases are consistent with our conclusion that
  Notably, this comment was made in the context of an attack on Linkletter's prospective approach as inconsistent with the idea that
  But that is entirely consonant with the proposition that

- support
  No facts in the record support any suggestion that
  Our decisions lend no support to the notion that
  affirming the pragmatic view that

Signalling a standpoint

The report contains no suggestion that
Judge Sloviter wrote separately to express her view that
My conclusion that … is reached

It has become clear that these roles or functions do not occur with equal frequency with each of the nouns concerned. The following generalizations have emerged from an earlier study (Goźdź-Roszkowski 2018) as well as from the present study.

All these nouns – *argument, conclusion, idea, notion, suggestion* and *view* – are associated with EVALUATION. In more than 30% of their occurrences in the corpus, their function is to signal attitudinal meaning. With four of these – *argument, idea, notion* and *suggestion* – the proportion of evaluative uses exceeds 60%. Two status nouns, *conclusion* and *proposition*, mostly occur in the context of CONFIRMATION. As we saw above, the way these nouns are patterned points to the essence of justification: propositions are evaluated and then those assessments are confirmed. This is a defining feature of justificatory discourse, even when a judge rejects a previous decision and then confirms their own. However, conclusions are not only evaluated, but they also need support or justification. Conclusions are truly a 'site of contention' which, especially when presented by lower court judges or other interactants, must be defended in appeal proceedings.

Status nouns in Polish justifications show some striking similarities to the US data in their behaviour. Propositions labelled as *argumenty* ('arguments') or *twierdzenie* ('claim') are assessed overtly using value-laden lexical items, such as negatively charged adjectives (*mylne* ('wrong'), *nieuzasadnione* ('unjustified'), *nie mające podstaw* ('baseless'), *niedopuszczalne* ('inadmissible')). If judges want to express their (dis)agreement, they tend to refer to *twierdzenie* and *tezy* ('propositions'). Interestingly, these last two nouns refer to propositions which are usually discoursed in terms of whether they are justified (*uzasadniona jest teza, iż* ('justified is the proposition that'), *dotychczasowe rozważania uzasadniają tezę, iż* ('the argumentation presented so far justifies the proposition that')). In addition, the noun *założenie* ('assumption') closely follows the pattern identified for its US counterpart, in which marking causal relations remains the prevalent function.

There are also some surprising differences. The most salient difference is connected with a much stronger focus placed on signalling standpoints adopted both by judges authoring an opinion or other actors advancing their arguments. For example, unlike its English counterpart, *przekonanie* ('belief') is almost exclusively used to signal standpoints averred, usually in separate opinions (*wyrażam przekonanie, że* ('I express my belief that')) or attributed (*Trybunał Konstytucyjny wyraził przekonanie, że* ('Constitutional Tribunal expresses its belief that')). In the same vein, the nouns *pogląd* ('view'), as we saw in (22) and (23), and *argument* are associated with this role in justifications. Incidentally, it is also surprising to find that Polish judges use the label 'argument' less frequently than US judges to mark propositions in their justifications. As already indicated, the salience of this discourse function can be attributed to particular institutional requirements, according to which Polish justifications need to acknowledge and address all relevant standpoints adopted in a given case (cf. Rzucidło 2020; Grochowski 2015). This practice is particularly conspicuous in the 'historical part' of the justification, which is generally characterized by the strategy of meticulous reporting of all its components (Rzucidło 2020). In other words, there is evidence of a positive correlation between the occurrence of standpoint signalling language devices and a specific part of the justification. This stands in opposition to the other parts of the justification, in which discursive and monologic strategies prevail.

In addition, conclusions (*konkluzje*) are usually construed as being caused by something prior. Of the 28 instances of *konkluzja, że* ('conclusion that'), most report that a conclusion has been 'reached' as an end goal: *prowadzi to do konkluzji, że* ('this leads to the conclusion that'), *do identycznej konkluzji prowadzi także analiza* ('The analysis ... leads to the identical conclusion that'). As seen in Chapter 2, Polish justifications display a much more clearly marked internal organization. Legal justifications usually contain a separate section designated as *Konkluzja and skutki orzeczenia* ('Conclusions and the effects of the ruling'), in which the reader can find propositions not labelled linguistically as conclusions but which, from a formal perspective, should be regarded as such. What is shared by both Polish and US justifications is that conclusions can be evaluated and confirmed, a feature which might be restricted to judicial opinions.[6]

Case study: arguments in US Supreme Court and Constitutional Tribunal justifications

One limitation of the analyses presented above is that they are based on the exploration of a single pattern that may seem unduly restrictive, raising questions about its validity for understanding the use of status nouns considered in their entirety. For example, the lemma *argument* is used 1,043 times in the US Supreme Court corpus (636.33 per million times). The *N that* pattern accounts for as many as 20% of all the uses of *argument*. In comparison, Polish judges use *argument* 338.69 times per million words, of which only 10% are used in the *N that* pattern.

In addition, as we have seen, another difference between how arguments in US and Polish opinions are used is that in the latter, the evaluative function does not come to the fore. It is, therefore, necessary to extend the study of *the argument that* and *argument, że* reported in the preceding section by considering further corpus evidence of their use.

More insight into this question can be afforded by using the software Sketch Engine to generate a Word Sketch, which is a summary of the word's collocational and grammatical behaviour. In the Word Sketch generated for this data, the output is organized into categories based on grammatical relations, such as

6 For example, in science writing conclusions are rarely evaluated or disconfirmed (Hunston 2011).

arguments that serve as an object of the verb, arguments that serve as a subject of the verb, words that modify arguments and so on. But our concern here is more with the lexical semantics of *argument*.

Even a cursory look at Figure 4.2 corroborates the observation that there is a strong connection between argument and evaluation. When considering the most frequent adjective predicates of *argument*, arguments are assessed in dichotomous terms: they are *right/correct* or they are *wrong/incorrect*; they can also be *persuasive* or *unpersuasive*. Several verbs with *argument* in subject position also signal that arguments are assessed negatively: *the argument fails*, *the argument confuses*, *that argument ignores*. There seems to be another nuanced correlation between the grammatical position and the evaluative function, indicating that arguments are more likely to be evaluated negatively if they are found in subject position. Even if a co-occurring word has a neutral prosody, as in the case of the lemmas *rest* or *base*, which reference the source of an argument, it turns out that the evaluation of the sources is usually negative (*its argument* ***rests on a number of mistakes*** *about the record*, *this argument* ***is based on an unjustified assessment*** *of the way in which courts do their work*). It is, therefore, not surprising that when judges refer to a proposition as 'argument' they do so in order to reject it, the lemma 'reject' being marked in the

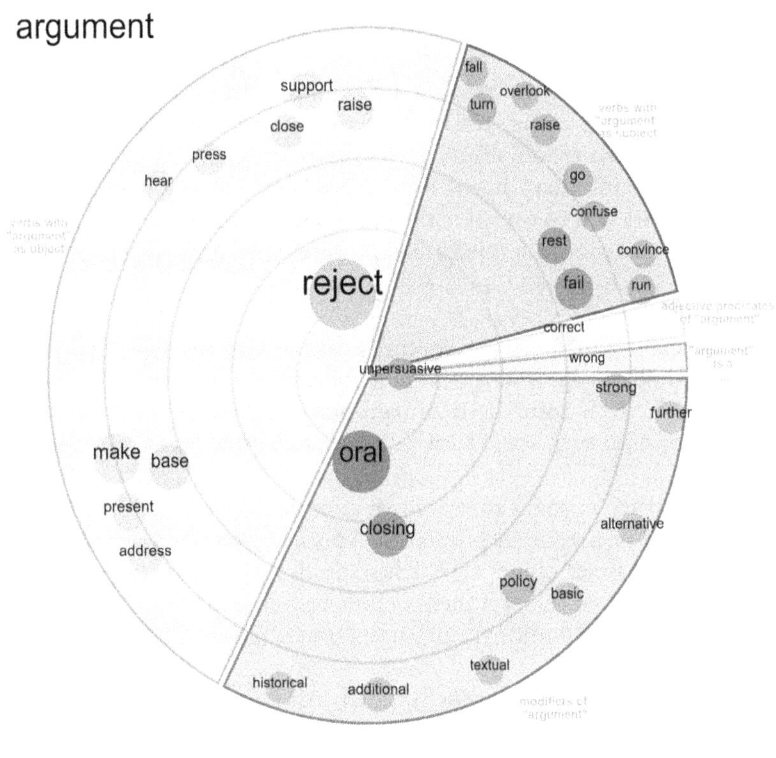

Figure 4.2 A Word Sketch visualization for the noun 'argument' in the US Supreme Court.

Word Sketch as another salient collocate of 'argument'. In the larger study, it becomes clear that arguments in US Supreme Court justifications are far more likely to be evaluated negatively than positively. More evidence can be gleaned from considering a pattern in which *argument* is preceded by the demonstrative adjective *this/that*.

The analysis of the concordance lines reveals an astonishing variety of ways in which the evaluation can be coded in language across different parts of speech. Some verbal elements include the following: *but that argument stretches too far*, *that argument suffers from at least three unjustified leaps of logic* (not shown in Figure 4.3), *this argument is flawed on a number of levels* (Line 5), *this argument is unavailing* (Line 6), *this argument fails because* (Line 13). There are very few counter-examples in which this pattern provides a neutral to positive evaluation (*this argument echoes Justice Black's dissent in Prima Paint*, *this argument seems to rest on a distinction*).

The picture here is not uniform, however, because the Word Sketch shows the relevance of certain verbs with *argument* as object – *make, raise, address* and *present* – which confirm the relevance of the standpoint-signalling function described in the previous section. Examples include *the state presents three main arguments for*, *Hamdan raises a substantial argument that* and *the majority makes essentially three arguments against this interpretation.* These show that occurrences of the word *argument* also contribute to textual cohesion (Halliday & Hasan 1976) by serving as conjuncts, thus having a text-structuring function. In the example below, taken from the majority opinion in *Puckett v. United States*, Justice Scalia organizes Part III of the opinion around the argumentation advanced by the petitioner. The 'several possible reasons' Scalia names have been construed as *four distinct arguments* for the purpose of clarity and to organize the court's justification. Note that the petitioner's argumentation is immediately interpreted by assigning it into specific categories of 'doctrinal' and 'practical' arguments.

> (24) 'Puckett puts forward several possible reasons why plain-error review should not apply in the present context. We understand him to be **making** effectively **four distinct arguments**: two doctrinal, two practical. We consider each set in turn' (*Puckett v. United States*).

The judicial writer engages in a kind of commentary on the progress of the discourse itself. The reader is primed to expect certain types of argument and to recognize the exact points at which a specific argument starts and finishes because evaluation of the arguments tends to occur at boundary points in a discourse, providing additional clues to its organization.

> (25) 'Puckett's primary precedent-based argument proceeds as follows'.
>
> (26) 'Puckett's second doctrinal attack rests on our decision in *Santobello*'.

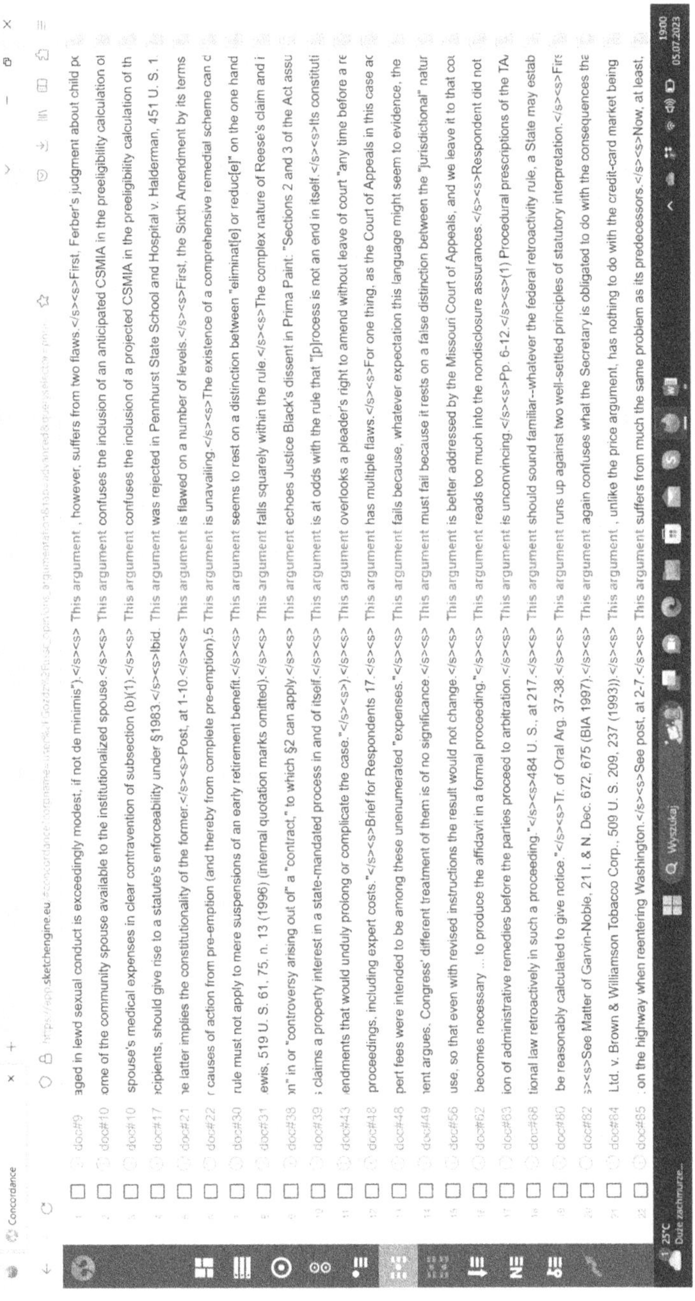

Figure 4.3 A Sketch Engine visualization showing 20 concordance lines with the phrase *This argument*.

Characteristically, there seems to be a distinct pattern whereby the argumentative discourse elaborating on the argumentative propositions is punctuated with evaluation. For example, the petitioner's argument introduced in (25) is evaluated at the start of the next paragraph, and the evaluation is supported immediately by the counter-arguments.

> (27) This **elaborate analysis** *suffers from at least two defects.* First, there is *nothing to support* **the proposition that** the Government's breach of a plea agreement retroactively causes the defendant's agreement to have been unknowing or involuntary. Any more than **there is anything to support the proposition that** a mere breach of contract retroactively causes the other party's promise to have been coerced or induced by fraud.
>
> (*Puckett v. United States*)

Note how the judge uses different status nouns to label the content of the petitioner's arguments. Puckett's argument, reified as 'elaborate analysis', is assessed negatively as *suffering from at least two defects* and is then dissected into two *propositions.* Each proposition is critically evaluated as lacking in support. It is interesting to note that in another example, (26), the judge turns to address Puckett's argument as an 'attack'. This lexical 'label' – to use the terminology of Francis (1994) – can certainly be interpreted as constituting evidence of Justice Scalia's negative evaluation of the petitioner's argument, but this choice of a lexical item might also remind us of the pragma-dialectical approach to legal argumentation. In the pragma-dialectical approach, argumentation is seen as a critical exchange of discussion moves aimed at putting the point of view under discussion to a critical test (Feteris 2017). In this case, the dialectical goal of the discussion was to establish whether the protagonist, the Court of Appeals, defended its decision successfully against the attacks of the antagonist, the petitioner. Needless to say, the judgment of the Court of Appeals was affirmed.

In another, less elaborate, example, the dissenting judge provides a 'wholesale' negative evaluation of the majority's arguments. The arguments are not evaluated separately but jointly.

> (28) The majority **makes** essentially **three arguments** against this interpretation. It says that the statute's purpose and 'legislative history is simply not enough' to overcome: (1) the fact that this is a Spending Clause case; (2) the text of the statute; and (3) our prior cases which hold that the term 'costs' does not include expert costs. *I do not find these arguments convincing.*
>
> (Justice Breyer dissenting in *Arlington Central School District Board of Education, Petitioner vs. Pearl Murphy*).

Both examples are illustrative of what could be termed 'evaluative coherence'. The use of the word 'argument' at different points in the text not only helps keep the text coherent by serving as signposts to help the reader to keep track of the progression of the argumentative discourse, but it also marks off the boundaries of what amount to discrete argumentative units. In this way, coherence is obtained from the logical connections made explicit for the readers as they are trying to make sense of the propositional content. Cohesion is seen in the 'explicit textual signalling by the writers of this potential logical coherence' (Thompson & Zhou 2000: 122). In other words, cohesion refers to the relationship between different lexical items in a text that contribute to the text's coherence (cf. Hoey 2017). It is the interaction between various unspecific nouns which, as we have said, are also known as 'labels' (Francis 1994) that results in logical and argumentative coherence. In so doing, the significance of the argumentative propositions and their interconnectedness are underscored by means of evaluation.

Turning to the Word Sketch of arguments in the Constitutional Tribunal justifications, we can note that, in structural terms, most are modified by participle forms: *argumenty przemawiające za* ('arguments advocating'), *przytoczone argumenty* ('arguments advanced'), *przedstawione argumenty* ('arguments presented') and *argumenty podniesione* ('arguments raised'). This use is similar to the non-evaluative function of signalling standpoints and the creation of cohesive links already observed in the US Supreme Court data. These participle forms are derived from communication and reporting verbs *przedstawić* ('present'), *sformułować* ('formulate'), *wskazywać* ('indicate'), *przytoczyć* ('advance'), *podnieść* ('raise') and *przywołać* ('refer'), reflecting a strong concern with presenting, rather than evaluating, the contents of prior arguments. This use can be attributed to the fact that 'reporting' is regarded as one of the major functions of legal justification in the Constitutional Tribunal decisions (Królikowski 2015). The importance of reporting is reflected in the considerable space afforded to 'procedural history' in the first two parts of the justification.

As noted in Chapter 2, the distinct parts of the justification, named 'historical' and 'at the trial', refer to all documents deemed relevant to the case, as well as to all the documents which have been filed at different stages of the proceedings and to documents that provide a detailed account of the constitutional complaint. In these parts, the arguments advanced by each of the parties to the case are also summarized.[7]

As we see in Figure 4.4, there are few recurrent evaluative adjectives. One worth nothing, however, is the occurrence of *przekonujący* ('persuasive'), a use paralleled by *unpersuasive* in the US Supreme Court data. This

7 See Goźdź-Roszkowski (2020[b]) for a detailed discussion of a move structure of Constitutional Tribunal justifications and how a common core of rhetorical structure is realized by means of recurrent functional segments of text.

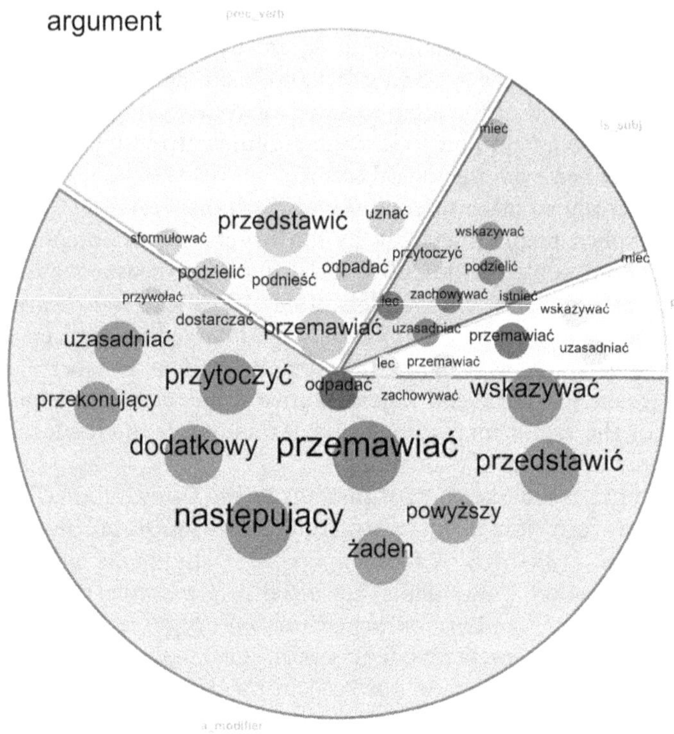

Figure 4.4 A Word Sketch visualization for the noun 'argument' in Constitutional Tribunal justifications.

underscores the fact that one of the major functions of argumentation is to persuade audiences so that arguments are accepted. Indeed, in the context of Polish justifications, the persuasive value of argument is often discussed in terms of its absence: *Nie ma logicznych i przekonujących argumentów na poparcie rozwiązania* ('there are no logical and persuasive arguments to support the solution'), *Brak przekonujących argumentów na rzecz zaistnienia takiego pominięcia czyni skargę – w zasadniczym jej wymiarze – bezzasadną* ('The absence of convincing arguments renders the complaint groundless'). More examples of such evaluation come from cases in which argument is the object in a clause (coded as prec_verb in Figure 4.4). Here, evaluation is expressed by pointing out the absence of arguments.

(29) 'Odmiennie stanowisko zajął Wojewoda Kujawsko-Pomorski oraz Wojewódzki Sąd Administracyjny w Bydgoszczy, jednak w uzasadnieniach wydanych przez siebie rozstrzygnięć organy te **nie przedstawiły żadnych argumentów** uzasadniających takie stanowisko'.(SK 43/07)

> A different standpoint was adopted by the governor of the province and the administrative court in [the city of] Bydgoszcz but in the justifications of their decisions, these institutional bodies **did not present any arguments** to justify this position].

In (29), the writer signals a standpoint adopted by the institutional interactants (the governor and the Court) while also evaluating its validity. The evaluation is negative because the justification of their positions is not supported by any argumentation. It is the applicants' constitutional complaints that are most often assessed as not grounded in any, or in any valid, argumentation. The use of argument seen in '*Tymczasem skarżący nie przedstawili argumentów , że*' ('Yet, the complainants failed to present arguments that') and '*Wnioskodawca musi przedstawić przekonujące argumenty*' ('The applicant must present persuasive arguments that') also shows how different discourse roles can intersect: the functions of signalling standpoints, evaluating status nouns and indicating disconfirmation can all be found simultaneously within a single sentence or a paragraph.

Summary and conclusions: status nouns as sites of contention

By now, it should be apparent that evaluation of status is particularly important to legal justification because the status of propositions comprises an essential aspect of legal reasoning and persuasion. Evaluation of status essentially reifies propositions into the objects of which legal argumentation is comprised: arguments, conclusions, assumptions, notions and so on. We have seen how status can be intrinsically linked with dichotomous evaluations of 'good' and 'bad' and how these are crucial in legal justification which ultimately seeks to elicit acceptance through various techniques of persuasion. The use of status nouns is one prominent technique among several, and this chapter has demonstrated how the choice of a linguistic resource can modify the assessment of an argumentative proposition. The enormous rhetorical potential found in applying this grammar pattern in argumentative discourse stems from the duality of the evaluative function. The act of evaluation is realized at two levels: Level 1 consists in selecting a particular noun, depending on how the judge interprets the object of evaluation – i.e., the propositional content of arguments made by other interactants – and how committed or not they feel towards it; Level 2 involves evaluating the object in positive or negative terms, leading to its acceptance or rejection. An assignment of status is usually both subjective and evaluative, and writers can choose how categorical, confident or conciliatory they want to be in their orientation towards the propositions discussed. In addition, status nouns perform other roles that are equally crucial to argumentative discourse: marking cause–result relations, providing confirmation for claim-making and signalling legal standpoints.

The generalizations highlighted above have been shown to hold true for both US Supreme Court and for Constitutional Tribunal justifications, even where some differences have also been discovered. Accordingly, I argue that the nexus between evaluation and argumentation embodied in the use of status nouns in the *N that* pattern is unique to the genre of legal justification. The link between negative evaluation and argumentation is particularly conspicuous. We have noticed that when a proposition is challenged or contested, it is likely to be labelled with such terms as *argument, notion* or *suggestion* in the US Supreme Court corpus, or *teza, twierdzenie or założenie* in the Polish Constitutional Tribunal decisions. But it is possible to take this point even further and to argue that status nouns contribute to the identification of 'sites of contention'. That is, they identify the part or segment of a legal justification in which the reader is most likely to encounter a formulation of, or reference to, an argument which assumes the form of its assessment. An analogy could be drawn here to Scollon's 'sites of engagement' (1998), understood as critical moments of interaction performed according to assigned roles in a specific professional context. In line with the perception of legal justification as an argumentative activity type, the professional role of a judge is to resolve the difference of opinion in a legal context (cf. Feteris 2017). The judge performs this role by checking whether the claim of the protagonist (the petitioner in court proceedings) is acceptable in the context of the critical reactions of the other party. In other words, the essence of the judicial role is to assess the arguments and counter-arguments within the constraints imposed by the institutional conventions of legal proceedings. Assessment is achieved during the argumentation stage of legal justification, and the status nouns in the *N that* pattern belong to the linguistic toolkit available for fulfilling this institutional role and discursive goal.

The term 'contention' is used in its neutral sense (an opinion or statement that something is true), but, as the analyses in this chapter have shown, in most cases, a more suitable sense of the term refers to misalignment between different points of view. Recall from Chapter 2 that one way of understanding argumentation is that it is accompanied by reasoning and conflict (Baumtrog 2018: 90). The conflict may be manifested in the expression of doubt or disagreement. Of course, this may not be true for all contexts in which argumentation occurs, but it stands as a fitting description of what occurs in the argumentation found in legal justification. Consider yet another example:

> (30) Not only does the Court's **opinion** in Boyde *fail to support* the **improbable argument** that respondent's mitigating evidence falls within factor (k)'s purview, but its **reasoning** is entirely consistent with the Court of Appeals' *contrary* **conclusion**.
>
> (Justice Stevens dissenting in *Supreme Court of the United States Ayers, Acting Warden v. Belmontes*)

Apart from the rather obvious fact that conflict is inherent in virtually any legal case, there is clearly a conflict between the majority opinion and dissent. In (30), the stakes were high because the case concerned a death penalty judgment. The ruling only narrowly allowed Belmontes's death sentence to go forward.[8] Linguistically, the conflict in (30) is coded in negatively charged lexis: *fail to support, improbable argument, contrary conclusion*. The key word is *argument*, which not only refers to an argument advanced in the majority opinion encapsulating its content but also points to elements representing crucial points of reference for the argument: the court's opinion in Boyde, its reasoning, and the Ninth Circuit Court of Appeal's conclusion. The immediate co-texts of the status noun mark out a textual territory in which an argument is embedded. The persuasive value of status nouns may be found in their anaphoric and cataphoric properties. That is, they refer to and label propositions embedded in a stretch of discourse, to align them with the ongoing argument as a final example will show:

> (31) The State's **argument** that the jury was properly informed of the law on parole ineligibility by the trial court's instructions and by defense counsel's own **argument** is *unpersuasive*. To support that *contention*, the State sets out defense counsel's closing pleas that […]
>
> (*Shafer v. South Carolina*)

Status nouns, thus, have a predictive as well as an organizing function, indicating to the reader how the argumentative discourse is to be interpreted on both ideational and interpersonal levels. The presence of 'sites of contention' helps solidify the judge's argument as the best alternative or, indeed, as the only reasonable solution to resolve a given issue.

Bibliography

Aarnio, A. (1987). *The rational as reasonable: A treatise of legal justification*. Reidel.

Baumtrog, M. (2018). Reasoning and arguing, dialectically and dialogically, among individual and multiple participants. *Argumentation, 32*(1), 77–98.

Biber, D., Stig, J., Leech, G., Conrad, S., & Finegan, E. (1999). *The Longman grammar of spoken and written English*. Longman.

Charles, M. (2007). Argument or evidence? Disciplinary variation in the use of the noun *that* pattern in stance construction. *English for specific purposes, 26*(2), 203–218.

Coxhead, A. (2000). A new academic word list. *TESOL Quarterly, 34*(2), 213–238.

Du Bois, J.W. (2007). The stance triangle. In R. Englebretson (Ed.), *Stancetaking in discourse: Subjectivity, evaluation, interaction*. John Benjamins Publishing.

Feteris, E.T. (2017). *Fundamentals of legal argumentation: A survey of theories on the justification of judicial decisions*. Springer.

8 'Ayers v. Belmontes'. *Oyez*, www.oyez.org/cases/2006/05-493. Accessed 3 Apr. 2023. *Boyde v. California*, a case in which the Justices ruled that there was no reasonable likelihood that the jury had misunderstood the instruction.

Flowerdew, J., & Forest, R. (2015). *Signalling nouns in English: A corpus-based discourse approach*. Cambridge University Press. https://doi.org/10.1017/CBO9781139135405

Francis, G. (1986). *Anaphoric nouns*. Discourse Analysis Monographs 11. University of Birmingham Printing Section.

Francis, G. (1994). Labelling discourse: An aspect of nominal-group lexical cohesion. In M. Coulthard (Ed.), *Advances in written text analysis* (pp. 83–100). Routledge.

Gardner, D., & Davies, M. (2013). A new academic vocabulary list. *Applied linguistics, 35*(3), 305–327.

Goźdź-Roszkowski, S. (2018). Facts in law: A comparative study of 'fact that' and its phraseologies in American and Polish judicial discourse. In S. Goźdź-Roszkowski & G. Pontrandolfo (Eds.), *Phraseology in Legal and institutional settings: A corpus-based interdisciplinary perspective* (pp. 143–159). Routledge.

Goźdź-Roszkowski, S. (2019). "It is not just a fact that the law requires this, but it is a reasonable fact": Using the Noun-that pattern to explore stance construction in legal writing. In F. Teresa & P. Rodriguez-Puente (Eds.), *Corpus-based research on variation in English legal discourse* (pp. 123–146). John Benjamins Publishing.

Goźdź-Roszkowski, S. (2020a). Communicating dissent in judicial opinions: A comparative, genre-based analysis. *International Journal for the Semiotics of Law, 33*(2), 381–401. https://doi.org/10.1007/s11196-020-09711-y

Goźdź-Roszkowski, S. (2020b). Move analysis of legal justifications in Constitutional Tribunal judgments in Poland: What they share and what they do not. *International Journal for the Semiotics of Law, 33*(3), 581–600. https://doi.org/10.1007/s11196-020-09700-1

Goźdź-Roszkowski, S., & Pontrandolfo, G. (2013). Evaluative patterns in judicial discourse: A corpus-based phraseological perspective on American and Italian criminal judgments. *International Journal of Law, Language and Discourse, 3*(2), 9–69.

Greenberg, M. (2004). How facts make law. *Legal Theory, 10*(3), 157–198.

Grochowski, M. (2015). Uzasadnienie zdania odrębnego [The justification of separate opinions]. In I. Rzucidło-Grochowska & M. Grochowski (Eds.), *Uzasadnienia decyzji stosowania prawa* [Justification in judicial decision-making process] (pp. 38–169). Wolters Kluwer.

Halliday, M., & Hasan, R. (1976). *Cohesion in English*. Longman.

Hoey, M. (2017). Cohesion and coherence in a content-specific corpus. In M. Pace-Sigge & K.J. Patterson (Eds.), *Lexical priming: Applications and advances* (pp. 1–38). John Benjamins Publishing.

Hunston, S. (2011). *Corpus approaches to evaluation: Phraseology and evaluative language*. Routledge.

Ivanič, R. (1991). Nouns in search of a context: A study of nouns with both open- and closed system characteristics. *International Review of Applied Linguistics in Language Teaching, 29*(2), 93–114. https://doi.org/10.1515/iral.1991.29.2.93

Jiang, F., & Hyland, K. (2015). "The fact that": Stance nouns in disciplinary writing. *Discourse Studies, 17*(5), 529–550.

Królikowski, J. (2015). Uzasadnienia orzeczeń Trybunału Konstytucyjnego. In M. Rzucidło-Grochowska (Ed.), *Uzasadnienia decyzji stosowania prawa* (pp. 427–439). Wolters Kluwer.

Mahlberg, M. (2009). Local textual functions of *move* in newspaper story patterns. In U. Römer & R. Schulze (Eds.), *Exploring the lexis-grammar interface* (pp. 265–287). John Benjamins Publishing.

Mazzi, D. (2007). "The rhetoric of judicial texts": The interplay of reported argumentation and the judge's argumentative voice. In G. Garzone & S. Sarangi (Eds.), *Discourse, ideology and specialized communication* (pp. 379–399). Peter Lang.

Rzucidło, I. (2020). *Uzasadnienie orzeczenia sądowego: Ujęcie teoretyczne a poglądy orzecznictwa*. Wolters Kluwer.

Schmid, H. (2000). *English abstract nouns as conceptual shells: From corpus to cognition*. De Gruyter. https://doi.org/10.1515/9783110808704

Scollon, R. (1998). *Mediated discourse as social interaction: A study of news discourse*. Longman.

Sinclair, J. (1987). *Mirror for a text*. (Unpublished ms.), University of Birmingham.

Solan, L. (1993). *The Language of judges*. The University of Chicago Press.

Thompson, G., & Zhou, J.L. (2000). Evaluation and organization in text: The structuring role of evaluative disjuncts. In S. Hunston & G. Thompson (Eds.), *Evaluation in text: Authorial stance and the construction of discourse* (pp. 121–141). Oxford University Press.

Part III

Uncovering evoked and less obvious evaluative meanings

One limitation of corpus studies of evaluation and status is that methods based on search and quantification rely on linguistic features named *explicitly* in texts and, ideally, features occurring *frequently*. And yet, evaluation is all about meaning, or different types of meaning, rather than form. Evaluation can be marked by a variety of explicit lexico-grammatical features, but successfully identifying evaluation as a practice involves more than just locating particular verbal forms associated with evaluation. Equally, interpreting the role of evaluation in discourse, especially judicial discourse, may call for a deeper understanding of discourse than can be gained by scrutinizing the immediate context of a given lexical item.

Part III of this book marks a transition from corpus-*based* to corpus-*assisted* method of analysis. The latter does not treat corpus data as the only source of input for the analysis. Rather, quantitative results are used as a starting point for carrying out detailed case studies and close readings, the aim being to become as conversant as possible with the discourse type at hand. In addition, the macro-context of the institutional environment in which the argumentative discourse of legal justification occurs is taken into account.

Chapter 5 shifts the focus from evaluative language understood in terms of lexico-grammatical patterning to evaluative language expressed as lexemes. This change of *unit of analysis* entails a change in functional perspective. While the former is used to *assess* argumentation and signal judicial stances, the latter is operationalized as value-based lexis *constitutive* of argumentation. The lexis is value-based because it denotes values and principles – for example, *dignity, equality, fairness* – which are used as argumentative premises (legal *topoi*). The major difference between these uses of evaluative language is brought to life by analyzing two cases based on value judgment, concerning a conflict between the right to life and the right to liberty and bodily integrity. One of the cases was heard by the US Supreme Court and the other by the Constitutional Tribunal of Poland.

Chapter 6 demonstrates how the use and role of evaluative language can be described more systematically by adopting the pragma-dialectical approach to legal justification (Feteris 2017). In the pragma-dialectical approach, the

DOI: 10.4324/9781003333302-7

argumentation of the litigants and the judge are reconstructed as a contribution to a critical discussion – an exchange of arguments and counter-arguments. Legal justification takes the form of a ***regulated*** critical discussion, one constrained by rules of procedural and substantive law regarding the procedural and material starting points appropriate and specific to a particular legal system or even a given court of law. The constraints on how justifications are written affect both argumentation and evaluative language. In my analysis of justifications, I apply the four-stage ideal model of critical discussion (IM) as a heuristic tool. The IM allows me to identify relevant points in an argumentative discussion in which argumentation and standpoints are staged and contribute to the resolution of a difference of opinion. In the course of the analysis, the close interrelatedness of argumentation and evaluative language becomes increasingly apparent. I interpret evaluative language by considering how it contributes to each stage of the critical discussion but also in light of *strategic manoeuvring* (van Eemeren 2010) – that is to say the overall strategy adopted by judges to ensure that their argumentation is rhetorically effective enough to be accepted as valid. Evaluative language can, therefore, be analyzed not only at the micro-level of an utterance (as demonstrated in Chapters 3 and 4) but also at the macro-level of an IM discussion stage. Chapter 6 first maps the four stages of the critical discussion model onto the different rhetorically oriented parts of justifications given by the Constitutional Tribunal of Poland. It then applies the model to compare argumentation and the evaluative language in the unique and specific contexts of two cases heard by the Constitutional Tribunal of Poland and the US Supreme Court.

Bibliography

Feteris, E.T. (2017). *Fundamentals of legal argumentation. A survey of theories on the justification of judicial decisions.* Springer.

van Eemeren, F.H. (2010). *Strategic maneuvering in argumentative discourse. Extending the pragma-dialectical theory of argumentation.* John Benjamins Publishing.

5 Value-based lexis and argument in morally sensitive issues

The previous two chapters have demonstrated how judges make conscious choices about which arguments they want to pay most attention to and which arguments they choose to emphasize or deemphasize. In doing so, judges rely on certain tried and tested evaluative language patterns. Scrutiny of both adjectival and noun-centred patterns has brought to light how the concepts of evaluation, positioning and alignment are used simultaneously in acts of evaluation and how these acts of evaluation are enacted in legal argumentation. In this chapter, the focus is on value-based lexis and ascriptions of value accomplished without overt indications of subjectivity or stancetaking. I propose to make a distinction between evaluative language used for *discourse about* arguments by assessing argumentative propositions and indicating judicial stances and evaluative language operationalized as value-based lexis which is *constitutive* of arguments. The central claim made in the present chapter is that the analysis of this type of evaluative language provides useful insights into judicial reasoning based on value judgment. Expressed as lexemes, rather than phraseologies, value-based lexis indicates major argumentative premises (*topoi*), values and principles.[1]

The perception of the role of this type of evaluative language is related to the rhetorical approach to legal argumentation and justification. Informed by Perelman's 'New Rhetoric' (Perelman & Olbrechts-Tyteca 1969: 83), Toulmin's 'Argumentation Model' (1958) and Viehweg's 'Topical Approach' (1993), these models share a concern with the content of arguments and the context-dependent aspects of acceptability. The logical approach, with its emphasis on formal proof, is deemphasized. Instead, as an alternative criterion of validity, priority is given to the acceptability of argumentation directed at

1 The term 'lexis' is problematic because it can have different meanings even within the discipline of linguistics. In general, 'lexis' refers to vocabulary of a language in all its aspects: words and their meanings (lexical semantics), how words relate to one another (collocation) and how they may combine with one another (Malmkjaer 2004). In this chapter, 'lexis' denotes lexemes, a group of word forms that share the same basic meaning and belong to the same word class.

DOI: 10.4324/9781003333302-8

a specific audience (Perelman & Olbrechts-Tyteca 1969[2]). In order to gain acceptance, the judge, as an arguer, must convince the audience of the acceptability of a legal decision. Acceptance can be gained by choosing generally accepted legal values, such as *equality* or *fairness*, as starting points for the ensuing argumentation (Feteris & Kloosterhuis 2013). The argumentation is then structured using specific legal argumentation schemes.

The rhetorical approach seems to be particularly fitting for hard cases that are defined by a fundamental conflict of incommensurable constitutional principles. That is, the rhetorical approach is particularly fitting for cases which involve a comparison among goods, values, principles and rights that cannot be ranked on a single scale of measurement (da Silva 2011). For example, in cases in which businesses deny services to same-sex customers on religious grounds, as in *Masterpiece Cakeshop v. Colorado Civil Rights Commission*, constitutionally protected freedoms of conscience, religion and speech inevitably clash with the equally protected right to non-discrimination and the protection of minority groups. Also relevant to this context are other morally sensitive issues, such as abortion, euthanasia, medically assisted dying or medically assisted procreation, which invariably give rise to cases that are fundamentally about collisions of competing principles, values and rules. Solutions to the question of whether one right should be protected at the expense of the other are sought outside the standard methods of pure logic and legal syllogism. Deductive reasoning, even if procedurally necessary, is very rarely sufficient to justify a decision in such cases (MacCormick 2009). Rather, judicial decisions in such cases are the result of balancing rights, values and social goods. Value-judgment, therefore, proves to be necessary. The role of argument in such cases is to persuade rather than to prove, demonstrate or refute. Judges need to establish a hierarchy of different values, making an explicit value choice in each case. One way of understanding how judges make such choices is by examining the way key lexis denoting values is used in the justifications of judicial opinions.

In this chapter, I explicate how value-based lexis is used in the argumentation of two cases concerning a conflict over the right to life versus the right to liberty and bodily integrity. These two cases show a striking similarity in that the changes limiting access to abortion have arrived not via legislation or referenda but through litigation before the respective apex courts: the Constitutional Tribunal of Poland and the US Supreme Court (USSC).[3] Yet, they differ radically in the way evaluative language is used in the justification

2 See, however, Feteris (2017) (Chapter 2 Section 2.5) for a critique of views which discount the role of formal logic in legal argumentation.

3 It is often thought that constitutional courts should be examined separately from supreme courts. However, it is not uncommon to compare the case law and the mechanisms of European constitutional courts with supreme courts functioning in countries belonging to the common law tradition, especially the US Supreme Court (Kelemen 2018).

of these decisions.[4] Based on a corpus-assisted discourse studies approach (Partington et al. 2013), I identify statistically salient lexis denoting potential values in the texts of both decisions. The selected lexis is then analyzed in terms of its co-occurrences and within the wider context of the entire opinion to establish whether a given lexeme, indeed, indicates a value. In the process, we see how language choice affects the argumentative framing of the judicial decisions.

To summarize briefly, my findings are that the argumentation in the Polish decision is heavily axiological, with Polish judges relying on value-based lexis to engage fundamental values and principles. In contrast, the USSC opinion considered here, generally, avoids broad, abstract reasoning, and it uses evaluative language to focus on flaws and weaknesses identified in the reasoning of the previous landmark cases in reproductive rights (*Roe vs. Wade* and *Planned Parenthood v. Casey*) that were reversed as a result of the ruling.

Legal *topoi*, values and forms of argument

Value-based lexis offers a way of identifying and reconstructing argumentation based on value judgment. In such cases, lexemes are used to refer to values, value hierarchies and legal *topoi*, all of which can be employed by arguers as starting points or common points of departure for constructing argumentation schemes. According to classical legal rhetoric (Frost 2016), *topoi* (also known as *loci*) are places where available legal arguments can be discovered. The idea goes back to Greco-Roman classical rhetoric, which devised a system of topics (*topica*) 'to discover a method by which we shall be able to reason from generally accepted opinions about any problem set before us and shall ourselves, when sustaining an argument, avoid saying anything self-contradictory' (Aristotle 2009). In a legal context, *topoi* or topics are generally accepted legal values which judges choose carefully in order to help them gain the acceptance of a legal audience. Legal *topoi* usually draw on general legal principles, such as *fairness* or *equity* (Feteris & Kloosterhuis 2013), principles regarded as fundamental to the legal and social order and in need of (constitutional) protection.[5] Perelman and Olbrechts-Tyteca use the term *loci* to denote 'premises

4 Clearly, coming from two very different legal jurisdictions, the cases differ in a number of ways, and it is not the aim of the analysis to provide their systematic and comparative description. Rather, these two cases have been selected with a view to highlighting how evaluative language used in those contexts can contribute to the persuasive and justificatory force of arguments.

5 Some authors use the term '*topoi*' in the sense of methods of interpretation generally accepted in a given legal culture. In their comparative study of argumentation and legal interpretation in the decisions of the Polish Supreme Court and the German Federal Court of Justice, Małolepszy and Głuchowski (2022) list, for example, linguistic *topoi*, systematic *topoi*, references to the legal literature and judicature and so on, as belonging to the category of 'formalistic arguments'. This understanding of *topoi* can be useful in distinguishing between formalistic and substantive ('value-oriented) legal cultures. *Topoi* have also been treated as a method for problem-solving in law. Viehweg argues that 'legal prudence can be understood as a permanent

of very general nature' (1969: 83) which can function as bases for values and hierarchies. They insist that a distinction should be made between abstract values (e.g., justice, truth) and concrete values related to a specific object and viewed as something unique. In the course of argumentation, both abstract and concrete values may be invoked, depending on the type of argument and the type of audience the judge seeks to persuade. In addition, argumentation not only relies on values but also on their hierarchical ordering, as some values will be considered as superior (or preferable) to others. Commonly accepted legal values are very useful as starting points in judicial argumentation, precisely because their general and vague nature makes them amenable to a variety of interpretations. For example, as we will see in the next section, the Polish justification relies on human dignity as a general value. However, the reliance on this value does not stop the tribunal from making a distinction between two categories of dignity. In an overview of Perelman's 'Legal Argumentation Theory', Feteris (2017) points to the advantage of relying on general legal principles as common starting points in legal argumentation – the advantage being that their universal acceptance helps to win approval for a specific but controversial legal standpoint. As demonstrated in the next section, this is exactly the kind of strategy adopted in the Polish case to justify its decision to restrict access to abortion.

According to Perelman (1976), the choice of particular values, whether abstract or concrete, and the subsequent hierarchical ordering, must be justified and explained. The justification is effected by applying various forms of argument in order to convince the audience that the decision is sound and legally correct. In other words, the function of the argumentation is to exploit the audience's acceptance of the starting points, transferring that acceptance to the expression of a judicial standpoint as formulated in a legal decision. Perelman describes different starting points and forms of argument used in law to convince an audience of the acceptability of a legal decision (e.g., *argumentum a contrario*, argument from analogy, teleological argument and so on). The choice of a particular form or forms of argument may depend on the conception of law and the preferred *topoi* in a given legal culture or even a given court. In the case of the Polish Constitutional Tribunal, the principle of proportionality (balancing of interest) is usually the default solution.[6]

Finally, the lexis referencing legal *topoi* or values can be also construed as ethical or emotive words characterized by the close relationship between value judgments and emotions. According to Macagno and Walton (2016: 31),

---

discussion of problems', and 'problems elicit the recurring search for *topoi* that can serve as solutions' (1993: 89). The understanding of law as a system of *topoi* continues to attract legal scholars. More recently Soboleva argues that sources of law 'can be represented as commonplaces (*topoi*) of legal reasoning' (Soboleva 2022: 166).

6 See Śledzińska-Simon (2019) for a book-length exploration of proportionality analysis in Constitutional Tribunal cases.

ethical words can become a powerful instrument of persuasion because they are effectively value judgments and are, thus, capable of affecting attitudes. If values and *topoi* are treated as sources or premises for argument, then analyzing value-based lexis and their collocates should help identify certain patterns of argumentation used by judges in a given case. Assuming that the value-based lexis and its collocates reveal the association of certain values or principles and, possibly, methods of interpretation, it should be possible to gain some insight into judicial reasoning in a given case. In addition, a comparative, cross-language analysis should shed light on similarities or differences in the use of value-based language or, broadly, evaluative language in the justification of decisions perceived as morally and socially sensitive.

The Constitutional Tribunal of Poland and the unconstitutionality of abortion

On 22 October 2020, the Constitutional Tribunal of Poland ruled that a clause in the *Act on Family Planning, Protection of Human Foetus and the Admissibility of Pregnancy Termination* allowing the termination of pregnancy in the event of a fatal foetal abnormality was unconstitutional.[7] As a result, abortion law in Poland has become one of the strictest in Europe. Poland now allows abortion in only two cases: when a woman's life or health is at risk and in the case of rape or incestuous pregnancy. The ruling led to a public outcry and mass protests against what was viewed as a blatant violation of human rights, all of which occurred at the peak of the COVID-19 pandemic in Poland.

Among the many functions of legal justification, its most essential function is to legitimize a judicial decision so that it is not only legally sound but also so that it gains social and political acceptance. According to Polish legal doctrine, a constitutional review of abortion admissibility must involve identifying and balancing all relevant constitutionally protected values, and it should express a broad social and political consensus (Grabowska-Moroz & Łakomiec 2021). Yet, legitimacy has become a thorny issue for a court in the wake of a rule of law crisis in Poland (see Sadurski 2019). As a result of the rule of law crisis, the credibility of the Constitutional Tribunal has been severely undermined, and the validity of the ruling on abortion was questioned by leading legal scholars in Poland. These scholars pointed towards some formal and procedural defects originating with the institution itself (Gliszczyńska-Grabias & Sadurski

7 The original and full name of this legislative act is *Ustawa z dnia 7 stycznia 1993 o planowaniu rodziny, ochronie płodu ludzkiego i warunkach dopuszczalności przerywania ciąży* [Act on Family Planning, Protection of Human Foetus and the Conditions to the Admissibility of Pregnancy Termination of January 7, 1993] (Official Journal of the Republic of Poland 1993 Vol. 17, Item 78). The Tribunal's decision designated as case no. K 1/20 is available from the internet database at https://ipo.trybunal.gov.pl/ipo/Sprawa?cid=1&dokument=20359&sprawa=22412 (27.04.2023).

2021).[8] The judgment was given by a panel of 13 judges, and five judges issued separate opinions (two dissenting opinions, three concurring).

From word use to *topoi* and values

In a large-scale, quantitative study spanning the period between 1989 and 2009, Matczak and Łajszczak (2015) analyze lexical items referencing the principles, values and interpretative methods most frequently used by Constitutional Tribunal judges. Their findings suggest that the Tribunal's constitutional interpretation is characterized by clear axiological concerns, as evidenced by the co-occurrences of the term *wartość* ('value') (as in *wartość konstytucyjna* ('constitutional value'), *wartości i zasady* ('values and principles') and *wartość życia* ('value of life')). Yet, according to the same study, references to specific values are rare (2015: 152). The axiological system is autonomous in the sense that it is based on legal provisions without necessarily referring to other external systems, such as Christian values or ethics. Concepts such as *dobro* ('good') or *moralność* ('morality') are only found in contexts derived from legislative provisions: *dobro wspólne* ('common good') and *moralność publiczna* ('public morality'). According to Matczak and Łajszczak (2015), this may suggest that the Constitutional Tribunal's adjudication is either marked by judicial passivism (as no other values than those introduced by the legislator are invoked) or that the judges only refer to other values by projecting them as constitutional values. In conclusion, the authors call for a more context-sensitive and qualitative analysis as complementary to large-scale quantitative analyses. The findings documented in this section are intended as a step towards filling that gap in the legal–linguistic research.

As a first step, I used a frequency analysis to identify the potentially value-indicating words underlying the tribunal's justification in both its majority and dissenting opinions. Fifty of the most frequent nouns were taken into account, based on lemmas rather than word forms so as to include inflectional forms. Appendix A lists the lexical items along with their English translations. This stage was followed by a close reading of co-texts surrounding these words to determine their semantic content and the function they perform in the analyzed texts.

In the Polish justifications, the primary axiological focus appears to be on *życie* ('life'), which is overall the most frequent term, and on *godność* ('dignity') (the twentieth most frequent word). The frequencies of words such as *prawo* ('right') and *ochrona* ('protection') suggest that the judges discuss *life* mainly

8 For example, some legal experts argue that the ruling was given by a panel of judges which included judges who had been improperly appointed and were not qualified to adjudicate. The same complaint of improper appointment is raised with regard to the president (Chief Justice) of the Constitutional Tribunal. In addition, the ruling was published well after its statutory deadline, which breached a constitutional requirement. In Poland, constitutional court rulings must be officially published to take effect.

in terms of its *protection* and the *right to life*. Worth noting is the occurrence of words denoting categories of protected persons. The word *dziecko* ('child') is used twice as frequently as *kobieta* ('woman') or *matka* ('mother'), indicating that the focus in the justifications tends to be more on the child's or the foetus's rights to life and dignity rather than on the mother's rights.[9] The view that Polish justifications exhibit a major concern with axiology is corroborated by the occurrences of the word *wartość* ('value'), which are relatively frequent in comparison with the findings reported in Matczak and Łajszczak (2015). Below, I start by considering the co-occurrence patterns for this term.

Overall, the frequency of *wartość* ('value') shows that values are often invoked explicitly rather than implied. Analysis of the concordance lines can reveal some of the ways in which judges use values in their argumentation. If we consider how the *wartość* ('value') is modified, it becomes clear that the reasoning relies on high, abstract values and generalizations. The co-occurring words modifying *wartość* indicate that the axiological basis consists of three major types of value: constitutional values (*wartości konstytucyjne*), values which are universal (*uniwersalny*) and inalienable (*niezbywalne*) and values related to common humanity (*ogólnoludzkie*). Many comparative forms occur in phrases such as *niższa wartość* ('lower value'), *większa wartość* ('greater value'), *najwyższej wartości* ('the highest value') and verbs related to measurement and weight, *mierzyć* ('measure') and *ważyć* ('weigh').

These lexical items signal that the identification of the relevant values and principles provides a necessary context for balancing and weighing (cf. Sieckmann 2013; Alexy 2002, 2003).

The Word Sketch of *wartość* also shows that the term is often found in coordinated noun phrases (see the section below marked as 'coord'). The presence of these co-occurrences is evidence of values being discussed in conjunction with other principles: *zasady* ('rules'), *reguły* ('rules'), *norma* ('norms'), *dobra* ('goods'), and *interesy* ('interests'). In addition, it becomes clear that values interact with one another when they are juxtaposed. The two explicitly named values are *wolność* ('freedom') and *godność* ('dignity'). Interestingly, the most frequent term, *życie* ('life'), is not found in the Word Sketch. On closer examination, it turns out that when referred to explicitly as a 'value', *życie* is found as the object of most of the verbs provided in Figure 5.1 (sections marked as post_verb and prec_verb), such as *mierzyć* ('measure'), *odznaczać się* ('be characterized by'), or *zważyć* ('weigh'). Example (1) is just one instance, indicative of how the argumentation revolves around the values of *life* and *dignity* and how the two are interconnected. More specifically, it expresses an argument that life is not amenable to any form of measurement because of its inherent dignity.

9 Note that the word *płód* 'foetus' is also more frequent, albeit slightly, than *kobieta* and *matka*.

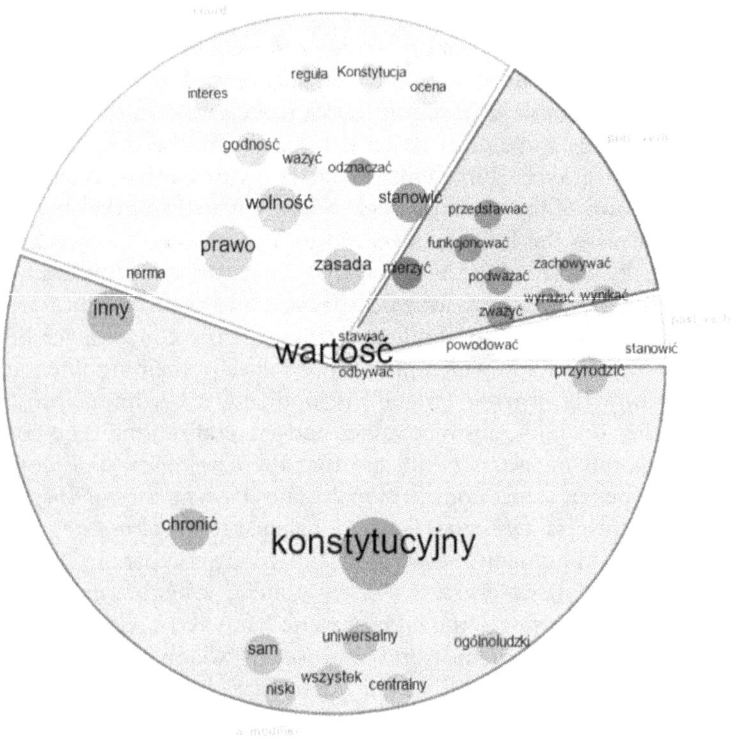

Figure 5.1 A Word Sketch visualization of the most frequent collocates of *wartość* ('value') in the justifications of the Constitutional Tribunal of Poland.

> (1) W moim przekonaniu, eksponowana w Konstytucji przyrodzona, niezbywalna i nienaruszalna **godność człowieka** nie pozwala **mierzyć wartości życia ludzkiego** (i zakresu jego ochrony prawnej) długością tegoż życia.
>
> [In my view, the inalienable, inherent and inviolable **human dignity** does not allow one to **measure the value of human life** (and the scope of its legal protection) by referring to its length.][10]

We now turn to focus on the term *życie* ('life') and its connection with *godność* ('dignity'), as the two appear to constitute the axiological basis for the ensuing argumentation. The arguments in both majority and dissenting opinions are structured around this pair of values.

10 The examples taken from the Constitutional Tribunal's opinions and used in this chapter were translated by the author, unless otherwise indicated.

A Word Sketch created for the term *życie* shows in more detail the context in which the term is used. As we see in Figure 5.2 (the section marked as 'coord'), *życie* co-occurs with other abstract nouns: *zdrowie* ('health'), *śmierć* ('death') and, indeed, with *godność* ('dignity'). The way the word is modified (see the section marked as 'a_modifier') reveals differing views on *life* that appear in both majority and separate opinions, but which can be traced to different types of opinion. For example, the words *prywatny* ('private'), *swój* ('own') and *osobisty* ('personal') are mostly found in dissenting arguments, ones which raise the question of the woman's right to privacy and to make her own decisions regarding her personal life. The life of foetus, especially its viability, is discussed using words such as *rozwijać* ('develop'), *samodzielny* ('independent') or *prenatalny* ('prenatal'). The other sections of the Word Sketch highlight the most frequent verbal collocates: *zagrażać* ('threaten'), *chronić* ('protect'), or *stawać się* ('become'), as in the following example.

(2) Od momentu powstania **życie ludzkie** staje się więc **wartością chronioną konstytucyjnie**.

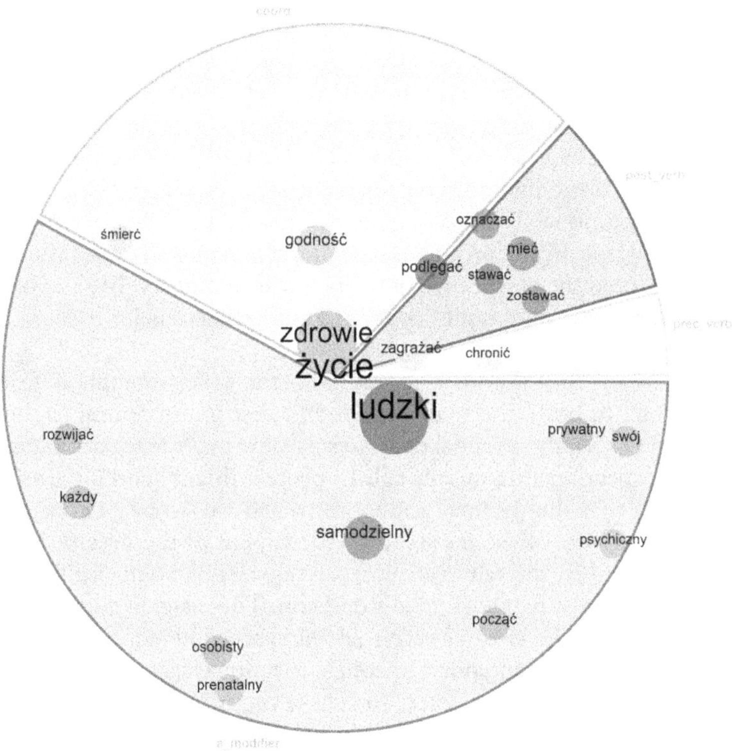

Figure 5.2 A Word Sketch visualization of the most frequent collocates of the term *życie* ('life') in the justifications of the Constitutional Tribunal.

[Since its inception, **human life** becomes a **constitutionally-protected value**.]

Example (2) validates *life*, or more precisely *human life*, as a constitutional value. In addition, it marks the temporal aspects of the protection afforded, which, as we shall see later, turns out to be a contentious point. There are 18 instances in which *life* and *dignity* are found juxtaposed in conjoined noun phrases, as in the following two examples.

(3) Wobec powyższego należało uznać, że poprzez ingerencję w istotę godności człowieka, ustawodawca art. 4a ust. 1 pkt 2 oraz art. 4a ust. 2 zdanie pierwsze ustawy o planowaniu rodziny naruszył swoje konstytucyjne obowiązki dotyczące prawnej ochrony **godności i życia**, a kwestionowana norma jest niekonstytucyjna.
(niezgodna z art. 30 i art. 38 Konstytucji)

[Given the foregoing, it should be emphasized that the legislator has violated its constitutional duty to provide legal protection of dignity and life by interfering with the nature of human dignity and the contested norm [contained in the Act on Family Planning] is unconstitutional.]

(4) Trybunał Konstytucyjny] uwzględnił tylko jedną perspektywę – perspektywę ochrony życia w fazie prenatalnej. Pominął jednocześnie perspektywę kobiet, których **godność,** życie i zdrowie są niewątpliwie **wartościami** objętymi konstytucyjną ochroną.
[The Constitutional Tribunal (…) took into account only one perspective – the perspective of protecting life in the prenatal phase. At the same time, it ignored the perspective of women whose **dignity, life** and health are undoubtedly values under constitutional protection.]

While (3) comes from the majority opinion, the other example is from one of the dissents. In both, the values of *life* and *dignity* are central to the arguments made. In (3), the tribunal expresses its view that the legislation in question is unconstitutional because it fails to protect dignity and life. In (4), the dissent argues that the tribunal unduly restricted the scope of constitutional protection to the life of the foetus to the detriment of the dignity and life of women. Importantly, the values are accepted as starting points for formulating the arguments to justify the tribunal's decision. The dissents do not challenge the values *per se*. In Perelman's terms (Perelman & Olbrechts-Tyteca 1969), these are abstract values intended to appeal to a universal audience. However, what the dissenting opinions object to is how the concepts of life and dignity are *concretized* in the majority reasoning by confining it to one category. In addition, it is worth pointing out that a threat to life is mentioned mainly in the context of a child's or a foetus's life. The infrequent references to the life or health of the woman are only made when judges cite the relevant law on abortion. In sum, the value-based words and their collocates serve as useful 'entry' into the argumentation contained in the justifications. What follows in the next section is an attempt at reconstructing in greater detail the argument made in the majority opinion based on what the initial analyses above have shown.

The values of *human dignity* and *human life* in the majority and dissents' arguments

It can be reasonably assumed that (apart from human life itself) it is human dignity that serves as the major starting point and *topoi* in the majority reasoning. The Constitutional Tribunal devotes one section of its justification to the concept of human dignity. Entitled *Godność człowieka* ('human dignity'), Section 3.1 opens with a reference to Article 30 of Poland's constitution.

> (5) The inherent and inalienable dignity of the person shall constitute a source of freedoms and rights of persons and citizens. It shall be inviolable. The respect and protection thereof shall be the obligation of public authorities.[11]

Citing also its own previous case law, the majority asserts that human dignity as such is not a right. Rather, it is the foundation and the source from which all rights are derived. Because dignity is the source of rights, it cannot be in any way restricted by them. It does not need to be legitimized by means of a normative act. The majority opinion applies a value hierarchy whereby it places human dignity at the top of the constitutional axiological system, prioritizing human dignity and projecting it as a value that needs to be respected and protected (K 1/20, Sec. 3.1). According to the majority, dignity is a point of reference for the constitutional system of values underpinning the entire legal order.

While acknowledging the universal nature of human dignity, the majority sets out to distinguish two aspects of human dignity, which are in fact two different senses of the term *dignity*. First, the majority argues, dignity is regarded as an inalienable and inherent human right. Second, citing its earlier decision, the opinion connects dignity with personal rights (*prawo osobistości*) that should be linked with the 'value of human psychological life and all those values that define an individual's position in society and which are worthy of respect'.[12] The distinction is crucial because, as the majority insists, it is only

11 The English translation of the Polish constitution used in this chapter comes from the official website of the Polish parliament available at https://www.sejm.gov.pl/prawo/konst/angielski/kon1.htm (last viewed 20 April 2023). The original text reads: '*Przyrodzona i niezbywalna godność człowieka stanowi źródło wolności i praw człowieka i obywatela. Jest ona nienaruszalna, a jej poszanowanie i ochrona jest obowiązkiem władz publicznych*'.

12 The original text reads as '*wartości życia psychicznego każdego człowieka oraz te wszystkie wartości, które określają podmiotową pozycję jednostki w społeczeństwie i które składają się,*

dignity in the first sense that must always remain intact, while dignity in the second sense could, in practice, be affected by the actions of other people or by other legal provisions.[13] The tribunal expresses its preference for the first understanding of dignity because, in its view, the first has its roots in the existence of a human being and not merely in a sense of well-being. This understanding of dignity then paves the way for reinforcing the link between human dignity and the legal protection of life as such. Invoking Article 38 of the Constitution, the majority further asserts that 'it is not possible to talk about protecting human dignity if there is no sufficient basis for the protection of life.[14].

Arguably, the viability of the causal link between the protection of dignity and the protection of life is made possible by exploiting one sense of the term *dignity* and modifying the meaning of the other crucial term ***human*** in the context of ***human life*** (K 1/20, Sec. 3.3.3). In a rare originalist turn,[15] the Constitutional Tribunal referred to the files of the Constitutional Commission of the National Assembly, which was tasked with drafting the Constitution of 1997, to determine the legislator's intention regarding the meaning of the term ***human***. The outcome of this reference is surprising. Rather than use the files to disambiguate the meaning of the term, the tribunal construed the politically situated parliamentary debate in such a way that it is left to the authority of the tribunal to establish a legal definition of ***human***.

> (6) Given the foregoing, the Tribunal accepts that it was the legislator's intention – in the absence of any express reference to the temporal limits of human life and its protection in the Constitution [...] – to leave it up to the Tribunal to determine the meaning of the term ***human*** as used in the wording of Article 38 of the Constitution.[16]

The tribunal then asserted that human life includes both the prenatal stage and the stage following birth. As a consequence, constitutional protection

---

według powszechnej opinii, na szacunek należny każdej osobie' taken from Constitutional Tribunal's ruling of 5 March 2003, case no. K 7/01.

13 The original text in Polish: *'godność rozumiana jako „prawo osobistości" może być w praktyce przedmiotem naruszenia – „może być «dotknięta» przez zachowania innych osób oraz regulacje prawne'*, taken from Constitutional Tribunal's ruling of 5 March 2003, case no. K 7/01.

14 The legal protection of life is enshrined in Art. 38 of the Constitution which reads: 'The Republic of Poland shall ensure the legal protection of the life of every human being'.

15 This move has attracted criticism pointing towards the tribunal's undue judicial activism to the detriment the legislative power (e.g., Bucholc 2022; Gliszczyńska-Grabias & Sadurski 2021: 141).

16 The original text: '*Mając na uwadze wszystkie powyższe wypowiedzi, Trybunał przyjął, że intencją ustrojodawcy było – wobec braku wskazania expressis verbis w Konstytucji granic temporalnych życia człowieka i jego prawnej ochrony lub wyłączenia w tym zakresie kognicji Trybunału – pozostawienie do rozstrzygnięcia Trybunałowi kwestii dotyczącej wiążącego ustalenia znaczenia pojęcia „człowiek' na gruncie art. 38 Konstytucji*' (K 1/20, Section 3.3.3).

must be extended to cover prenatal life. As we can see, the way the meanings of dignity and human life are construed in the majority opinion illustrates the central importance of such definitions, and it plainly shows how arguers can steer the argumentation in the direction they favour by modifying the definition of a central term. Typically, such modifications are possible because of the open-ended and general nature of legal *topoi*, as well as, in this instance, the generality of the constitutional provisions related to the concepts of life and dignity. It is fair to say that the tribunal's line of argumentation has been the object of very critical comments in the legal literature. It has been pointed out that a close reading of Article 30 posits dignity as a source of *all* rights and freedoms not solely the *right to life*.[17] In addition, it has been pointed out that there is a logical fallacy in the tribunal's argument: if dignity itself is a source rather than a right, then it cannot be invoked as a basis for the legal determination of a right. Instead, dignity can only be used as an 'interpretive tool for rights analysis' (Gliszczyńska-Grabias & Sadurski 2021: 141). In the context of this case, the choice of such an interpretation of dignity carries vital implications for other constitutional rights, especially the right to equality before the law and to non-discrimination (Article 32), bodily inviolability (Article 41) and privacy (Article 47). Indeed, the wording of Article 30 should not be construed to suggest the primacy of the right to life as such.

In the dissenting opinions, the way in which the majority opinion interprets dignity and connects it to rights of the foetus, at the expense of the mother's rights, is directly contested. We saw this in (4), which I reproduce again here for ease of reference:

> (4) The Constitutional Tribunal [...] took into account only one perspective – the perspective of protecting life in the prenatal phase. At the same time, it ignored the perspective of women whose **dignity, life** and health are undoubtedly values under constitutional protection.

The majority opinion interprets *dignity* as inextricably linked to the sheer existence of a human being, in effect relegating other aspects of dignity to an inferior position. This hierarchy of values then allows the tribunal to disregard the dignity of women, a point further raised in another excerpt from the dissenting opinion.

> (7) In the name of protecting life in the prenatal phase – which is not absolute – the Constitutional Tribunal imposed on women the obligation to have a heroic attitude, i.e., the obligation to assume responsibility in all circumstances – regardless of the nature and degree of pathology of the foetal development or the possible consequences for their **life** and

17 Article 30 of the Constitution reads: 'The inherent and inalienable dignity of the person shall constitute a source of freedoms and rights of persons and citizens'.

> **health** with the continuation of pregnancy – sacrifices and hardships far exceeding the usual measure of limitations related to pregnancy, childbirth and raising a child.[18]

It is noteworthy that the counter-argument provided in the dissent is structured around value-based lexis which draws on values that enable the assessment of the legal decision from outside the system: *heroic attitude, sacrifices* and *hardships*. The dissent rebuts the majority's argument based on the value *life*, concretized as the protection of foetal life, by invoking the value of women's life and health. Interestingly, the dissent's counter-argument draws attention to the value *life* by foregrounding possible negative consequences of pregnancy and childbirth for the mother's life and health. The consequences are, again, reified as *heroism, sacrifices* and *hardships*.

In sum, the examination of value-based lexis is useful because it brings to light the foundations of the arguments used in the justifications. The justifications consist of arguments based on common legal starting points, such as the protection of life and dignity, as well as arguments based on moral values commonly accepted in the relevant legal community and culture. At the same time, the abstract values, when concretized, become sites of contention. As we have seen, the dissenting opinions invoke the concrete value of women's lives in order to challenge the acceptability of the majority arguments and to challenge the views of life and dignity those arguments express.

USSC and *Dobbs v. Jackson Women's Health Organization*

This section considers the use of value-based lexis and evaluative language in another case in which the right to life and the right to liberty are in conflict. *Dobbs v. Jackson Women's Health Organization* is a landmark case that was argued before the USSC on 1 December 2021 and decided 24 June 2022. The case is related to a Mississippi state law, passed in 2018, that bans abortions after 15 weeks of pregnancy except in cases of medical emergency or severe foetal abnormality. The Jackson Women's Health Organization, the only abortion clinic in Mississippi, sued the state over the 2018 law, arguing that it violates the right to access abortion established by *Roe v. Wade*. The case made its way to the USSC, which agreed to hear the case in May 2021. The question addressed by the USSC concerned the constitutionality of Mississippi's 2018 law. The majority opinion of the court, authored by Justice Alito, concludes that the Constitution does not confer the right to abortion access. The USSC thereby reversed two earlier landmark decisions, *Roe v. Wade* and *Planned Parenthood of Southeastern Pa. v. Casey*, which had recognized the fundamental right to abortion access. There were as many as six separate opinions: three concurring, three dissenting.

18 Judge Pszczółkowski's dissent, introductory section at Page 70; translation provided after Gliszczyńska-Grabias & Sadurski (2021).

The same analytical technique used to examine the previous case was applied here in order to identify the most frequent words likely to denote values in both the majority and separate opinions. Appendix B provides a list of the 50 most frequent nouns. There are two terms most associated with abstract axiological concepts: *life* appears as the tenth most frequent word and *liberty* is found as twenty-fifth. Other abstract concepts include *history* and *time* and, given that there are also two other references to time (*year* and *today*), their presence signals the strong temporal orientation in the discourse of the opinions. Topping the frequency list is the term *abortion*, which, incidentally, does not emerge as a frequent term in the Polish case. Note also the very high occurrence of references to *woman* rather than to *foetus* or *child* or even to *mother*. This finding is in stark contrast to the Polish justifications, and it could be taken as indicative of a stronger concern with women as a category of persons affected by the issue of abortion. Two other frequent terms, *Roe* and *Casey*, refer to the two prior landmark cases (*Roe vs Wade* and *Planned Parenthood v. Casey*). Combined with the presence of *precedent* and *stare decisis,* these terms underscore the central importance of precedent, in general, and of the two landmark cases, in particular, in the legal arguments provided in the *Dobbs* case.

In addition, it is worth noting the frequent occurrence of two terms: *issue* and *question*. The examination of their concordance lines suggests that they do not only carry the rather obvious discourse function of signalling topic change in the text of the opinion (e.g., *The Court therefore turns to the question that, address this issue*), but they are also used to signal axiological content. This can be seen in the co-occurrences of *moral* and *question* or *issue* (e.g., *critical moral question, fundamental moral question, underlying moral question, profound moral issue*). For example, the court, in its primary holding, refers to abortion as 'presenting a profound moral question'. One possible explanation for this is that this is the preferred way for the judges to address the axiological aspect of the case. Unlike the Polish case, in which the term *wartość* ('value') is relatively frequent, the *Dobbs* opinion avoids framing the issue explicitly in terms of 'value'.[19] Note also another 'discourse-oriented' term, *reason*, which contributes to the justificatory tone of the text (*for reasons already explained, that is not correct for reasons we have already discussed*). Its frequent occurrence signals that Justice Alito, who drafted the majority opinion, not only explains the legal choices made in the decision but also attempts to convince others that this choice was sound.

This brief overview suggests that the discourse of justification in the *Dobbs* case is not replete with general values at a high level of abstraction, even if *life* and *liberty* are also salient lexical items (which we will examine in some detail below). Bearing in mind that, in the *Dobbs* case, the USSC set out to determine whether the Constitution protects the right to abortion access, then the

19 The lexeme value appears in the entire case only 12 times.

term *right*, the fifth most frequent word, can provide a useful point of entry into what forms the bedrock of the argumentation. It seems natural, therefore, to begin a more detailed analysis by considering the lexical co-occurrences of this term, summarized and visualized in Figure 5.3.

The co-occurring lexis which modifies 'right' shows that the term is used in multiple contexts: constitutional right to abortion access, other fundamental rights (for example those including marriage and intimacy), a broader right to bodily autonomy (invoked to justify the right to abortion access), substantive rights (for example, those rights guaranteed by the first eight Amendments to the Constitution), reproductive rights and unenumerated rights. The last category, unenumerated rights, is discussed in terms of the conditions for recognizing and protecting rights unknown at the time when the Constitution was created (as was clearly the case with the right to abortion access) and the question of creating new rights and liberties.

The next biggest category groups verbs with *right* as object. Several verbs found in this category signal major issues raised in both majority and separate opinions. The frequent occurrence of *confer*, *protect*, *support* or *recognize* reflects

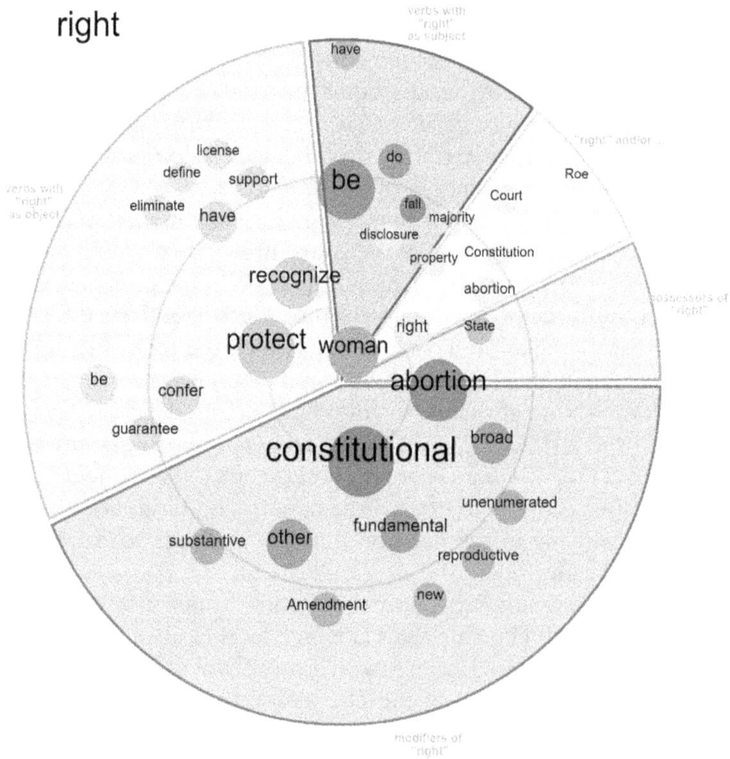

Figure 5.3 A Word Sketch visualization of the most frequent collocates of 'right' in the justification of the *Dobbs* case.

the disagreement on whether the Constitution affords the right to abortion access and protects that right and the extent to which this right is similar or dissimilar to other rights recognized and mentioned in the Constitution and in past decisions. The combination of *have* and *right(s)* alludes to the argument that prenatal life has rights (but the argument is nowhere near as robust as in the Polish case discussed above) and the competing right to choose to terminate a pregnancy. The same issues are addressed using another category of verbs with *right* as subject. For example, the arguments focus on *whether the right is 'deeply rooted in [our] history and tradition'*, or whether *the abortion right is an integral part of a broader entrenched right* (right to privacy).

One could expect to uncover a broader axiological basis for the argumentation by considering the co-occurrences of *right* with other, possibly value-based nouns, but there were no such findings. As we see in Figure 5.3, *right* or *rights* are discussed in the context of the Constitution, and, more precisely, the first eight Amendments to the Constitution. The term *property* is mentioned in the context of assessing the consequences of the ruling, in particular of assessing whether overruling *Roe* and *Casey* would upend concrete reliance interests (such as those involving property and contract rights). The last category of possessors of *right* confirms what was already mentioned earlier as contributing to the greater emphasis on women in the US justifications. The collocational analysis shows sharply divided views on *woman's right*, as reflected in highly polarized language. The woman's right is *invaded, curtailed, removed, not recognized, withdrawn* but also *protected, safeguarded* (until the time of the ruling, at least) and it is *the most central principle*. The *right to abortion* serves as a starting point for the arguments used in the reasoning of both the majority and dissenting opinions.

As we recall, *życie* ('life') is one of the major value premises in the Polish majority opinion, and it is the tenth most frequent noun in the *Dobbs* case. In what follows, the focus shifts to consider collocates of *life*. There are some similarities in how the terms are modified (both as *human life* or *prenatal life*) and how they are made the object of *protecting* and *preserving* life. In the *Dobbs* case, the term *life* appears in contexts alluding to certain concrete values (*women* as the centre of *home and family life*, the ability of women to participate equally in the *economic and social life of the nation*), even if it is never explicitly named as a value. Interestingly, as the category of *possessors of life* shows, *women's life* and *mothers' life* are also statistically salient, unlike the Polish opinion in which the focus is predominantly on prenatal life. In the *Dobbs* case, the picture is much less uniform. The life of the mother and of the woman is mentioned in terms of it being saved and preserved. As we see in Figure 5.4, these references are not infrequent. Yet, *life* is not linked to the concept of *dignity*, as is typical in human rights cases (Valentini 2017; McCrudden 2008). Instead, there is an association with *liberty*, which can be accounted for by references to the Fourteenth Amendment's guarantee that no state shall 'deprive any person of life, liberty, or property without due process of law'. In addition, most references to the term *life* are found

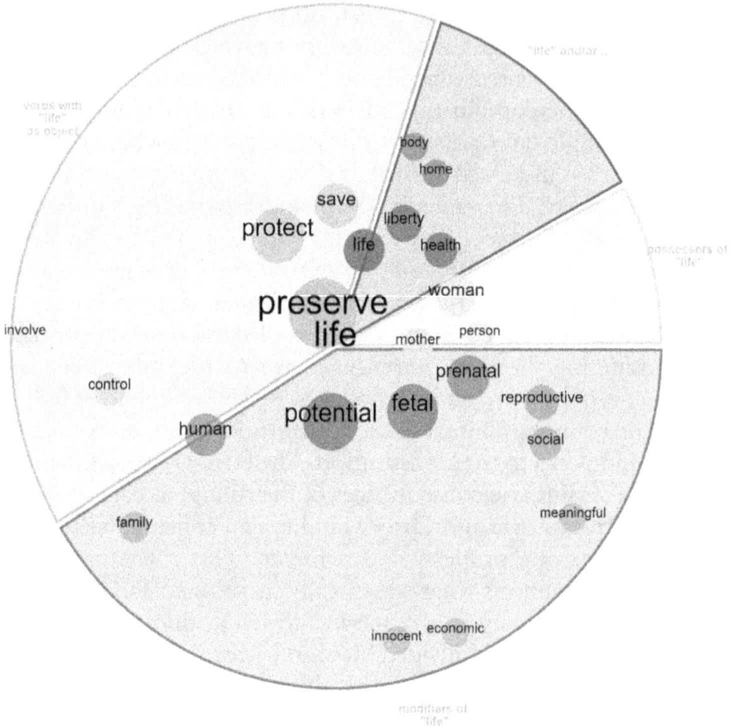

Figure 5.4 A Word Sketch visualization of the most frequent collocates of 'life' in the justifications of the *Dobbs* case.

in dissenting opinions. This asymmetry suggests that neither *life* nor *liberty* should be treated as forming common lines of argument or common starting points.

This analysis points towards *rights* as a pivotal point in the opinions and in the underlying premises of the arguments. The reluctance to apply value-based argumentation that involves the balancing of competing rights, as was done in the Polish case, can be attributed to the nature of the *Dobbs* case. *Dobbs v. Jackson* states that the Constitution does not confer a right to abortion access and that the authority to regulate abortion is 'returned to the people and their elected representatives'.[20] To arrive at this conclusion, the court reversed its own precedents, *Roe v. Wade* and *Planned Parenthood of Southeastern Pennsylvania v. Casey*, which asserted the fundamental right to abortion access. The majority opinion indicates that the method of interpretation is textualist (and some would argue originalist).

20 See the description of the case available from https://www.law.cornell.edu/wex/dobbs_v._jackson_women%27s_health_organization_%282022%29

(8) Constitutional analysis must begin with 'the language of the instrument, which offers a 'fixed standard' for ascertaining what our founding document means. The Constitution makes no express reference to a right to obtain an abortion, and therefore those who claim that it protects such a right must show that the right is somehow implicit in the constitutional text.

(*Dobbs*, No. 19-1392, slip op. at *9)

It is striking the extent to which evaluative language, rather than value-based lexis, is used to assess the reasoning in the two overturned cases here. It is, therefore, instructive to look at the first two paragraphs of the court opinion delivered by Justice Alito[21] (emphasis mine).

(9) Abortion presents a profound moral issue on which Americans hold sharply conflicting views. Some believe fervently that a human person comes into being at conception and that abortion ends an innocent life. Others feel just as strongly that any regulation of abortion invades a woman's right to control her own body and prevents women from achieving full equality. Still others in a third group think that abortion should be allowed under some but not all circumstances, and those within this group hold a variety of views about the particular restrictions that should be imposed.

For the first 185 years after the adoption of the Constitution, each State was permitted to address this issue in accordance with the views of its citizens. Then, in 1973, this Court decided Roe v. Wade, 410 U.S. 113. *Even though* the Constitution *makes no mention of* abortion, the Court held that it *confers a broad right to obtain one.* It did not claim that American law or the common law had ever recognized such a right, and its survey of history ranged from the *constitutionally irrelevant* (e.g., its discussion of abortion in antiquity) to the *plainly incorrect* (e.g., its assertion that abortion was probably never a crime under the common law). After cataloging a wealth of other information *having no bearing on the meaning of the Constitution*, the opinion concluded with a numbered set of rules *much like those that might be found in a statute enacted by a legislature.*

These two paragraphs provide a good illustration of the overall strategy adopted in the majority's justification. In the first, Justice Alito recognizes that abortion is a matter of enormous moral import and that diametrically opposed views on abortion are widespread. It is the freedom to hold different views, as

21 This excerpt was taken from https://supreme.justia.com/cases/federal/us/597/19-1392/#tab-opinion-4600822

reflected in the right of each state to decide, that the opinion prioritizes. *Roe v. Wade* is framed as a case that broke with the age-old tradition of granting each state that freedom. What follows is a clear indication that the negative evaluation of *Roe v. Wade* (and also of *Planned Parenthood v. Casey*) is the true engine of argumentation in *Dobbs*. The evaluation starts when the decision in *Roe* to confer a right to abortion is contrasted with the textualist argument that the Constitution does not mention abortion. This is followed with some negatively charged evaluative statements (here italicized) which are directed at the way *Roe* embraced the historical perspective, which is further assessed as *constitutionally irrelevant* and *plainly incorrect*. The assertion of irrelevance is strengthened by the statement that the information contained in it has *no bearing on the meaning of the Constitution*. Neither can the final statement in the paragraph, which compares the conclusion in *Roe* to a legislative act, be regarded as favourable.

To illustrate the role of negatively charged evaluative language in the majority opinion, concordance lines have been created for the term *reasoning*.

As we see in Figure 5.5, the term *reasoning* is used only with reference to *Roe*, and it is marked with clearly negative valuations. There are *glaring deficiencies* in *Roe's* reasoning (Line 14), *Roe's* reasoning was *exceedingly weak* (Line 11), the *weaknesses* in *Roe's* reasoning are *well-known* (Line 10), *Roe's* reasoning quickly drew *scathing scholarly criticism* (Line 8). A critical assessment of *Roe's* reasoning is also linked to its lack of argumentative support: *Casey did not even attempt to bolster Roe's reasoning* (Line 13), *very little of Roe's reasoning was defended or preserved* (Line 12), *pointedly refrained from endorsing most of its reasoning* (Line 9), *even abortion supporters have found it hard to defend Roe's reasoning* (Line 1).

The majority in *Dobbs* focuses on a critical appraisal of *Roe* which held that the right to abortion access is part of a right to privacy that comes from the First, Fourth, Fifth, Ninth, and Fourteenth Amendments. The appraisal includes the opinion, in *Planned Parenthood of Southeastern Pa. v. Casey*, which grounded its decision solely on the theory that the right to obtain an abortion is part of the 'liberty' protected by the Fourteenth Amendment's Due Process Clause. The majority argues that the opinion in *Casey* did not delve into the question of whether the Constitution confers a right to access abortion, and that *Casey* reaffirmed *Roe* solely on the basis of the doctrine of *stare decisis*. A proper application of *stare decisis*, the majority in *Dobbs* insists, requires an assessment of the strength of the grounds on which *Roe* was based. That is why *Roe's* reasoning was subjected to such scrutiny, and this may help account for the density and intensity of the explicitly negative language.

It is interesting to note that the evaluation of *Roe* and *Casey* is shared in both the majority and dissenting opinions. Examination of the contexts in which the term *Roe* is found in the dissenting opinions reveals positive appraisals of *Roe* and *Casey* (Examples (10)–(14), with emphasis added). Interestingly, the appraisal in (10) relies on invoking the values of liberty and equality and on

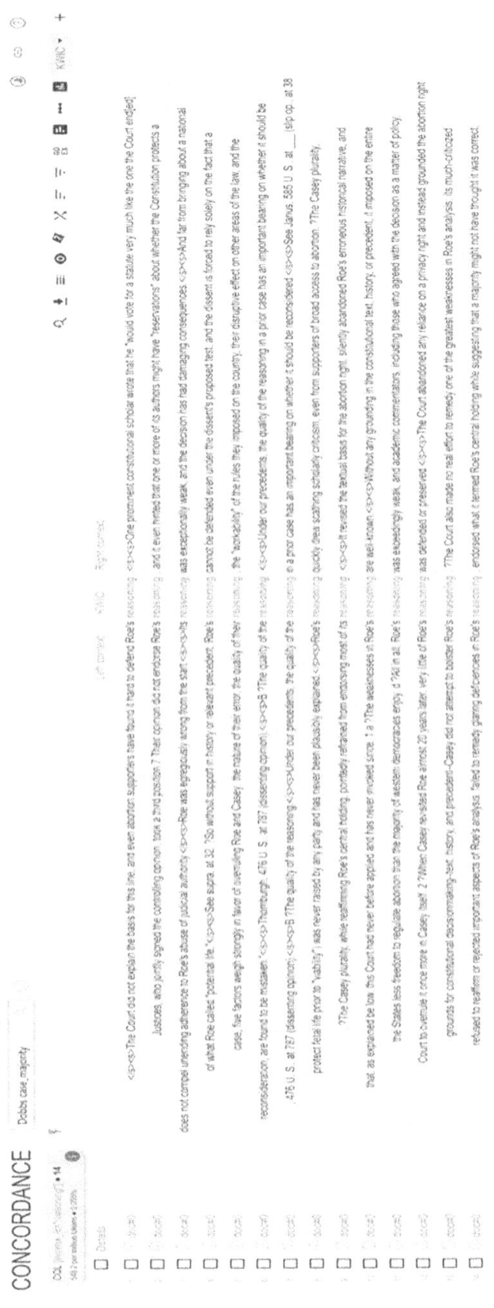

Figure 5.5 A Sketch Engine visualization showing concordance lines with 'reasoning' as keyword in context.

acknowledging the instrumental role played by *Roe* and *Casey* in guaranteeing a woman's right to autonomy and bodily integrity.

> (10) For half a century, Roe v. Wade, 410 U. S. 113 (1973), and Planned Parenthood of Southeastern Pa. v. Casey, 505 U. S. 833 (1992), have **protected** the **liberty** and **equality** of women. Roe held, and Casey reaffirmed, that the Constitution **safeguards** a **woman's right to decide for herself** whether to bear a child.
>
> (11) The legal framework Roe and Casey developed to balance the competing interests in this sphere has **proved workable** in courts across the country.

It also demonstrates how the positive evaluation interacts with the majority's arguments, which are, in turn, the object of negative assessment (italicized).

> (12) '*The majority has no good reason for the upheaval in law and society it sets off.* Roe and Casey have been the law of the land for decades, shaping women's expectations of their choices when an unplanned pregnancy occurs'.
>
> (13) '*To hear the majority tell the tale,* Roe and Casey are aberrations: They came from nowhere, went nowhere–and so are easy to excise from this Nation's constitutional law. *That is not true*'.
>
> (14) A multitude of decisions supporting that principle led to Roe's recognition and Casey's reaffirmation of the right to choose; and Roe and Casey in turn supported additional protections for intimate and familial relations. *The majority has embarrassingly little to say about those precedents.*

In (12) the dissent focuses on the consequences of the court's ruling and the reversal of *Roe* and *Casey*. The consequences are assessed negatively as *upheaval in law and society*. Framed as unwelcome change, the impact is contrasted with an evaluation of *Roe* and *Casey* as established and time-honoured law which has provided legal certainty for women in relevant matters. In sum, my analysis shows that it is the evaluation of the reasoning in these cases and the impact of these now overturned landmark cases that constitutes the major site of contention around which the arguments of the majority and the dissenting opinions are centred. In each instance, language plays an indispensable role. The major difference between these uses of evaluative language is brought to life by analyzing two cases based on value judgment concerning a conflict between the right to life and the right to liberty and bodily integrity. One of the cases was heard by the USSC, the other by the Constitutional Tribunal of Poland.

Summary and Conclusions

Two very important cases concerning the morally sensitive issue of abortion have been explored here to demonstrate how the examination of evaluative language can provide useful insights into judicial argumentation. Corpus-assisted analysis can help identify values or general principles as potential legal *topoi* and starting points used in argumentation schemes. Using widely accepted values or principles as starting points is a rhetorical strategy that helps judges persuade audiences of the soundness of their decisions. It should be stressed that quantitative analysis only provides a list of potentially relevant terms and that their relevance as values underlying rules, principles and legal institutions must be corroborated by means of a close reading of their contexts and the entire text of the opinion. In other words, value-based lexis can provide linguistic clues to help in the reconstruction of arguments. The present chapter has shown that this method can be applied in very different linguistic and legal contexts.

In the Polish case, the majority opinion adopts *human life* and *dignity* as explicitly named constitutional values that form the bedrock of its reasoning. Both represent commonly accepted legal values evoked in order to gain audience acceptance in a case that is highly controversial. The majority applies a value hierarchy which prioritizes *human dignity* within the constitutional axiological system. It also distinguishes two senses of the term *dignity*. One sense of *dignity* is conceptualized as an inalienable and inherent human value which is constitutionally protected; the other sense of *dignity*, associated with personal rights, could in practice become affected by the actions of other people or by legal provisions. The meaning of *dignity* is, therefore, context-specific. Instead of providing a basis for principled decision-making, such a protean concept seems open to significant judicial manipulation. Further, the majority modifies the meaning of *human life* to include prenatal life in order to give foetuses full constitutional protection. In other words, the majority attributes a specific argumentative role to the legal principle of protecting human life and dignity. The collocational analysis of the term *wartość* ('value') signals that the majority opinion uses the argumentative scheme of balancing and weighing, and the principle of proportionality in particular, to resolve the conflict between competing rights. The dissenting opinions accept human life and dignity as general principles and starting points, but they object to the way the majority interprets them in its argumentation.

In the *Dobbs case*, the corpus-assisted analysis of value-based lexis helps to identify 'life' and 'liberty' as axiological concepts relevant to the argumentation. But it is the term 'right', and the broader concept of 'right to abortion access', that is both the starting point and site of contention around which the arguments of the majority and dissenting opinions revolve. Interestingly, the evaluation of the reasoning in *Roe* and in *Casey* produces another site of contention. The majority opinion chooses textualism as its method of interpretation, and it devotes considerable attention to the critical assessment of the reasoning in *Roe* and *Casey*. In contrast, the dissenting evaluations are favourable, and their evaluations of *Roe* and *Casey* are to engage critically with the majority arguments.

Bibliography

Alexy, R. (2002). *A theory of constitutional rights* (J. Rivers, Trans.). Oxford University Press. (Originally published 1985)

Alexy, R. (2003). On balancing and subsumption: A structural comparison. *Ratio juris*, *16*(4), 433–449.

Aristotle. (2009). *The basic works of Aristotle* (R. McKeon, Trans.). Random House. (Originally published 1941)

Bucholc, M. (2022). Abortion law and human rights in Poland: The closing of the jurisprudential horizon. *Hague Journal on the Rule of Law, 14*(1), 73–99.

da Silva, V.A. (2011). Comparing the incommensurable: Constitutional principles, balancing and rational decision. *Oxford Journal of Legal Studies, 31*(2), 273–301. https://doi.org/10.1093/ojls/gqr004

Feteris, E.T. (2017). *Fundamentals of legal argumentation: A survey of theories on the justification of judicial decisions*. Springer.

Feteris, E.T., & Kloosterhuis, H. (2013). Law and argumentation theory: Theoretical approaches to legal justification. SSRN: https://ssrn.com/abstract=2283092 or http://dx.doi.org/10.2139/ssrn.2283092

Frost, M. (2016). *Introduction to Classical Legal Rhetoric*. Routledge.

Gliszczyńska-Grabias, A., & Sadurski, W. (2021). The Judgment that wasn't (but which nearly brought Poland to a standstill) "judgment" of the Polish Constitutional Tribunal of 22 October 2020, K1/20. *European Constitutional Law Review, 17*(1), 130–153.

Grabowska-Moroz, B. and Łakomiec, K. (2021) Glosa do wyroku TK z 22.10.2020, K 1/20. *Państwo i Prawo 8*, 251-56.

Kelemen, K. (2018). *Judicial dissent in European Constitutional Courts: A comparative and legal perspective*. Routledge.

Macagno, F., & Walton, D. (2014). *Emotive language in argumentation*. Cambridge University Press.

MacCormick, N. (2009). *Rhetoric and the rule of law: A theory of legal reasoning*. Oxford University Press.

Malmkjaer, K. (2004). *The linguistics encyclopedia* (2nd ed.). Routledge.

Małolepszy, M., & Głuchowski, M. (2022). Argumentation and legal interpretation in the criminal decisions of the Polish Supreme Court and the German Federal Court of Justice: A comparative view. *International Journal for the Semiotics of Law, 35*(5), 1797–1815. https://doi.org/10.1007/s11196-021-09843-9

Matczak, M., & Łajszczak, Sz. (2015). Wartości, zasady i typy wykładni w orzecznictwie Trybunału Konstytucyjnego: Badanie ilościowe słownictwa użytego w uzasadnieniach orzeczeń. In T. Stawecki & J. Winczorek (Eds.), *Wykładnia konstytucji. Inspiracje, teorie, argumenty* (pp. 461–482). Warszawa.

Macagno, F. and Walton, D. (2016). *Emotive Language in Argumentation*. Cambridge University Press.

McCrudden, Ch. (2008). Human dignity and judicial interpretation of human rights. *European Journal of International Law, 19*(4), 655–724. https://doi.org/10.1093/ejil/chn043

Partington, A., Duguid, A. & Taylor, Ch. (2013). *Patterns and meanings in discourse: Theory and practice in corpus-assisted discourse studies (CADS).* John Benajmins Publishing.

Perelman, Ch. (1976). *Logique juridique: Nouvelle Rhétorique.* Dalloz.

Perelman, Ch., & Olbrechts-Tyteca, L. (1969). *The new rhetoric: A treatise on argumentation*, University of Notre Dame Press.

Sadurski, W. (2019). *Poland's Constitutional Breakdown.* Oxford University Press.

Sieckmann, J. (2013). Is balancing a method of rational justification sui generis? In Ch. Dahlman & E. Feteris (Eds.), *Legal argumentation theory: Cross-disciplinary perspectives* (pp. 189–206). Springer.

Śledzińska-Simon, A. (2019). *Analiza proporcjonalności ograniczeń konstytucyjnych praw i wolności: Teoria i praktyka.* E-Wydawnictwo, Prawnicza i Ekonomiczna Biblioteka Cyfrowa.

Soboleva, A. (2022). Law as a system of *topoi*: Sources of arguments v. sources of law. In A. Condello (Ed.), *New rhetoric for contemporary legal discourse* (pp. 156–170). Edinburgh University Press.

Toulmin, S.E. (1958). *The uses of argument.* Cambridge University Press.

Valentini, L. (2017). Dignity and human rights: A reconceptualisation, *Oxford Journal of Legal Studies, 37*(4), 862–885. https://doi.org/10.1093/ojls/gqx011

Viehweg, T. (1993) [1953]. *Topics and law: A contribution to basic research in law.* Peter Lang. (Originally published 1953)

Appendix A 50 most frequent lemmas in the Constitutional Tribunal justifications in case no. K 1/20

Frequencies are provided as absolute frequencies (the actual number of occurrences in the corpus). There was no need to provide a number of occurrences (hits) of an item per million tokens because the Polish and US datasets are similar in size.

	Lemma	*Frequency*		*Lemma*	*Frequency*
1.	życie 'life'	1,075	26	kobieta 'woman'	202
2.	prawo 'right'	783	27	ustawodawca 'legislator'	199
3.	trybunał 'tribunal'	699	28	matka 'mother'	191
4.	konstytucja 'constitution'	682	29	prenatalny 'prenatal'	186
5.	ochrona 'protection'	578	30	wynikać 'result from'	186
6.	konstytucyjny 'constitutional'	561	31	dotyczyć 'concern'	182
7.	państwo 'state'	499	32	wartość 'value'	174
8.	punkt 'item' (legal provision)	470	33	przesłanka 'premise'	172
9.	prawny 'legal'	468	34	faza 'phase'	172
10	ciąża 'pregnancy'	458	35	zasada 'rule'	169
11	dziecko 'child'	425	36	stanowić 'constitute'	162
12	przepis '(legal) provision	421	37	sposób 'way''	160
13	móc 'may'	379	38	powinien 'should'	159
14	człowiek 'human (being)'	377	39	uwaga 'draw attention to'	159
15	wyrok 'judgment' (verdict)	324	40	wniosek 'application'	159
16	sprawa 'case'	316	41	zdrowie 'health'	154
17	ustawa 'an act of Parliament'	313	42	przypadek 'in case of'	153
18	mieć 'have'	306	43	zostać 'become'	148
19	ludzki 'human'	281	44	orzeczenie 'ruling'	148
20	godność 'dignity'	265	45	istota 'nature'	147
21	uzasadnienie 'justification'	253	46	podstawa 'basis', 'grounds'	146
22	zdanie '(part of) provision'	230	47	wskazać 'indicate'	143
23	przerwać 'terminate'	229	48	dopuszczalność 'admissibility'	141
24	zakres 'scope'	228	49	norma 'norm'	140
25	płód 'foetus'	220	50	sytuacja 'situation'	138

Appendix B 50 most frequent lemmas in the justifications of *Dobbs v. Jackson Women's Health Organization*

Lemma		*Frequency*		*Lemma*	*Frequency*
1.	abortion	647	26	health	106
2.	court	539	27	today	105
3.	woman	482	28	part	95
4.	right	464	29	ante	95
5.	roe	432	30	issue	93
6.	casey	363	31	process	90
7.	state	351	32	decisis	89
8.	law	310	33	section	87
9.	decision	259	34	stare	85
10	life	219	35	time	85
11	majority	197	36	brief	78
12	case	188	37	identification	77
13	states	167	38	history	77
14	opinion	160	39	question	76
15	child	151	40	number	75
16	precedent	149	41	united	72
17	pregnancy	149	42	emphasis	71
18	amendment	147	43	intent	70
19	constitution	144	44	people	68
20	year	143	45	instrument	67
21	person	133	46	clause	67
22	rule	129	47	miscarriage	66
23	interest	122	48	reason	65
24	viability	110	49	line	64
25	liberty	108	50	see	64

6 Evaluative language

The model of critical discussion and strategic manoeuvring

The preceding chapters have shown how an examination of evaluative language can furnish clues which enable the researcher to identify specific starting points, single arguments or chains of arguments as manifested in an argumentative pattern. It turns out that linguistic items signalling evaluative attitudes and ascription of value to propositions are often sites of legal contention. That is to say, they are the focal points around which institutional actors, as arguers, formulate their standpoints. One limitation of this approach to the analysis of legal argumentation is that evaluative language can be found in relatively isolated and unconnected instances of argumentative discourse. Consider the following two excerpts from the justifications of the decisions in which courts point to the negative consequences of accepting a rule that moral and religious beliefs can be treated as a valid reasons for denying services or goods.[1]

(1) And any decision in favor of the baker would have to be sufficiently constrained, lest all purveyors of goods and services who object to gay marriages for moral and religious reasons in effect be allowed to put up signs saying 'no goods or services will be sold if they will be used for gay marriages,' **something that would impose a serious stigma on gay persons**.

(2) Stanowisko to zaakceptował Sąd odwoławczy, który uznał, że przekonania religijne danej osoby nie mogą stanowić uzasadnionej podstawy odmowy wykonania usługi, ponieważ mogłoby to **doprowadzić do kompletnego chaosu w stosunkach gospodarczych**.

[This standpoint was accepted by the Appeals Court which was of the opinion that religious beliefs of an individual cannot form a justified

1 The two cases are *Masterpiece Cakeshop, Ltd., et al.* v. *Colorado Civil Rights Commission et al* heard by the US Supreme Court and Case no. II KK 333/17 *Refusal to Provide Services on the Grounds of Freedom of Conscience and Religion* adjudicated before the Supreme Court in Poland.

DOI: 10.4324/9781003333302-9

basis for refusing to provide service because **this could lead to complete chaos in economic relations**.][2]

In both excerpts, evaluative language manifested in the negatively charged *serious stigma* in (1), and *complete chaos* in (2) is used to construct the same type of argumentation, i.e., consequentialist argumentation,[3] in which the judges assess the potential real world consequences of making a particular decision or adopting a particular standpoint. Clearly, in each case, the consequentialist argumentation is embedded within a distinct institutional context.[4] In (1), Justice Kennedy, who authored the majority opinion, signals that the application of the ruling given in favour of the business provider should be limited. Kennedy's argument is used as part of a more general strategy to avoid resolving the fundamental question of whether a business's freedom to choose its customers is more important than preventing discrimination.[5] In (2), the Polish Supreme Court judge reconstructs the consequentialist argumentation used by the lower courts. The argumentation in the appeal procedure, thus, becomes more complex because certain additional differences of opinion must also be reconstructed. In doing so, the Supreme Court is constrained by the requirements of the cassation procedure, which specifies that the judge must verify whether the lower courts correctly applied the legal rules and principles. Arguments and evaluative language invariably occur in specific institutional contexts which delineate the boundaries of the argumentative space within which justification is expressed. Argumentation is not only an inferential procedure, it is also a (communicative) act involving various legal actors. Furthermore, argumentation is embedded in a specific cultural–social (historical) context (van Eemeren & Grootendorst 2004: 52). To overcome its limitations, analysis which focuses on discrete evaluative items used in unrelated instances of argumentative discourse should be expanded to account not only for argumentative patterns used by the arguers but also the overall strategy of an institutional arguer (i.e., the judge) and the relevant extrinsic constraints on the argument. In sum, what is needed is a more holistic and multifaceted view of how evaluative language and legal justification are interrelated. The next sections show how the study of evaluative language can be approached in a way that better reflects the full argumentative reality of legal justification.

2 All the examples from the Polish justification were translated by the author.

3 This type of argument is also known as a 'pragmatic argument or an argument about the desirability or undesirability of a certain proposition' (Bustamante 2013).

4 See Goźdź-Roszkowski (2022[b]) for a detailed comparison of these two cases in which evaluative language is identified in four 'sites of evaluation' corresponding with critical points of judicial argumentation.

5 See Goźdź-Roszkowski (2021) for a detailed analysis of this case from the perspective of the pragma-dialectical theory of argumentation and the concept of 'strategic manoeuvring'.

The pragma-dialectical approach to legal argumentation

In Goźdź-Roszkowski (2021, 2022[a]), I propose to adapt certain concepts from the pragma-dialectical approach (PDA) to legal argumentation to account, in a more systematic way, for the complex interrelation between evaluative language and argumentation. This approach belongs to the dialogical tradition which considers legal argumentation from the perspective of a critical discussion (Aarnio 1987; Alexy 1989; Peczenik 1989). In the dialogic tradition, argumentation is considered rational if it meets certain formal and material standards of acceptability (Kloosterhuis 2013). The pragmatic element in this approach assumes that argumentation is a 'goal-oriented form of language use' and analyzes discussion moves as discrete speech acts. The dialectical component of the theory concurrently treats argumentation as part of a critical exchange of discussion moves, putting the points of view under discussion to a critical test (Feteris 2017: 205).[6] In other words, the justification of a legal standpoint is perceived to be part of a critical discussion 'in which a protagonist defends a standpoint against the anticipated or actual reactions of an antagonist', and argumentation is analyzed as 'an exchange of arguments and counter-arguments' (Kloosterhuis 2013: 73). In most argumentative contexts, the difference of opinion occurs between two parties, but in the legal argumentative contexts, the critical discussion, first and foremost, involves a judge. While paying attention to claims and counter-claims made by the interactants participating in the case, the focus of analysis, therefore, needs to be on the judge, who uses argumentation to solve a legal problem and to convince 'implicit and explicit antagonists of the correctness of his [sic] decision' (Kloosterhuis 2013: 74). This means that legal argumentation should not be viewed as abstracted from the communicative and interactional context in which it is embedded. Nor should it be seen as an abstract argumentative product of a single user, i.e., the judge.

In numerous publications, Feteris (2009, 2012, 2015) has demonstrated how the pragma-dialectical theory can help account for the complexities of argumentative practices in the justifications of judicial decisions.[7] Applied to judicial discourse, the pragma-dialectical theory aims to reconstruct the argumentation of the parties and of the judge, treating these as contributions to a critical discussion which is subject to rational controls. Importantly, this approach takes into account the macro-context of the institutional environment in which the argumentative discourse of legal justification occurs. Legal justification is viewed as a type of communicative activity which has become

6 See Feteris (2017: Chapter 10) for an introduction and an overview of the pragma-dialectic approach to legal argumentation.

7 Pragma-dialectics, as a theory of argumentation, was developed by Frans van Eemeren and Rob Grootendorst in a series of their joint publications (1984, 1992) and with Sally Jackson and Scott Jacobs (1993).

conventionalized in response to specific institutional requirements.[8] It has become conventionalized in order to better fulfil its major goals of administering justice and accounting for how the law has been applied in the present case and in prior cases. Legal justification, thus, represents a *regulated* discussion constrained by rules of procedural and substantive law. The law regulating legal justification regards the procedural and material starting points specific to either a particular legal system as a whole or to a given court of law. All of these constraints strongly affect the structures of the argumentation and the choice of argumentation schemes used to resolve any given difference of opinion.[9] The constrained nature of legal justification – the constrained ways that argumentative discourse is expressed – corresponds to what genre studies terms 'allowable contributions' within highly structured and conventionalized genres (e.g., Aplevich 2011). Arguably, the choices of evaluative language made by judges when they account for their decisions must also fit within the limits of allowable contributions: there are generic limits on how a judge can express evaluations. Judges' evaluative language choices are intertwined with their choice of a specific form of argument or argumentative scheme.

The pragma-dialectical theory offers what it terms the 'ideal model of critical discussion' (IM). The IM is a heuristic tool used to identify relevant points in an argumentative discussion. That is, the IM helps identify points at which argumentation and standpoints are staged and the points which contribute to the resolution of a difference of opinion. The model also functions as a critical tool by specifying the rules for critical discussion and ascertaining whether the discussion 'has been conducive to the resolution of the dispute and for identifying the factors in the discussion process which offer a positive and a negative contribution' (Feteris 2017: 205).[10] The IM distinguishes four stages. First, in the *confrontation stage*, the difference of opinion is established by delineating the scope and content of a dispute. Second, the *opening stage* determines the common legal starting points and the discussion rules, which are understood as a procedure and a system of rules for conflict resolution in a legal case. Third, in the *argumentation stage*, the dialectical goal for the arguers is to determine whether the argumentation is acceptable in terms of the given starting points and methods of evaluation. It is at this point, in the *argumentation stage*, that different arguments and standpoints of the parties are presented.

8 For example, findings reported in Goźdź-Roszkowski (2020) show how justifications of the decisions issued by the Constitutional Tribunal in Poland are becoming more and more uniform and conventional in response to certain institutional requirements. The Constitutional Tribunal now formulates the constitutional problem raised in a complaint in constitutional language. Earlier, the tribunal would typically only reiterate the content of the complaint or charge as phrased by the petitioner.

9 For example, the Constitutional Tribunal judges are bound by the rule that they do not consider facts of a case or resolve issues related to an individual person, whether natural or legal. This means that the Constitutional Tribunal primarily engages in abstract judicial review.

10 These rules have been formulated as the code of conduct for reasonable discussants.

The judge's role is now to decide whether the arguments are acceptable in terms of given legal principles and rules, precedents, interpretation methods and other factors. Finally, in the *concluding stage*, the result of the discussion is presented in the form of the judge's decision. Here, the judge specifies which position in the discussion is justified based on the common legal and factual starting points (Feteris 2017: 221–225).

The IM has the advantage of offering a solid basis on which argumentation can be reconstructed in its entirety. The model not only provides for the argumentative space *per se* but also includes other institutional and external factors which impact the type and structure of the argumentation. In addition, the model takes into account the role of language by considering what type of speech act is involved in realizing a particular argumentative move. For example, Feteris (1989) demonstrates that the final judicial decision, located in the *concluding stage*, is expressed as an assertive declarative speech act.[11] I argue that evaluative language can be analyzed as occurring at several different stages of the critical discussion not only in the *concluding stage*. The use of evaluative language is, however, subordinate to the goal of each stage and the overall common goal of the dialogue. The analytical advantage in the IM can be seen in how it helps us to determine the ways that evaluative language contributes to the realization of each argumentative move in the different stages of the discussion. The pragma-dialectical model can characterize a given justification as an argumentative activity type, allowing, on the one hand, for the universal nature of the four stages (that is, the stages can be hypothesized to occur in most, if not all, judicial justifications) and, on the other hand, their unique realization in a given case. Because of differences in the institutional context and the argumentative reality, the four stages are always realized in distinctive ways. The specific language used in actualizing these stages is a key factor in making every realization unique. However broad and varied they are in real life interactions, I argue that the IM stages can serve as stable points of reference for achieving a functional characterization of the evaluative language used. The guiding points of reference that the IM provides are invaluable because evaluation occurs not only at the micro-level of an utterance but also at a macro-, or textual, level. In addition, evaluation as a discursive practice can be compared across cases that originate in disparate institutional contexts, wherever the rules of the critical discussion are respected.

One of the challenges in adopting the universal IM is in how to apply it to the precisely specific institutional and argumentative contexts of a given legal decision and its justification. To start with, the logical, clear chronological, ideal order of the IM often does not always map onto the argumentative stages found in an actual justification. Before discussing two different cases heard by the Constitutional Tribunal and the Supreme Court, I will first attempt to

11 See Kloosterhuis (2013) for a discussion on reconstructing judicial standpoints in legal decisions.

address a more general question regarding the extent to which it is possible to map the IM stages onto the various, rhetorically oriented parts of justifications. I intend to thereby concretize the IM stages by linking them with specific parts of the justification within the specific institutional context of Constitutional Tribunal adjudication. Unlike US Supreme Court opinions, justifications of the Constitutional Tribunal are examined below to identify specific rhetorical structures realized by means of recurrent functional segments of text (Goźdź-Roszkowski 2020).

The ideal model of a critical discussion (IM) and the legal justification of a Constitutional Tribunal decision

The structure of legal justifications given by the Constitutional Tribunal in Poland reflects Polish court practice, which distinguishes between two major elements: the historical and the legal (Rzucidło-Grochowska 2017). The first two parts (referred to as Part I: *historyczna* 'historical' and Part II: *na rozprawie*, literally 'at the trial') together correspond to what is known as 'procedural history' in common law jurisdictions. The third part, (*uzasadnienie prawne* 'legal justification'), should be seen as justification proper, in which judges provide their reasoning and enunciate in detail the reasons behind their decisions. No specific form is prescribed for this part of the justification, no fixed structure the judge must adhere to.[12] Predictably, judges exercise their own discretion in choosing how to the present their reasons for a decision. However, a study reported in Goźdź-Roszkowski (2020) demonstrates that there are certain recurring elements found in virtually all Constitutional Tribunal justifications.[13] These elements are:

A. Evaluation of the admissibility of an application;
B. Delineating the object of the constitutional review and specifying the constitutional issue in question;
C. Determining the standard of constitutional review;
D. Determining material circumstances in light of the evaluation of whether an application is legitimate;
E. Evaluating the legitimacy of a complaint;
F. Evaluating the effect of a ruling.

12 In terms of their layout (their formal textual organization), the justifications are organized into sections,
but only half of these are given headings. In the remainder of the cases, texts are structured into sections and subsections marked only with Arabic numerals.

13 The analysis is based on a dataset containing 20 justifications (totalling 242,487 words) randomly sampled from the period between 2017 and 2019 that focus on the legal justifications (Part III). The first stage of the analysis seeks to corroborate the occurrence of functional elements identified by legal practitioners (Królikowski 2015).

Several of these elements can be linked to the stages of the IM. The scope and content of the dispute in the IM's *confrontation stage* corresponds to the first two elements, A and B. Depending on how a case is initiated, the tribunal determines whether a legal question, an application or a constitutional complaint fulfils the criteria of admissibility[14]. In pragma-dialectical terms, the tribunal needs to ensure that 'the procedural and substantive rules for presenting and formulating a legal claim are observed' (Feteris 2017: 221) and establish that the tribunal is competent to address a given question or complaint. The tribunal uses relatively formulaic and restricted language to evaluate the admissibility of a case. The key terms here are *przesłanka* ('premise') and *zakres* ('scope').[15] The former is used in the sense of a criterion, and its most frequent collocate is *spełnić* ('fulfil'), as illustrated in the following example, (3), in which the performative *stwierdził* ('find') is combined with a positive evaluation (*spełnia przesłankę* ('has fulfilled the premise/criterion')).

> (3) Wziąwszy powyższe pod uwagę oraz uwzględniwszy okoliczności faktyczne i prawne w sprawie toczącej się przed pytającym sądem, **Trybunał stwierdził, że pytanie prawne Sądu Okręgowego spełnia przesłankę funkcjonalną** (P7/16) [Having taken into account and considered the factual and legal circumstances of the case heard by the petitioning court, **the Tribunal finds that the Circuit Court's legal question has fulfilled the functional premise.**[16]]

Note that the tribunal's evaluation may turn out to be negative if the tribunal rules that a given application, legal question or complaint does not comply with all or some of the admissibility criteria. When the criteria are only partially met, the tribunal tends to limit the scope of admissibility. At this stage, the word *zakres* ('scope') becomes crucial. The word's importance is reflected in headings or subheadings that signal the scope of adjudication and/or discontinuance of an action regarding those parts of an application that were found inadmissible (Goźdź-Roszkowski 2020: 593), for example:

> (4) *Zakres dopuszczalnego orzekania merytorycznego*
> [The scope of permitted adjudication on the merits.]

14 There are basically three ways in which a case can be initiated before the Constitutional Tribunal: applications for deciding a competence dispute, legal questions concerning the compliance of a normative act with the Constitution and constitutional complaints for determining whether legal provisions given by state authorities comply with the Constitution, ratified international treaties and parliamentary statutes. Constitutional complaints are filed with the Constitutional Tribunal once appellate procedures have been exhausted (Garlicki 2007: 57).

15 Both terms are very frequent. The term *przesłanka* is found 821 times in the corpus (665.23 per million tokens and 0.067% of the whole corpus), while the term *zakres* occurs 3,769 times (3,053.89 per million tokens and 0.31% of whole corpus).

16 All the English translations are literal and have been provided by the author.

(5) *Umorzenie postępowania*
[Dismissal of an action.]

(6) *Częściowe umorzenie*
[Partial dismissal of an action]

The second element in the *confrontation stage* specifies the object of the constitutional review and the constitutional issue that the tribunal has to resolve. This move in the argumentation is realized by indicating whether the entire legal provision or only a part of the provision is subject to review. The move may involve describing the content of a challenged legal provision that the tribunal has been petitioned to examine. As seen in (7), the description usually includes verbatim citation of the challenged provision:

(7) **Przedmiotem kontroli Trybunału w niniejszej sprawie jest** art. 245 § 1 ustawy z dnia 6 czerwca 1997 r. – Kodeks postępowania karnego (Dz. U. Nr 89, poz. 555, ze zm.; dalej: k.p.k.). Przepis ten stanowi: 'Zatrzymanemu na jego żądanie należy niezwłocznie umożliwić nawiązanie w dostępnej formie kontaktu z adwokatem, a także bezpośrednią z nim rozmowę; zatrzymujący może zastrzec, że będzie przy niej obecny'. **Zakwestionowany przepis wzbudza zdaniem wnioskodawcy wątpliwości konstytucyjne** w części zawierającej słowa 'zatrzymujący może zastrzec, że będzie przy niej obecny'. Zatem tylko w tej części art. 245 § 1 k.p.k. podlega kontroli konstytucyjnej w niniejszej sprawie.

['**The object of the Tribunal's review in the present case is** Art. 245 §1 of the Act (Code of Criminal Procedure). This provision stipulates that 'the person detained must be allowed to contact a lawyer as soon as possible in a manner deemed accessible, including a direct conversation. The officer making the arrest may insist that they be present during it'. According to the applicant (petitioner), **the challenged provision raises constitutional doubts** regarding its part which includes the words 'The officer making the arrest may insist that they be present during it'.]

In addition, (7) shows how the tribunal can reconstruct the difference of opinion based on doubts expressed by one of the parties. Some forms of doubt and critique can be expressed as standard 'critical questions' routinely posed in a given institutional context. In its current practice, the Constitutional Tribunal tends to reformulate the constitutional problem raised by an applicant by 'translating' it into the language of constitutional norms. In earlier cases, the court merely repeated the contents of an application already described in Part I (historical) of the justification (Królikowski 2015).

In pragma-dialectical terms, all these elements combined contribute to determine the exact difference of opinion. The difference of opinion emerges from a dialogue between the court and the parties. The dialogue is evident in how the tribunal refers to and reacts to the standpoints adopted by the applicants and other actors.

If the *confrontation stage* establishes the object of the dispute, then the *opening stage* sets out to determine rules for conducting the discussion. In the context of judicial argumentation, the dialectical goal at this stage is to ensure that the common legal starting points are all in place. These starting points usually include the rules of substantive and procedural law. Determining the standard of constitutional review, specified above as Element C, belongs to the *opening stage* of the IM. An applicant filing a constitutional complaint must indicate the standard of review, i.e., which constitutional freedoms or rights have become violated, and which constitutional provision can address the substance of these violations. Determining the standard of review becomes a starting point for the next stages of the critical discussion. In practice, however, this can become an area of disagreement among the parties. As such, it can be a major disputed issue that the tribunal is forced to resolve through its own argumentation and by references to legal standpoints adopted by the parties. Example (8) illustrates this practice.

> (8) **Powołanie jako wzorca kontroli** zaskarżonego przepisu art. 2 Konstytucji **opiera się na nieporozumieniu**, ponieważ z przepisu tego nie wynika zasada jawności życia publicznego w znaczeniu, jakie nadali mu wnioskodawcy. Nie może on zatem stanowić właściwego wzorca dla jego kontroli. 43 **W ocenie Marszałka Sejmu**, również art. 61 ust. 1 Konstytucji **nie jest właściwym** wzorcem kontroli.
>
> [Adopting Art. 2 of the Constitution as **standard of review** for the challenged provision **is based on misunderstanding** because the principle of the transparency of public activity cannot be derived from this constitutional provision. Therefore, it cannot constitute an adequate standard of constitutional review. According to the Speaker of the Sejm (lower house of the Polish parliament), Art. 61, Sec. 1 of the Constitution is **not a proper** standard of review either.]

Here, as elsewhere, determining the standard of review involves the use of both argumentative and evaluative language. At times, it may be difficult to draw a clear line between indications of the difference of opinion and the determination of the starting points. It is also in this stage that the tribunal may reveal the methods it uses to carry out its analyses and interpretations. The tribunal's choices of interpretative method are often rationalized with reference to general legal commonplaces. Their choices may themselves also become objects of justification. Example (9) shows one such instance. In (9), the choice of the principle of proportionality as a starting point is justified by referring to the standpoint adopted by the tribunal in its earlier decision.

(9) Za punkt wyjścia prowadzonych rozważań Trybunał Konstytucyjny przyjął **zasadę demokratycznego państwa prawnego**, z której wynikają reguły i zasady, współkształtujące system prawny. Jedną z nich jest zasada proporcjonalności. Zgodnie ze stanowiskiem utrwalonym w orzecznictwie, **zasada proporcjonalności** ma na gruncie Konstytucji ściśle sprecyzowany charakter związany z ochronną funkcją konstytucyjnych praw i wolności człowieka i obywatela (zob. wyrok TK z 31 stycznia 2013 r., sygn. K 14/11).

['*As a starting point for its reasoning,* the Constitutional Tribunal has adopted the **principle of the rule of law** from which are derived rules and regulations constituting the legal system. One of them is the **principle of proportionality.** *According to the position adopted in previous cases,* the principle of proportionality is of a very specific nature connected with the protective function of constitutional rights and freedoms. (see the Constitutional Tribunal decision of 31 January 2013, case no. K 14/11)

(Source: 49/A/2019)'.]

Justifications may vary in the extent to which interpretation and argumentation methods are explicitly named. In many instances, the methods can only be retroactively reconstructed by scrutinizing the text of a justification. In some cases, such as in (10), the tribunal provides additional explanation regarding the rules of what procedures must be followed to adjudicate a case.

(10) Trybunał nie bada stanów faktycznych, ani nie rozstrzyga spraw indywidualnych pod-miotów. Może się odnieść do praktyki stosowania danych przepisów tylko w takim zakresie, by zrekonstruować treść normy prawnej oraz wtedy, gdy przeprowadza test proporcjonalności i ocenia skuteczność i przydatność danej regulacji do realizacji jej celów.

['As a rule, the Constitutional Tribunal does not consider facts of a case, nor does it resolve issues related to individual entities. The Constitutional Tribunal may refer to the actual practice of applying specific provisions to such an extent as to reconstruct the content of a legal norm and in order to carry out the proportionality test and to assess the effectiveness and usefulness of a given regulation regarding the implementation of its goals (CT K 16/17 justification section 3.1)'.]

The tribunal's explanation of the essence of abstract judicial review is intended to clarify the institutional (procedural) constraints imposed on the tribunal, constraints which affect the scope of adjudication and the choice of interpretation or argumentation method.

In terms of the dialogic goal to determine the acceptability of the argumentation, the *argumentation stage* corresponds to the recurring Element E of the Constitutional Tribunal justification. Element E, recall, evaluates the legitimacy of the application or constitutional complaint. Exactly how this move of the justification is realized depends on how the tribunal determines the question of unconstitutionality raised in an application. If the tribunal does not find for the applicant, its argumentation will focus on demonstrating that the application is groundless and unjustified.

> (11) *Przedstawiona* w tym zakresie *przez skarżącą* **argumentacja** wskazująca, że pełnienie funkcji płatnika to praca narzucona przez państwo pod przymusem – tj. pod groźbą kary i pozbawienia wolności – jest, *w ocenie Trybunału*, oczywiście **bezzasadna**.
>
> [*The* **argumentation** *advanced by the Applicant* claiming that [...] is, *according to the Tribunal*, of course **baseless**.]

In general, the Tribunal's argumentation depends on the type of complaint or charge brought by the applicant and the nature of the challenged legal provision. In the case of decisions which rule for the unconstitutionality of a legal provision, the tribunal focuses on describing the process of weighing and balancing the values protected and violated by the provision (Królikowski 2015). The *argumentation stage* of the justification will, therefore, depend on the choice of a particular argumentative scheme as an evaluation method used by the judge to establish the acceptability of the arguments put forward by the parties. At this stage, evaluative language is used to assess argumentation put forward by the petitioner or complainant and to refer to values and general legal principles as the object of a specific argumentation pattern (e.g., weighing and balancing, teleological-evaluative argumentation).

The *conclusion stage* corresponds to the part of a justification in which the judge determines the result of the discussion. It usually coincides with a formal disposition of a case announcing its ruling. The language is, therefore, formulaic, and it carefully indicates the specific legislative provision which has been found unconstitutional, noting whether the provision does not comply with the constitution in its entirety or in part.

> (12) Ze względu na powyższe Trybunał Konstytucyjny **orzekł**, że art. 35 ust. 1 i 4 u.o.z. w zakresie, w jakim przewiduje odpowiedzialność karną za poddawanie zwierząt ubojowi w ubojni (rzeźni) według szczególnych metod wymaganych przez obrzędy religijne, **jest niezgodny** z art. 53 ust. 1, 2 i 5 Konstytucji w związku z art. 9 Konwencji.
>
> [In light of the foregoing, the Constitutional Tribunal **adjudicates** that art. 35 section 1 and 4 of the Act on the Protection of Animals, with regard to criminal responsibility for slaughtering animals using methods required by religious rituals, **is not in compliance** with art. 53, section 1, 2 and 5 of the Constitution and art. 9 of the Convention.]

Judges may justify the result with reference to the outcome of their chosen interpretation or argumentation method. In those cases in which a challenged provision has been found to be unconstitutional, the tribunal can assess the effect of its ruling. The purpose of such evaluation is to address potential ambiguities arising from a tribunal's decision. These may include the effects of the new ruling on previous cases in which the challenged provision was applied, effects on the admissibility of the provision during adjournment (transition) or changes triggered in the legislative sphere by the ruling.

Table 6.1 summarizes the relations between the stages of the IM and the recurrent elements found in the Constitutional Tribunal. At a minimum, the correspondences show that legal justifications can be successfully mapped onto the IM. The presence of a shared core of rhetorical structure, often signalled explicitly in the headings of the sections (Goźdź-Roszkowski 2020), makes it easier to apply the IM to the institutional and argumentative contexts of Constitutional Tribunal decisions.

As we can see, argumentative discourse is not confined to the *argumentation stage*. Establishing certain starting points, such the standard of review, can be far from non-argumentative and may involve the use of negatively charged language. The different stages rely on specific performatives for their realization. Depending on the given stage, and its goal in the overall framework of

Table 6.1 The stages of the Ideal Model of Critical Discussion (IM) and the recurrent elements in a justification of a Constitutional Tribunal (CT) decision

IM stage	*Recurrent element of justification*	*Type of language*
The confrontation stage	Evaluation of the admissibility of an application, delineating the object of the constitutional review and specifying the constitutional issue.	Neutral reporting language; non-evaluative use of language to reconstruct legal standpoints.
The opening stage	Determining the standard of constitutional review; indicating methods of interpretation, type of reasoning; clarification of procedural constraints.	Evaluative language to determine the standard of constitutional review; value-based language to denote legal principles as starting points.
The argumentation stage	Evaluating the legitimacy of an application or constitutional complaint.	Evaluative language used to assess the legitimacy of a complaint or application. Value-based language applied in balancing of values.
The concluding stage	Announcing the decision; providing the outcome of an interpretation or argumentation method; assessing the effect of the decision.	Highly formulaic using fixed expressions.

the critical discussion, evaluative language is used to directly assess the argumentation advanced by various institutional actors and to indicate the choice of the goals and values which legal rules are designed to promote. It may also be used to assess the consequences of certain interpretations and the potential effects of the tribunal's decision. However, it is important to bear in mind that the stages of the IM do not necessary unfold in a specific order and that some stages may only occur implicitly. The relative stability of the elements identified in the tribunal's justifications provides a limited case for perceiving the stages of the IM as corresponding to specific textual segments. In practice, it is important to refer to the complexity of real-life interactions by considering specific cases in their entirety. With this background in mind, we turn to the next section, in which we compare two cases: one from the Constitutional Tribunal in Poland and one from the US Supreme Court.

Between animal sacrifice and religious freedom: A case study in *Church of the Lukumi Babalu Aye v. City of Hialeah* (1993)

In the following section, we will see how the IM can be applied to enable a comparative analysis of two cases heard by the Constitutional Tribunal in Poland and the US Supreme Court. Using the IM, the two cases can be compared directly in terms of their argumentation and the role of evaluative language in each. The *Church of the Lukumi Babalu Aye v. City of Hialeah* is a landmark US Supreme Court case decided in 1993. The case arose after the city of Hialeah, Florida passed several ordinances that effectively banned the practice of animal sacrifice as a form of worship by the Santería religion.[17] The ordinances prohibited possession of animals for sacrifice or slaughter, with specific exemptions for state-licensed activities. The case eventually made its way to the Supreme Court, which ruled in favour of the Church of the Lukumi Babalu Aye, holding that the city's ordinances were unconstitutional.[18]

In Poland, the Constitutional Tribunal, in its decision (K52/13 2014), ruled for the admissibility of ritual slaughter so that animals could be consumed by people of various religious denominations, especially Judaism and Islam. The case was initiated by the Union of Jewish Communities in Poland which challenged the *Act on the Protection of Animals* insofar as it banned and penalized the killing of animals, even though such sacrifices were required by certain rituals in Judaism and Islam. The Constitutional Tribunal found the law unconstitutional.

17 Santería is an Afro-Caribbean religion that combines elements of Catholicism with the West African religion of Yoruba. The sacrifice of animals, especially of chickens, goats and sheep, is a traditional part of worship in Santería.

18 See facts of the case summarized at https://www.oyez.org/cases/1992/91-948 (12 May 2023) and the syllabus of the case at https://www.law.cornell.edu/supct/html/91-948.ZS .html (12 May 2023).

Both cases address the fundamental conflict between freedom of worship and the right of the state to exercise some control over how faith is practiced. While granting freedom of worship, the state retains some rights to control or restrict forms of worship which, arguably, may cause suffering to humans or animals. The disputes in these cases involve fundamental and competing values and principles. Finding common ground and compromise between such values remains elusive. Both decisions resolved the dispute by giving priority to freedom of worship, but each constructs the rationale behind their decisions in distinctly different ways. In the following sections, both justifications are analyzed in terms of the different stages of the IM and in terms of the role language plays in their gaining the approval of legal and non-legal audiences.

The *confrontation stage* (Constitutional Tribunal)

To begin, it should be noted that, in Poland, a detailed presentation of legal standpoints adopted by the parties is routinely provided in Part I, the *historyczna* ('historical') part of a justification. However, unlike Part III (the justification part), Part I does not provide any conclusions about the scope and content of the dispute. The justification (Part III) of the Constitutional Tribunal summarizes the scope and content of the dispute in the very first section, named explicitly as the *przedmiot i zakres kontroli* ('object and scope of review'). Interestingly, the tribunal starts by reiterating the rule (based on the statutory law regarding the Constitutional Tribunal) which regulates how the scope of its adjudication should be determined.

> (13) Trybunał Konstytucyjny, orzekając, **jest związany granicami** wniosku, pytania prawnego lub skargi (art. 66 ustawy z dnia 1 sierpnia 1997 r. o Trybunale Konstytucyjnym, Dz. U. Nr 102, poz. 643, ze zm.; dalej: ustawa o TK). Żądanie wniosku, przez wskazanie zaskarżonych przepisów i powołanych wzorców kontroli oraz uzasadnienie postawionych zarzutów, **wyznacza zakres orzekania** Trybunału, poza który Trybunał nie jest legitymowany wykraczać (art. 7 Konstytucji).
>
> ['In its adjudication, the Constitutional Tribunal **is bound by the limits of** an application, a legal question or constitutional complaint (based on relevant provision of the law on the Constitutional Tribunal not cited in full here). The claim made in an application which indicates challenged enactments, the standard of review and its justification **determines the scope** of the Constitutional Tribunal's adjudication beyond which the tribunal is not legitimized to move.]

This excerpt illustrates how the procedural rules can affect the scope and content of the dispute. In the subsequent paragraphs, the tribunal provides a meticulous description of the enactments challenged by the applicant in the complaint. The Union of Jewish Communities in Poland challenged certain legislative provisions of the *Act on the Protection of Animals*[19] which provides that a vertebrate animal in a slaughterhouse may only be killed if it is first stunned and that the animal must be killed by a qualified person. The same rule applies to hoofed animals killed in domestic slaughter. The application also questioned the provision which provided for a criminal liability for people who engage in this type of slaughter. The applicant drew attention to the absolute nature of the ban, which made no exception for ritual slaughter and its use of special methods (without stunning the animal). It should be borne in mind that, under Jewish and Islamic law, to produce kosher and halal meat, animals must be healthy and uninjured at the time of slaughter. The requirement that the animal be uninjured rules out stunning the animal before slaughter. The scope and content of the dispute is limited by the tribunal, which dismisses the part of the application concerning domestic slaughter. The evaluation of the admissibility of the claim is expressed in formal and neutral language, listing what the applicant failed to do in its justification. For example, the applicant in their justification did not refer in detail to the content of Article 34, Section 3 of the Act, especially regarding the concept of 'domestic slaughter'; the applicant did not analyze the normative meaning of this provision; the applicant did not justify their claim and so on.

How the constitutional issue and the object of review are determined is another factor that contributes to establishing the scope and content of the dispute:

> (14) Analiza wniosku prowadzi do stwierdzenia, że w niniejszej sprawie wnioskodawca przedstawił Trybunałowi do rozstrzygnięcia **zasadniczy problem**, czy w świetle wolności religii (wyznania), gwarantowanej przez art. 53 Konstytucji i art. 9 Konwencji, dopuszczalny jest obwarowany sankcjami karnymi bezwzględny zakaz uboju zwierząt według szczególnych metod wymaganych przez obrzędy religijne.
>
> ['The analysis of the application leads to the conclusion that, in this case, the Applicant has submitted to the tribunal the **fundamental problem** whether, in light of the freedom of religion safeguarded by Article 53 of the Constitution and Article 9 of the Convention, an absolute ban (including criminal sanctions) on animal slaughter using special methods required by religious rituals is permissible'.]

Here the *confrontation stage* ends, and the start of the *opening stage* is signalled by the tribunal's reference to the content of the application as a major factor in constraining the scope of its adjudication. The scope and content of the

19 Pol. art. 34 ust. 1 i 3 oraz art. 35 ust. 1 i 4 ustawy z dnia 21 sierpnia 1997 r. o ochronie zwierząt (Dz. U. z 2013 r. poz. 856; dalej: ustawa o ochronie zwierząt. [Article 34, Section 1 and 3 and Article 35 Sections 1 and 4 of the Act from 21 August 1997 on the Protection of Animals]

dispute is finally established by formulating the question that the tribunal has agreed to resolve.[20]

(15) **Z uwagi na treść wniosku oraz związanie Trybunału Konstytucyjnego jego granicami**, należy już na samym początku podkreślić, że **zakres orzekania** w niniejszej sprawie obejmował wyłącznie odpowiedź na zasadnicze pytanie: **Czy obwarowany sankcjami karnymi, bezwzględny zakaz uboju rytualnego jest zgodny z powołanymi wzorcami kontroli, w tym art. 53 ust. 1, 2 i 5 Konstytucji i art. 9 Konwencji?**

['In view of the content of the application and the limits it imposed on the Constitutional Tribunal's adjudication, it should be emphasized that the scope of adjudication in the present case will only focus on answering the following question: does the absolute ban on ritual slaughter, with its criminal sanction, comply with the standards of review, including Article 53 of the Constitution and Article 9 of the Convention [European Convention on Human Rights]'.]

Fulfilment of the dialectical goal of the *confrontation stage* is the outcome of a process during which the judge decides on certain crucial points: whether to accept the application in full or only in part, what constitutes the object of the constitutional review and how the constitutional issue should be specified. To a considerable extent, the scope and content of the dispute can be reconstructed by identifying certain recurrent terms and phrases – *przedmiot i zakres kontroli* ('object and scope of review'), *(constitutional) problem* – and by analyzing their co-texts. Reconstruction of legal standpoints adopted by the parties and institutional actors is facilitated by searching for the terms *argument* or *argumentacja* ('argumentation') and *stanowisko* ('position'), especially in the *historyczna* part of the justification. We see that the co-texts of these terms reveal not only the standpoints adopted by the parties but also whether the tribunal has agreed with them. Examples (16) through (18) illustrate this practice.

(16) **Argumentacja wnioskodawcy** konsekwentnie koncentruje się na konfrontacji bezwzględnego zakazu dokonywania uboju rytualnego w rzeźni z wielorakimi aspektami wolności wyznania.

[The **applicant's argumentation** focuses consistently on the confrontation between the absolute prohibition on ritual slaughter in the slaughterhouse and the various aspects of freedom of religion.]

(17) Marszałek Sejmu **zajął stanowisko w imieniu Sejmu**, wnosząc o umorzenie postępowania.

20 It should be noted that the Tribunal specifies which matters will not be subject to its review, e.g., export of meat obtained as a result of the slaughter.

[The Speaker of the Sejm **took a position on behalf of** the Sejm filing for the proceedings to be dismissed.]

(18) Trybunał Konstytucyjny **nie podzielił stanowiska** Marszałka Sejmu, jakoby w niniejszej sprawie legitymacja wnioskodawcy budziła wątpliwości.

[The Constitutional Tribunal **did not share the position** adopted by the Speaker of the Sejm regarding (...).]

A search for the term *zakres* ('scope') is equally revealing. *Zakres* occurs as many as 96 times in its various declensional forms. Scrutiny of its co-texts also helps determine the legal standpoints adopted by the institutional actors, such as the Speaker of the Sejm,[21] and how the tribunal resolves a particular factor contributing to the scope of the dispute.

(19) Trybunał Konstytucyjny stwierdził, że w niniejszej sprawie **ograniczenie zakresu orzekania do sytuacji prawnej gmin wyznaniowych żydowskich** (postulowane przez Marszałka Sejmu), nie tylko nie znajdowałoby podstaw w świetle powołanych przepisów Konstytucji, lecz także mogłoby prowadzić do powstania stanu prawnego sprzecznego z art. 25 ust. 1 Konstytucji. Przepis ten określa zasadę ustrojową równouprawnienia kościołów i innych związków wyznaniowych.

['The Constitutional Tribunal finds that in the present case **limiting the scope of adjudication to the legal situation of the Jewish communities in Poland** (as advocated by the Speaker of the Sejm) would not only be baseless in light of the adopted constitutional provisions, but it could also result in creating a legal situation non-compliant with Art. 25, Section 1 of the Constitution. This constitutional provision provides for the principle of equality among churches'.]

The *confrontation stage* (US Supreme Court)

The difference of opinion in the Supreme Court decision is established by providing a summary of ordinances adopted by the city council to address the issue of religious animal sacrifice, the decision of the District Court which ruled for the city and the *per curiam* opinion of the Court of Appeals for the Eleventh Circuit which concluded that the ordinances were consistent with the Constitution. Using reporting (narrative) and neutral language, the majority opinion reconstructed the legal standpoints adopted by these institutional

21 The Sejm, the lower house of the Polish parliament, is presided over by an official known as the Speaker of the Sejm, or the Marshal of the Sejm. The Speaker/Marshal here represents the legislative body responsible for enacting the challenged provisions.

actors and the petitioner Church of the Lukumi Babalu Aye, Inc. In sum, ritual killing practised by the church is treated as a threat to public morals, peace or safety (Resolution 87 66). It is unnecessary and cruel (Ordinance 87 40) and 'possess[ion], sacrifice, or slaughter' of an animal if it is killed in 'any type of ritual' and not for purpose of food consumption is prohibited (Ordinance 87 52). Petitioners disagreed and filed a suit alleging that their religious rights were violated under, *inter alia*, the Free Exercise Clause of the First Amendment. The District Court's position is that, even if the ordinances are not religiously neutral, compelling governmental interests in preventing public health risks and cruelty to animals fully justified the absolute prohibition on ritual sacrifice. More generally, the difference of opinion can be equated with the conflict between the religious liberty of believers, who claim the right to be excused from laws that interfere with their religious practices and the interests of society.

The neutral summary provided in the opinion contrasts with the first two opening paragraphs of the majority opinion which seems to serve two major functions. First, it signals the scope and content of the dispute by specifying the constitutional principle that has been violated. Second, it already establishes the result of the ensuing critical discussion. The excerpts below are also noteworthy for the role played by evaluative language.

> (20) **The principle** that government may not enact laws that suppress religious belief or practice is so well understood that few violations are recorded in our opinions. Cf. McDaniel v. Paty, 435 U.S. 618, 98 S.Ct. 1322, 55 L.Ed.2d 593 (1978); Fowler v. Rhode Island, 345 U.S. 67, 73 S.Ct. 526, 97 L.Ed. 828 (1953). Concerned that this **fundamental nonpersecution principle** of the First Amendment was implicated here, however, we granted certiorari.
>
> (503 U.S. ----, 112 S.Ct. 1472, 117 L.Ed.2d 616 (1992))

> (21) Our review confirms that the laws in question were enacted by officials who **did not understand, failed to perceive, or chose to ignore the fact that their official actions** violated the Nation's essential commitment to religious freedom. The challenged laws had an impermissible object; and in all events the principle of general applicability was violated because the secular ends asserted in defense of the laws were pursued only with respect to conduct motivated by religious beliefs. **We invalidate the challenged enactments and reverse the judgment of the Court of Appeals.**

In (21), the content of the principle is described so as to suggest it should be taken for granted (*so well understood, few violations are recorded*). Assessed as *fundamental* and in terms of *non-persecution*, it introduces the First Amendment as the legal basis, a major point of reference for the discussion.

Recall that the First Amendment of the US Constitution safeguards freedom of religion, expression, assembly and safeguards the right to petition.[22] Example (20) can, thus, be said to establish a common starting point. In (21), the principle is qualified in abstract and evaluative terms, without explicit reference to the First Amendment, as 'the Nation's essential commitment to religious freedom'. The reference to the source of the violation is equally evaluative. The laws themselves (referring here to the city's ordinances against sacrifice) are named as the source, but the officials who enacted these ordinances receive the brunt of the court's negative assessment (*officials* [...] ***did not understand, failed to perceive, or chose to ignore***). Example (21) is also noteworthy for how it both provides the result of the judicial decision-making process (***we invalidate the challenged enactments and reverse the judgment*** *of the Court of Appeals*) and the rationale behind the decision (***the principle of general applicability was violated because***). Several paragraphs later in the opinion, Justice Kennedy curtly states: 'We must consider petitioners' First Amendment claim'.

The *opening stage* (US Supreme Court)

The general principle of religious freedom and non-persecution, embodied, in particular in the Free Exercise Clause of the First Amendment, is used as a legal commonplace (*topos*) and a starting point. The majority opinion identifies this principle as the standard of review. Citing the court's previous cases, the majority opinion points to the Smith test[23] as the method for testing constitutionality. The two-part Smith test specifies that the government may burden

22 https://constitution.congress.gov/constitution/amendment-1/ (12 May 2023)

23 The test was introduced in *Employment Division, Department of Human Resources of Oregon v. Smith*. The case involved two members of the Native American Church, Alfred Leo Smith and Galen Black, who were fired from their jobs as drug rehabilitation counsellors after they tested positive for a controlled substance, peyote. Peyote is a hallucinogenic substance that is used in religious ceremonies by certain Native American tribes, including the Native American Church. Smith and Black applied for unemployment benefits, but their applications were denied by the state of Oregon on the grounds that they were fired for work-related misconduct. They appealed the decision, arguing that the denial of benefits violated their First Amendment right to the free exercise of religion. The Supreme Court, in a majority opinion written by Justice Antonin Scalia, ruled against Smith and Black. The court held that the Free Exercise Clause of the First Amendment did not require the state to grant an exemption from generally applicable laws that incidentally burdened religious practices. In other words, the fact that the use of peyote was part of a religious ritual did not entitle Smith and Black to an exception from the state's drug laws. This decision significantly narrowed the scope of religious freedom protections under the First Amendment, shifting the legal standard from one that required the government to have a compelling interest to restrict religious practices to a more general standard of laws being generally applicable and neutral in their intent (National Constitution Center: https://constitutioncenter.org/the-constitution/supreme-court-case-library/employment-division-v-smith; Oyez: https://www.oyez.org/cases/1989/88-1213; see also Hutchison 2022.

religious practice if a law is neutral and generally applicable. The majority uses these two criteria of neutrality and general applicability to examine the challenged ordinances. In addition, as the opinion clarifies, a law that fails to satisfy these requirements must be justified by a 'compelling governmental interest' and must be 'narrowly tailored' to advance that interest. The court also uses the Smith test to establish the division of the burden of proof (cf. Feteris 2017: 222), finding that the government is required to show that there is a compelling interest which justifies the harm done by the alleged discrimination. In addition, the adoption of the two-part Smith test provides a clear structure to the *argumentation stage*. In applying the Smith test, the majority opinion must first determine whether the ordinances meet the requirements of neutrality and general applicability. It must then apply the compelling interest standard to determine whether the local government (the city council) has chosen a narrowly tailored and the least restrictive means to achieve a compelling governmental objective.

From the linguistic perspective, there are several linguistic clues which signal that the judge sets out to establish common starting points, testing methods and the division of the burden of proof. Among the clues are the use of terms, such as *principle*, or his direct reference to a constitutional provision, especially when applied in the context of the Court's previous cases.

> (22) **The Free Exercise Clause of the First Amendment**, which has been applied to the States through the Fourteenth Amendment, see Cantwell v. Connecticut, 310 U.S. 296, 303, 60 S.Ct. 900, 903, 84 L.Ed. 1213 (1940), provides that.
>
> (23) **In our Establishment Clause** cases we have often stated **the principle** that the First Amendment forbids an official purpose to disapprove of a particular religion or of religion in general. See, e.g., Board of Ed. of Westside Community Schools (Dist. 66) v. Mergens, 496 U.S. 226, 248, 110 S.Ct. 2356, 2370-71, 110 L.Ed.2d 191 (1990) (plurality opinion).

Another clue is when the co-text suggests the application of the principle in the Court's reasoning.

> (24) Petitioners allege an attempt to disfavor their religion because of the religious ceremonies it commands, and **the Free Exercise Clause is dispositive in our analysis**.

As we see in (25), the justification may not explicitly name the testing method applied as such. The adoption of the Smith test can be inferred from the reference to the landmark case in which it originated. Another clue is found in the judge's statement that the challenged enactments have not met 'the Smith requirements'.

(25) In addressing the **constitutional protection for free exercise of religion, our cases** establish the **general proposition that** a law that is neutral and of general applicability need not be justified by a **compelling governmental interest** even if the law has the incidental effect of burdening a particular religious practice. *Employment Div., Dept. of Human Resources of Oregon v. Smith, supra.* [...] A law failing to satisfy these requirements must be justified by a compelling governmental interest and must be narrowly tailored to advance that interest. These ordinances fail to satisfy the Smith requirements. We begin by discussing neutrality.

Example (25) shows that the justification not only determines which testing method has been adopted, but also specifies the procedural rule explaining what happens when the requirements of the Smith test are not met by the challenged enactments. This excerpt is also indicative of the non-linearity and contingent complexities of real-life interactions, even in institutional settings. The negative result of the test is revealed before the test is discussed. The final sentence then indicates the direction in which the argumentation will proceed.

The *opening stage* (Constitutional Tribunal)

As noted in the section above about the *confrontation stage*, the Constitutional Tribunal has formulated the question it had agreed to resolve (Example 14), thus determining the scope and content of the adjudication, while it also specifies the appropriate standard of review. The standard of review refers to Article 53 of the Constitution and Article 9 of the European Convention on Human Rights. This means that the principle of freedom of conscience and religion can be taken as the starting point for the next stages of the critical discussion, as per the IM.[24] Its importance and justification is reinforced by the tribunal, as illustrated in Example (26), with overtly value-based language:

(26) Wolność wyznania, określana w polskim porządku konstytucyjnym wolnością religii, jest fundamentalną (podstawową) wolnością człowieka. Już wstęp do Konstytucji podkreśla znaczenia wiary jako źródła *prawdy, sprawiedliwości, dobra* i *piękna*.

(K52/13, par. 224)

[Freedom of religion is a fundamental freedom of man. It is the preamble to the Constitution which emphasizes the importance of faith as a source of *truth, justice, good* and *beauty*.]

24 The term *wzorzec kontroli* ('standard of review') is found 20 times in the entire justification, including the historical part. The analysis of the historical part indicates disagreement over what constitutes standard of review. The Attorney General (*Prokurator Generalny*) argued that the standard or review as declared by the Applicant is 'inadequate'.

Freedom of religion is invoked here as the source of abstract values: *truth*, *justice*, *good* and *beauty*. Thus, freedom of religion is placed in the context of universal and absolute values, ostensibly valid and persuasive to a universal audience (Perelman & Olbrechts-Tyteca 1969). The concept of human dignity later serves as another common starting point. Just as in the Polish and US cases resolving the unconstitutionality of access to abortion (see Chapter 5), human dignity is established as a transcendental value that forms the axiological bedrock of the entire constitutional order (K52/13, par. 225).

(27) Obowiązek poszanowania wolności religii jest ściśle związany z ochroną przyrodzonej i niezbywalnej godności człowieka, która stanowi źródło wolności i praw człowieka i obywatela (art. 30 Konstytucji). Godność człowieka jest wartością transcendentną (zob. wyrok pełnego składu TK z 5 marca 2003 r., sygn. K 7/01, OTK ZU nr 3/A/2003, poz. 19, cz. III, pkt IV uzasadnienia). Stanowi aksjologiczną podstawę i przesłankę całego porządku konstytucyjnego (zob. L. Garlicki, komentarz do art. 30, [w:] Konstytucja Rzeczypospolitej Polskiej. Komentarz, t. 3, red. L. Garlicki, Warszawa 2003, s. 2-3).

[The obligation to respect freedom of religion is closely connected with the protection of the inherent and inalienable human dignity which is the source of freedoms and rights of people and citizens (Art. 30 of the Constitution). Human dignity is a transcendental value (see the judgement given by the full bench of the Constitutional Tribunal, case no. K 7/01, Part III of the justification. It constitutes the axiological foundation and premise of the entire constitutional order.]

Human dignity is used as a justification for respecting freedom of religion because it is the source of all other human freedoms and rights. Article 30 of the Constitution compels public authorities to respect and protect human dignity, and by extension, freedom of religion. The high status of the principle of freedom of religion is maintained by the tribunal which invokes Article 18 of the Universal Declaration of Human Rights and Article 9 of the European Convention of Human Rights. In addition, the tribunal refers to case law of the European Court of Human Rights which embraces freedom of thought, conscience and religion as the cornerstone of a pluralist and democratic society. In short, the starting points are framed in value-based language and invoke widely accepted legal values. But Article 53 of the Constitution is regarded as the main guarantor of the principle of freedom of religion.[25] In the justification, the principle is projected as a value that needs to be protected against interference from public authorities. Crucial to the ensuing discussion is the tribunal's acknowledgement that ritual slaughter carried out according to the

25 See the official English translation at https://www.sejm.gov.pl/prawo/konst/angielski/kon1.htm (16 May 2023)

special methods required by religious ritual can be considered an external manifestation of freedom of religion and, as such, it deserves protection.

The dialectical goal of determining testing methods is fulfilled by the tribunal in pointing to the limitation clause provided in Article 53, Section 5 of the Constitution.

> (28) Treść i znaczenie wolności religii, a także jej ścisły związek z przyrodzoną i niezbywalną godnością człowieka, determinują sposób uregulowania dozwolonych ograniczeń uzewnętrzniania tej wolności. Art. 53 ust. 5 Konstytucji stanowi, **że wolność uzewnętrzniania religii może być ograniczona jedynie w drodze ustawy i tylko wtedy, gdy jest to konieczne do ochrony bezpieczeństwa państwa, porządku publicznego, zdrowia, moralności lub wolności i praw innych osób**.
>
> [The content and meaning of freedom of religion, as well as its close connection with the inherent and inalienable human dignity, determine the manner or regulating permitted restrictions place upon the manifestation of this freedom. Article 53, Section 5 of the Constitution '[T]he freedom to publicly express religion may be limited only by means of statute and only where this is necessary for the defence of State security, public order, health, morals or the freedoms and rights of others'.[26]]

As in the case of the Smith test in the US Supreme Court justification, the limitation clause determines the direction in which the tribunal advances its arguments. As we will see in the *argumentation stage*, the tribunal's argumentation focuses on assessing whether the challenged legislative provisions are constitutional, based on the criteria found in the limitation clause.

The *argumentation stage* (Constitutional Tribunal)

As already indicated in the previous section, the tribunal's argumentation is organized around several criteria contained in the limiting clause, criteria which specify when the public manifestation of religion can be subject to restrictions. Worth noting is that only the first – that public expression of freedom of religion may be limited by means of a statute – is a formal criterion. The others are values: security, public order, health, morals, the freedoms and rights of other people. In the *argumentation stage*, the judge's task is to determine the acceptability of the arguments advanced by the parties in light of the common starting points and methods of evaluation (Feteris 2017: 222-223).

As we recall from Chapter 4, the Constitutional Tribunal uses the word 'argument' in its justifications for three dialectical goals: (1) it uses the word in a non-evaluative way to reconstruct legal standpoints adopted by institutional actors, (2) in an evaluative way to evaluate an argument and 3) to

26 https://www.sejm.gov.pl/prawo/konst/angielski/kon1.htm (16 May 2023)

structure argumentative discourse. These three basic uses of 'argument' are also found in this justification, and they help us reconstruct the tribunal's line of argumentation.

The first use can be seen when the justification reiterates the standpoint adopted by the applicant, as it argues that the challenged provision (Art. 34, Section 1 of the Act on the Protection of Animals) leads to a restriction of the public expression of religion and argues, furthermore, that it is not necessary to protect any of the values provided in Article 53, Section 5 of the Constitution. This standpoint is juxtaposed with that of the Attorney General.

> (29) Stanowisku wnioskodawcy przeciwstawił się Prokurator Generalny, powołując **argumenty** mające świadczyć o niezbędności zaskarżonego ograniczenia dla ochrony zdrowia, moralności, a także – w pewnym sensie – wolności i praw innych osób.
>
> [The applicant's position was contradicted by the Attorney General, who raised **arguments** which were supposed to demonstrate the necessity of the challenged provision to protect health, morality and, to some extent, the freedom and rights of other people.]

At this point, the justification does not evaluate the standpoints directly and explicitly. Rather, after their presentation, it responds to the two legal standpoints by declaring that there is no causal link between the ritual slaughter of animals and the protection of state security, public order and the freedoms and rights of other people. Worth noting is the absence of any justification for what amounts to a substantial reduction in the scope of the judicial review. The tribunal will now only examine the necessity of limiting freedom of religion for the sake of protecting public health and morality. Here, the justification follows a pattern of three discussion moves: (1) the presentation of the parties' argumentative stances on each of the relevant issues is followed by (2) the tribunal announcing how it has resolved the issue and (3) its justification. In Example (30) the reference to *arguments* serves the text-organizing function of structuring the tribunal's argumentation.

> (30) 'Trybunał Konstytucyjny **stwierdził, że** bezwzględny zakaz uboju rytualnego zwierząt gospodarskich w rzeźni nie jest niezbędny do ochrony zdrowia. Przemawiają za tym łącznie następujące **argumenty: po pierwsze**'.
>
> ['The Constitutional Tribunal **finds that** absolute prohibition of ritual slaughter in the slaughterhouse is not necessary for health protection. The following **arguments** jointly support that statement: first'.]

The third evaluative use of the term '*argument*' is found in the tribunal's argumentation assessing the parties' argument.

(31) **'Przekonujący** jest również **argument wnioskodawcy**, że o braku zagrożeń dla bezpieczeństwa i higieny żywności oraz zdrowia konsumentów świadczy dotychczasowa praktyka dokonywania uboju rytualnego, na tle której nie stwierdzono takich zagrożeń'.

['**Convincing** is also the **applicant's argument** that the absence of a threat to the safety and hygiene of food and consumers' health is supported by the existing practice of ritual slaughter where no dangers have been found'.]

The tribunal's justification fulfils the dialectical goal of establishing the acceptability of the argumentation in defence of the position adopted by the applicant in the dispute. The arguments advanced by the other party, the Attorney General, are assessed as unacceptable:

(32) 'Po czwarte, przedstawione przez Prokuratora Generalnego zagrożenia dla bezpieczeństwa i higieny żywności związane z dokonywaniem uboju rytualnego oparte zostały na **nieudokumentowanym przeświadczeniu** o wadliwej praktyce dokonywania tego uboju'.

['Fourth, the Attorney General described threats to the safety and hygiene of food related to ritual slaughter based on *a baseless belief that* the slaughter practice is faulty'.]

The justification does not refer to the proposition as 'argument' but uses another status-indicating noun (*belief*), assessed as *baseless,* in order to reject the Attorney General's argument.

In the course of its justification, the tribunal resorts to various forms of argumentation, one of which is teleological–evaluative argumentation. In this teleological–evaluative argument, the judge interprets a legal rule in the light of the goal and value the rule is intended to realize (Feteris 2017: 237). In doing so, the arguer needs to reconstruct the will of the historical legislator. Example (33) illustrates this argumentative practice as used by the Tribunal.

(33) Po pierwsze, nie ma żadnych podstaw, aby zakładać, że zakaz uboju rytualnego został wprowadzony do ustawy o ochronie zwierząt z uwagi na niezbędność (konieczność) ochrony zdrowia. Materiały legislacyjne wskazują, że jedyną **wartością, na którą powoływano się w pracach parlamentarnych, była troska o dobrostan zwierząt p**odczas uboju.

['There is no basis to assume that the prohibition of ritual slaughter was introduced to the Act on the Protection of Animals due to the necessity to protect health. The legislative documents (records) show that the only **value** invoked in the course of the parliamentary work was a concern for the **welfare of animals** during slaughter'.]

As the name of this type of argument suggests, the use of evaluative language is found with references to various legal, social and economic goals and values. A legal rule is seen as an instrument for realizing such goals and for promoting specific values.

The same sequence of discussion moves occurs when the tribunal addresses protection of morality as a premise for limiting freedom of religion. First comes the presentation of the parties' standpoints. The Attorney General's argument is based on the assumption that human attitudes towards animals influences ***moralna osobowość człowieka*** ('man's moral personality'). Citing scientific literature, the Attorney General argues that ritual slaughter exposes animals to additional suffering, pain and stress. According to the Attorney General, suffering inflicted on animals during slaughter is the result of actions considered glaringly immoral in present-day Poland. For its part, the applicant argues that the morality premise was itself influenced by Judeo-Christian religion and tradition and that it, therefore, cannot be used to justify restricting the religious freedoms of Jews and Muslims. Rather, it is the prohibition of ritual slaughter for religious purposes that represents a violation of moral norms. Both parties to the dispute formulate their arguments in language that expresses negative assessments revolving around the notion of morality, but they do so in exactly the opposite way. The tribunal acknowledges the vagueness of the notion of morality, and it points out that the established juridical understanding of morality refers to moral norms held as valid in a given society and concerning interpersonal relations. The justification questions the acceptability of the Attorney General's argumentation, arguing that the issue in this case is not whether the slaughter is moral but whether the prohibition is necessary to protect morality. In its questioning of the argumentation, the tribunal uses the testing method derived from the limitation clause contained in Article 53 of the Constitution. The tribunal uses the same language it did with the health premise, finding that the absolute prohibition of ritual slaughter is not ***necessary*** to protect morality. This discussion move is followed by the tribunal's arguments. Two arguments are mentioned as relevant to the present analysis. One argument is noteworthy because of its similarity to the requirement of the Smith test in the US Supreme Court justification. The tribunal argues that the legislative provision cannot specifically prohibit ritual slaughter while permitting the killing of animals in non-ritual contexts.

As a final illustration of the interplay between argument and evaluative language in the Constitutional Tribunal's justification, we turn to consider the other argument. The argument here applies a value hierarchy referring to the *loci* of quantity (Perelman & Olbrechts-Tyteca 1969). Its use is illustrated by the following excerpt.

(34) Zważywszy, że społeczeństwo polskie przywiązuje dużą wagę do religii oraz wolności jej uzewnętrzniania, **Trybunał uznał za przekonujący argument** wnioskodawcy, że wolność religii jest nie tylko

> gwarantowana konstytucyjnie i konwencyjnie, lecz jest także jedną z podstawowych wartości moralnych w polskim społeczeństwie. **Stanowisko to jurydycznie wzmacnia** wstęp do Konstytucji, który odwołuje się do wartości zakorzenionych w tradycji judeochrześcijańskiej. Z uwagi na powyższe nie zasługuje na poparcie **twierdzenie, że** w społeczeństwie polskim bezwzględny zakaz uboju rytualnego jest konieczny do ochrony szeroko rozumianej moralności. Należy raczej przyjąć, że zgodne z normami moralnymi podzielanymi przez zdecydowaną większość polskiego społeczeństwa jest jak najszersze poszanowanie wolności religii (wyznania).
>
> ['Considering that **the Polish society attaches considerable weight to** religion and the freedom of its expression, the tribunal **finds the applicant's argument convincing** that freedom of religion is not only safeguarded by the Constitution and the Convention, but it is also one of the fundamental moral values in the Polish society. This position is reinforced juridically in the preamble to the Constitution which invokes values rooted in the Judeo-Christian tradition. In view of the foregoing, **the contention that** absolute prohibition of ritual slaughter is necessary does not deserve support. Instead, it should be accepted that a broad respect for religion (faith) is shared by the overwhelming majority of the Polish society'.]

The strategy of using a value hierarchy can be seen in how the justification places freedom of religion not only as a constitutionally protected value but also as a fundamental moral value of Polish society rooted in the Judeo-Christian tradition. The elevated status of religious freedom is contrasted, elsewhere in the justification, with the competing value of animal welfare and protection. The *loci* of quantity can be found in the references to Polish society *as a whole* and its 'overwhelming majority' made by the tribunal in support and acceptance of the applicant's argument. Worth noting also is how the justification evaluates two status nouns: *argument* and *contention*. The petitioner's *argument* is assessed as *convincing*, and it is bolstered by the axiologically oriented preamble to the Constitution. The *contention*, on the other hand, attributed earlier to the Attorney General, is qualified as *not deserving support*.

The *argumentation stage* (US Supreme Court)

As we have noted, the argumentative space here is structured around the two parts of the Smith test: the neutrality and general applicability criteria. Our linguistic analysis, which seeks to determine how the judge establishes the acceptability of the argumentation, is aided by the identification of status nouns. It turns out that the justification relies on the term *conclusion* to signal the discussion move in which the judge responds to the criterion of neutrality.

(35) The record in this case compels the **conclusion that** suppression of the central element of the Santería worship service was the object of the ordinances.

(36) It is a necessary **conclusion that** almost the only conduct subject to Ordinances 87-40, 87-52, and 87-71 is the religious exercise of Santería church members.

(37) It suffices to recite this feature of the law as support for our **conclusion that** Santería alone was the exclusive legislative concern.

(38) In sum, the **neutrality inquiry** leads to one **conclusion**: The ordinances had as their object the suppression of religion.

The sequence of discussion moves differs from the sequence identified in the Constitutional Tribunal justification. The court's conclusions are usually placed at paragraph-initial positions, and they are followed by detailed text-based analysis of a given ordinance.

(39) **It is a necessary conclusion that** almost the only conduct subject to Ordinances 87-40, 87-52, and 87-71 is the religious exercise of Santería church members. The texts show that they were drafted in tandem to achieve this result. **We begin with Ordinance 87-71**.

The court's argumentative stance can also be marked using the certainty adjective '*evident*' with the noun *evidence* as a supporting proposition.

(40) **It becomes evident that** these ordinances target Santería sacrifice when the ordinances' operation is considered. Apart from the text, the effect of a law in its real operation is **strong evidence** of its object.

(41) We also find significant **evidence** of the ordinances' improper targeting of Santería sacrifice in the fact that they proscribe more religious conduct than is necessary to achieve their stated ends.

In (43), the court's finding that the challenged law is not neutral is justified by an argument introduced using the same *it v-link ADJ to-inf* grammatical pattern we saw in Chapter 3.

(43) **It is not unreasonable to infer**, at least when there are no persuasive indications to the contrary, that a law which visits "gratuitous restrictions" on religious conduct, McGowan v. Maryland, 366 U.S., at 520, 81 S.Ct., at 1186 (opinion of Frankfurter, J.), seeks not to effectuate the stated governmental interests, but to suppress the conduct because of its religious motivation.

In both (40) and (41), the use of *target* and *targeting* is noteworthy for how, in the context of the court's argumentation, these otherwise evaluatively neutral lexical items express unfavourable evaluations. There are, in fact, as many as many as 18 instances in the justification in which *target* or its related form are used. In most cases, it co-occurs with the words *improper* or *impermissible.*

The court's concluding statement can also assume the form of rejecting an argument advanced by one of the parties. The justification uses the familiar *N that* pattern seen in Chapter 4. Here, *N that* is used to mark the proposition as 'contention'.

(42) 'We reject the **contention** advanced by the city, see Brief for Respondent 15, that our inquiry must end with the text of the laws at issue'.

There is one very interesting instance in which the petitioners make a linguistic argument, in which they argue that three of the ordinances fail the test of facial neutrality because they use the words '*sacrifice*' and '*ritual*', words which are acknowledged as having 'strong religious connotations' (Brief for Petitioners 16-17.). The Court responds:

(43) 'We agree that these words are consistent with the claim of facial discrimination, but the **argument is not conclusive**. The words "sacrifice" and "ritual" have a religious origin, but current use admits also of secular meanings'.

The frequent occurrence of words associated with the notion of '*scope*' is striking. Associated with *scope* we find: *only, alone, underinclusive, underinclusion, overinclusive, narrowly, narrow, overbroad.* Their role becomes salient in those parts of justification that address the general applicability requirement and the compelling interest standard. These words are used to determine the acceptability of the respondents' arguments by assessing whether the challenged enactments served the purpose of protecting public health and animal welfare.

> (44) Respondent claims that Ordinances 87-40, 87-52, and 87-71 advance two interests: protecting the public health and preventing cruelty to animals. The ordinances are **underinclusive** for those ends.

The same negative evaluation is reiterated with respect to the specific issue of animal disposal.

> (45) The ordinances are also **underinclusive** with regard to the city's interest in public health, which is threatened by the disposal of animal carcasses in open public places and the consumption of uninspected meat.

The court argues that the health risks posed by the improper disposal of animal carcasses are the same whether they result from Santería sacrifice or some nonreligious killing. The city does not, however, prohibit hunters from bringing their kill to their houses, nor does it regulate subsequent disposal of animal remains.

The lexis expressing various degrees of scope restriction is also found in the resolution of the compelling interest standard.

> (46) First, even were the governmental interests compelling, the ordinances are not drawn in **narrow** terms to accomplish those interests. As we have discussed, see supra, at 16-18, 21-24, all four ordinances are **overbroad** or **underinclusive** in substantial respects'.

The *concluding stage* (US Supreme Court)

The dialectical goal of this stage is to determine the result of the critical discussion. The judge's task is to specify which party is justified in maintaining its position in the dispute (Feteris 2017: 223). As seen in the previous section, Justice Kennedy drew several specific conclusions regarding the outcomes of the Smith test and the compelling interest standard. While these conclusions communicate the evaluation of the challenged local law, the court's final decision is preceded by a direct assessment of the respondent's argument.

> (47) Respondent **has not demonstrated**, moreover, that, in the context of these ordinances, its governmental interests are **compelling**.

The final determination is found in the disposition of the case, in which Justice Kennedy announces that 'The laws here in question were enacted contrary to these constitutional principles, and they are void. Reversed'. This means that the position of the respondent in this case, the City of Hialeah, is not justified. The city's ordinances prohibiting ritual animal sacrifices are found to have violated the First Amendment's Free Exercise Clause.

The *concluding stage* (Constitutional Tribunal)

The Constitutional Tribunal draws on a fixed formulaic expression to announce its decision, in which the challenged legislative provision is found to be unconstitutional. In effect, this means that the position of the petitioner, the Union of Jewish Communities in Poland, is justified, and it has been defended against the critique and doubt expressed by the Attorney General.

> (48) Z powyższych względów **Trybunał Konstytucyjny orzekł**, że art. 34 ust. 1 u.o.z. w zakresie, w jakim nie zezwala na poddawanie zwierząt ubojowi w ubojni (rzeźni) według szczególnych metod wymaganych przez obrzędy religijne, **jest niezgodny** z art. 53 ust. 1, 2 i 5 Konstytucji w związku z art. 9 Konwencji.
>
> ['In view of the foregoing, **the Constitutional Tribunal finds** that Article 34, Section 1 of the Act on the Protection of Animals with respect

to the prohibition of animal slaughter in the slaughterhouse using special methods required by religious rituals **does not comply with** Article 53, Sections 1, 2 of **the Constitution** in connection with Article 9 of the Convention'.]

This final disposition is preceded by a more specific reference to the principle of proportionality, which weighs the values of religious freedom against those of animal welfare. Given that no proportionality test was carried out by the tribunal in its argumentation, this may not be surprising. Yet, the unacceptability of the challenged provisions is justified by stating that the enactment incorrectly balances the proportion between these two values. The court also adds that it is the duty of the legislator to weigh the competing values in such a way as to provide effective protection to both freedom of religion and animal welfare.

Strategic manoeuvring in the justifications of the Constitutional Tribunal and the US Supreme Court

The analysis of the two cases has shown how reading a justification in terms of the pragma-dialectical IM can contribute to characterizing legal justification as an argumentative activity type. Our analysis has also shown how the use of evaluative language can vary across the four different IM stages of the discussion. For example, the *confrontation stage* in the Constitutional Tribunal justification uses stance-oriented language to reconstruct legal standpoints in a non-evaluative way and to mark the area of (dis)agreement between the parties and the court. In contrast, the language of the *confrontation stage* in the US Supreme Court opinion is adversarial, apportioning blame to local authorities which enacted the challenged ordinances.

Both justifications demonstrate that the IM stages need not unfold in linear order. Each different discussion move can be elicited at any point in the argumentative discourse of the justifications. This is particularly evident in the US Supreme Court justification in which the court's decision is announced right at the start of the text. The IM stages were easier to identify in the Constitutional Tribunal justification because of its more stable structure and the presence of the recurrent elements (e.g., *przedmiot i zakres kontroli* ('object and scope of review'), *problem konstytucyjny*, ('constitutional problem')). Importantly, reading the texts of the justification in terms of the IM stages helps show how the court's argumentative space is organized. In both cases, the choice of a specific method for testing constitutionality affects the direction taken by the judges in their argumentations.

In the extended pragma-dialectical theory, van Eemeren (2010) develops the concept of 'strategic manoeuvring' to account for the fact that, in real-life argumentative discourse, arguers want their argumentation to be both reasonable and rhetorically effective so that it will be accepted as valid. In the context of legal argumentation, this means that legal justification is a rational activity aimed at dispute resolution. It is, furthermore, a rhetorical practice during which judges steer the discussion 'in the direction that is desirable from the perspective of certain legal goals' (Feteris 2012). To adopt van Eemeren's terminology, strategic manoeuvring can be seen in the choices made from the 'topical potential' available at a particular point in the discourse, the adaption to 'audience demand' and the 'presentational devices' that are used at all stages in the IM. Viewed from this perspective, the focus in this analysis has been on the aspects of topical potential and on presentational devices which 'pertain to the communicative means that are used in presenting the argumentative moves constituting a piece of strategic manoeuvring' (van Eemeren 2010: 118). The concept is, thus, useful to account for how courts can manoeuvre strategically in their choice of arguments and presentational techniques, including evaluative language to convince a given legal audience of the acceptability of their decisions. It can also be used to attempt a direct comparison of the argumentation in the two cases. In both cases, the argumentation revolves around a conflict of fundamental values which is, therefore, difficult to resolve in a way that would be acceptable to all parties and, by extension, acceptable to the various audiences interested in the outcome of the judicial decision-making process. For example, it would be extremely unrealistic to expect religious Jews or Santería *creyentes* (believers) to abandon their ritual practices for the sake of animal welfare. Reaching a compromise in such a dispute is virtually impossible.

In both cases, the judicial decisions give priority to freedom of religion rather than to animal welfare, but the judges use very different forms of strategic manoeuvring in their justifications. From the perspective of topical potential, the Constitutional Tribunal chooses universal and abstract values (*truth, justice, goodness* and *beauty*) as well as specific values (*human dignity, freedom of religion, the rule of law, public morality, animal welfare*) as legal *topoi*. Most of these concepts are open-ended and hard to define. The tribunal leaves them largely undefined except for referring to its own previous decisions, in which it mentioned moral concepts. Crucially, ritual slaughter is subsumed within the concept of religion as its outward manifestation. Because freedom of religion is deemed a value equated with the overarching value of human dignity, values which deserve robust legal protection, the protection is extended to ritual slaughter. Adopting the strategy of modelling a value hierarchy enables the tribunal to deny the same level of protection to animal welfare that it extends to religious freedom. The tribunal concludes that protecting animals against unnecessary suffering is irrelevant for public morality because animal suffering is not harmful to public morality. The value hierarchy offered is explicitly rooted in the Judeo-Christian tradition in order to enhance the persuasive potential of the argument by including Christians, the religious majority in Poland. In sum, the tribunal steers the discussion in the direction of concluding that animal welfare is a value that does not justify legal interference with the higher value of religious freedom.

The strategic manoeuvring in the US Supreme Court opinion avoids relying on such general and abstract principles or values. The difference between the US Supreme Court and the Constitutional Tribunal justifications in the level of argumentation is reflected in the use of specific terms. For example, the lemma *wartość* ('value') appears 22 times and *moralność* ('morality') 38 times in the Constitutional Tribunal justification. The US Supreme Court justification has 26 instances of *principle*, nine instances of *standard* and only two of *value*. Apart from invoking the First Amendment as a protection against suppressing religious belief or practice, the court does not refer to abstract and universal values or constitutional principles. The justification duly reconstructs the legal standpoints, but it does not engage with the argumentation advanced by lower courts. It focuses on the texts of the ordinances. Finding that the challenged enactments interfere with freedom of religion, it uses the Smith test to determine whether the city's law meets the criteria of neutrality and general applicability. Using these criteria, the court considers whether the state has a compelling interest that would justify interference with religious freedom. Justice Kennedy steers the discussion towards resolving the dispute in terms of concrete outcomes rather than abstractions. In other words, the justification aims to determine and seek agreement that a certain legislative practice (in this case, the city's ordinances) is unconstitutional, even if the theories underlying the decisions differ radically.[27] Thus, the distinctive feature of strategic manoeuvring in this case is its reliance on low-level and medium-level principles in avoidance of large-scale theoretical conflicts. Low-level or mid-level principles assume the form of rules or standards derived from or referring to rules at a higher level of abstraction and generality.[28] The mid-level argument is that law prohibiting ritual killing is not an adequate means of preventing cruelty to animals. The low-level principle is operant when the justification uses the specific criteria of the Smith test – neutrality and general applicability – to determine that the Santería religion and its believers have been discriminated against. The concrete outcome of the test is then used to resolve the dispute between two abstract values: freedom of religion and animal welfare. In other words, the conflict between two abstractions is resolved at the point of application based on the specifics of the case.

Bibliography

Aarnio, A. (1987). *The rational as reasonable: A treatise of legal justification*. Reidel.

Alexy, R. (1989). *A theory of legal argumentation: The theory of rational discourse as theory of legal justification*. Clarendon Press.

27 The phenomenon of reaching agreements in constitutional cases of conflict and disagreement on the most fundamental matters by agreeing on constitutional practices, and even on constitutional rights, but without agreeing on constitutional theories, is discussed in the context of the concept of 'incompletely theorized agreement' in Sunstein (2007).

28 Sunstein (2007) refers to 'low-level principle' as something relative, not absolute, understood in comparative terms. The same approach is taken towards the terms 'theories' and 'abstractions', which he uses interchangeably.

Aplevich, N. (2011). Discourse communities and communicative genres. In S. Habscheid (Ed.), *Textsorten, Handlungsmuster, Oberflächen. Linguistische Typologien der Kommunikation* (pp. 98–122). De Gruyter.

Bustamante, T. (2013). On the *argumentation ad absurdum* in statutory interpretation: Its uses and normative significance. In Ch. Dahlman & E. Feteris (Eds.), *Legal argumentation theory: Cross-disciplinary perspectives* (pp. 21–43). Springer.

Feteris, E.T. (1989). *Discussieregels in het recht.: Een pragma-dialectische analyse van het burgerlijk process en het strafproces.* [Discussion rules in law: A pragma-dialectical analysis of the Dutch civil process and criminal process] Dissertation Amsterdam. Foris.

Feteris, E.T. (2009). Strategic maneuvering in the justification of judicial decisions. In F.H. van Eemeren (Ed.), *Examining argumentation in context: Fifteen studies on strategic maneuvering* (pp. 93–114). John Benjamins Publishing.

Feteris, E.T. (2012). Strategic manoeuvring in the case of the "Unworthy spouse". In F.H. van Eemeren & B. Garssen (Eds.), *Exploring Argumentative Contexts* (pp. 149–164). John Benjamins Publishing.

Feteris, E.T. (2015). The role of pragmatic argumentation referring to consequences, goals, and values in the justification of judicial decisions. In B.J. Garssen, D. Godden, G. Mitchell, & A.F. Snoeck Henkemans (Eds.), *International society for the study of argumentation: 8th international conference on argumentation: July 1–July 4, 2014, University of Amsterdam, The Netherlands* (pp. 414–425). Sic Sat.

Feteris, E.T. (2017). *Fundamentals of legal argumentation: A survey of theories on the justification of judicial decisions.* Springer.

Garlicki, L. (2007). Constitutional courts versus supreme courts. *International Journal of Constitutional Law, 5*(1), 44–68.

Goźdź-Roszkowski, S. (2020). Move analysis of legal justifications in Constitutional Tribunal judgments in Poland: What they share and what they do not. *International Journal for the Semiotics of Law, 33*(3), 581–600. https://doi.org/10.1007/s11196-020-09700-1

Goźdź-Roszkowski, S. (2021). Hostility to religion or protection against discrimination? Evaluation and argument in a case of conflicting principles. In J. Giltrow, F. Olsen, & D. Mancini (Eds.), *Legal meanings: The making and use of meaning in legal reasoning* (pp. 57–76). De Gruyter. https://doi.org/10.1515/9783110720969

Goźdź-Roszkowski, S. (2022a). Evaluative language and strategic manoeuvring in the justification of judicial decisions: The case of teleological-evaluative argumentation. In S. Goźdź-Roszkowski & G. Pontrandolfo (Eds.), *Law, language and the courtroom: Legal linguistics and the discourse of judges* (pp. 98–111). Routledge.

Goźdź-Roszkowski, S. (2022b). Evaluative language in legal professional practice: The case of justification of judicial decisions. In B. Lewandowska-Tomaszczyk & M. Trojszczak (Eds.), *Language use, education and professional contexts* (pp. 3–20). Springer.

Hutchinson, B.L. (2022). Revisiting employment division v. Smith. *University of Cincinnati Law Review, 91*(2), 397–436.

Kloosterhuis, H. (2013). The rule of law and the ideal of a critical discussion. In Ch. Dahlman & E. Feteris (Eds.), *Legal argumentation theory: Cross-disciplinary perspectives* (pp. 71–83). Springer.

Królikowski, J. (2015). Uzasadnienia orzeczeń Trybunału Konstytucyjnego [Justifications of Constitutional Tribunal decisions]. In I. Rzucidło-Grochowska

& M. Grochowski (Eds.), *Uzasadnienia decyzji stosowania prawa* [Justification in Judicial Decision-Making Process] (pp. 427–439). Wolters Kluwer.

Peczenik, A. (1989). *On Law and Reason*. Kluwer Academic Publishers.

Perelman, Ch., & Olbrechts-Tyteca, L. (1969). *The new rhetoric: A treatise on argumentation*. University of Notre Dame Press.

Rzucidło-Grochowska, I. (2017). Strategies and techniques used in the preparation of judicial opinions. *Ruch Prawniczy, Ekonomiczny i Socjologiczny, 79*(2), 59–72.

Sunstein, C. (2007). Incompletely Theorized Agreements in Constitutional Law. University of Chicago Public Law & Legal Theory Working Paper 14. https://chicagounbound.uchicago.edu/cgi/viewcontent.cgi?article=1149&context=public_law_and_legal_theory (last viewed 25 January 2023).

Van Eemeren, F.H. (2010). *Strategic maneuvering in argumentative discourse: Extending the pragma-dialectical theory of argumentation*. John Benjamins.

van Eemeren, F.H., & Grootendorst, R. (1984). *Speech acts in argumentative discussions*. Foris.

van Eemeren, F.H., & Grootendorst, R. (1992). *Argumentation, communication, and fallacies: A pragma-dialectical perspective*. Erlbaum.

van Eemeren, F.H., Grootendorst, R., Jackson, S., & Jacobs, S. (1993). *Reconstructing argumentative discourse*. University of Alabama Press.

7 Pulling the strands together

In closing, I would like to return to the beginning of this volume to draw together the different strands of my book's central theme: the closely related questions of how evaluative language and argumentation are closely intertwined in legal justification and of how evaluation serves to realize the goals of a legal justification. This book has attempted to bring the methodologies of linguistics together with theories of legal argumentation in order to show the rich, complex roles that evaluative language plays in the institutional discourse of legal justification. The various approaches to my research questions, suggested in each chapter of this book, should be useful for further research by other scholars who wish to explore the same areas. Some suggestions to that effect – possible directions for future research – are outlined below.

In Chapter 1, we noted that evaluation has many faces. Evaluation can be expressed using a diverse and seemingly indefinite range of linguistic resources. In the context of legal justification, the judicial writer faces many choices about how to construct their arguments. The selection of specific words, phrases and or extended patterns to effectively express their judgments are among the major choices they make. Chapters 3 and 4 examine evaluation understood as linguistic markers of evaluative meanings. Approaching from the perspective of corpus linguistics, these language resources are viewed in terms of predictable lexico-grammar patterns, a level of language description in which lexis (or vocabulary) and grammar (or syntax) combine into one. The findings in Chapters 3 and 4 bring to light two major points. First, evaluation in legal justification can indeed be seen as manifested in patterned verbal behaviour, but judicial writers, in particular, rely on a restricted range of language patterns to signal their assessments. Many of the patterns identified as evaluative and belonging to the local grammar of evaluation in other discourses (Hunston & Sinclair 2000) are simply not found in the corpora of judicial opinions with any salient frequency.[1] This means that while there are certain

1 For example, the pattern '*there link verb something/anything/nothing + adjective group + about or in + thing evaluated*', illustrated below, is extremely rare, with only five instances found in the entire corpus:

DOI: 10.4324/9781003333302-10

common, preferred forms for encoding attitudinal meanings, there is always room for idiosyncratic, creative and necessarily low-frequency forms of verbal expression. Such idiosyncrasies of judicial style are bound to be undetectable by quantitative methods. Although the two patterns discussed in detail in both chapters cannot offer an exhaustive account of evaluation in legal justification, they served here as viable models for the linguistic approach to evaluation in exploring how judicial voices tend to be operationalized and deployed in judicial prose.

Second, even though the adjectival and noun-centred grammar patterns are also found in other formal registers of writing (especially in academic writing), in some respects, their use seems to be unique to judicial prose. The high frequency of these patterns in judicial prose reveals something of the rhetorical dimension of legal justification. Adjectival patterns are the most obvious and overt linguistic means used by judges to signal their evaluative concerns. Like academic writers, judges adopt a 'voice' which gains its authoritativeness by demonstrating that every effort has been made to be appropriately fair, objective and reasonable. These lexico-grammar patterns offer judges a useful linguistic tool for ascribing value while, at the same time, preserving their persona of disinterested, objective authority through the obfuscating vagueness of 'it' used as a grammatical subject.

What makes their use in judicial discourse distinctive is best understood in terms of a distinction between the language of 'justification' and the language of 'persuasion' (Romano & Curry 2020). The former is selected by judges when they wish to emphasize that the decision reached is the only correct legal solution. Judges select arguments solely to demonstrate support for their decisions and assert that no other viable solution could have been found. In contrast, the latter relies on presenting multiple arguments, openly recognizing the existence of possible alternatives. 'Persuasion' is, thus, also dialogic in its attempt to show the superior merit of one argument by comparing it with others. The use of the patterns can be described as oscillating between justificatory and persuasive concerns, specifically in the presence of four major adjectival patterns (difficulty, desirability, importance and validity) that, together, reveal the underlying paradigm of legal justification. The corpus data from decisions of both the US Supreme Court and the Constitutional Tribunal of Poland were strikingly consistent in these respects. Judges' acts of evaluation are enacted by engaging, both formally and functionally, with evaluations and stances taken in other opinions of the same case (whether majority, concurring or dissenting) or in relevant prior opinions. Judges use the patterns strategically to include numerous standpoints and arguments, then apply their own

'While **there is something unique about** statutes whose pre-emptive force is closely patterned after that of the LMRA (which we had held to support removal), **there is nothing whatever unique about** a federal cause of action that displaces state causes of action' (*Beneficial Nat. Bank v. Anderson*).

reasoning to demonstrate which argument is correct and why. By appealing to commonsense notions of obviousness and by using the phraseologies of validity, judges may also focus on their own arguments and justify their choices by providing a definitive answer to the legal dispute in question. It appears that the justificatory and persuasive functions co-exist as trade-offs, the emphasis of the one always being, to some extent, at the expense of the other. However, more research is needed to establish this more securely and to investigate whether the type of opinion (majority or dissenting) is a factor.

The comparative approach taken in this book, which considered language patterns in Poland and the United States, provides evidence that legal justification is underpinned by the same rhetorical assumptions across, at least if not beyond, these two cultures and languages. For example, from the perspective of politeness theory, the phraseologies of difficulty are generally preferred because they enable the judges to signal non-acceptance of argumentation in a less face-threatening manner. Both US and Polish judges tend to adopt phraseologies of difficulty to avoid more direct, explicitly negative and potentially face-threatening evaluation. From the perspective of phraseological patterning, it is particularly noticeable that the regularities of occurrence are not confined to the patterns themselves but that they also cover the co-occurrence between the patterns and argumentative propositions (often named explicitly as 'argument'). For this reason, the adjectival patterns (or, rather, specific sequences realizing these patterns) represent 'argumentation pointers'. Their function is similar to what van Eemeren et al. (2007) refer to as 'argumentative indicators'. Their occurrence signals that a particular argumentative move might be in progress or is just about to appear. They are also used to advance a standpoint, mainly by means of sequences built around the idea of importance. These are often placed at clearly designated textual points in justifications, and their discursive function is to signal that the judge is making an important point in their reasoning and to introduce a supporting argument.

My analysis of how the other major noun-centred (*N that*) pattern is used in justifications reveals its crucial role in evaluating the epistemic status of argumentative propositions. We have seen how evaluation operates at two levels, providing the judicial writer with ample opportunity to make rhetorical choices. First, selecting a particular noun depends on how the judge interprets the object of evaluation (i.e., the propositional content of arguments made by other interactants) and on how committed or not s/he feels towards it. Second, once propositions have been reified into the objects of which legal argumentation is comprised (e.g., arguments, conclusions, assumptions and so on), the judge can evaluate them in positive or negative terms that point the way towards its acceptance or rejection. This type of evaluation occurs on the interactive plane, as the text of a justification reflects the ongoing interaction between writer and reader. The judicial writer signals to the reader what the role of any particular argumentative proposition is in the context of the case. An assignment of status is usually both subjective and evaluative, and the writers can choose how categorical, confident or conciliatory they want to be in the orientation towards the propositions discussed. In addition, linguistic resources, as encapsulated in the choice of status nouns, are of critical importance in performing other roles equally crucial to argumentative discourse: marking cause–result relations, providing confirmation for claim-making and signalling legal standpoints.

If the adjectival patterns are viewed as 'argumentation pointers', then the *N that* pattern represents a 'site of contention'. The *N that* pattern represents a part of a legal justification in which a formulation of, or a reference to, an argument is likely to be encountered in the form of its assessment. The strong co-occurrence between most status nouns and explicitly negative evaluation points to one of the hallmark features of judicial argumentation: judges focus their opinion on the reasons for their own decisions in the process of brushing aside any arguments to the contrary. These findings corroborate the perception of legal justification as an argumentative activity type in which the judge's professional role is to resolve a difference of opinion in a legal context (cf. Feteris 2017). The judge performs this role by checking whether the claim of the protagonist (the petitioner in court proceedings) is acceptable in the context of critical reactions of the other party. In other words, the essence of the judicial role is to assess arguments and counter-arguments within the constraints imposed by the institutional conventions of legal proceedings. This is achieved during the argumentation stage of legal justification. The status nouns in the *N that* pattern, as well as the adjectival patterns, are both part of the linguistic toolkit available for fulfilling this goal.

Chapters 3 and 4 also show how corpora and quantitative methods can be used to quantify markers of evaluation. They also show, however, that such quantitative work must be complemented by a more qualitative approach which treats linguistic figures as only the starting point of context-bound investigations. The advantage of qualitative analysis is that it can show typicality (and frequency) of use. In cross-language research, this reservation is particularly important because there is no formal one-to-one correspondence between the patterns. Their functional similarities across languages can only be ascertained by exploring comparable contexts of use. My analyses have identified markers of evaluation in Polish justifications that were previously unknown,[2] allowing direct comparisons with their English language counterparts. While undoubtedly useful and illuminating, the statistical data should be treated with caution; the statistical data only chart general trends in constructing evaluation. Although corpus-based methods might allow comparative quantitative analysis of evaluative meanings in English and Polish, the lack of one-to-one formal correspondence in the patterns across languages made it unfeasible to interpret the results in such terms. More importantly, the main goal was not to quantify forms in order to calculate comparative frequencies of co-occurrence; rather,

2 There is very little research into grammar patterns in Polish. See, however, Grabowski and Groom (2021) for an experimental study of patterns in English–Polish translation).

it was to identify sequences of forms that play a role in the evaluative act and indicate the presence of an argumentative move. The basic unit of analysis in comparative, cross-language studies of evaluation, therefore, needs to go beyond discrete language items or patterns. In addition, the interpretation of status nouns as indicating sites of contention in Chapter 4 has implications for comparative cross-language research. Analyses of evaluative language can centre around argumentative propositions targeting specific issues occurring in sufficiently similar cases to ascertain how judges handle such arguments linguistically. For example, in cases concerning the responsibility for refusing to provide certain business services (e.g., *Masterpiece Cakeshop vs. Colorado*, or very recently *Creative LLC v. Elenis*), citing freedom of conscience, religion and speech, issues likely to occur as points of contention include evaluating the nature of service, religious beliefs, solution to conflict principles and so on. While requiring careful selection, this type of comparative analysis of how evaluative language is used to construct arguments could be very fruitful both for linguists and argumentation scholars.

Chapters 5 and 6 demonstrate the advantage of complementing corpus-based studies with case studies and with widening the context to consider evaluative language against the backdrop of actual cases seen in their entirety. In Chapter 5, I argue for making a distinction between evaluative language used to *discourse about* arguments by assessing argumentative propositions and indicating judicial stances and evaluative language operationalized as value-based lexis *constitutive of arguments*. Viewed from this perspective, the language and argument are inseparable. The lexis is value-based because it denotes values and principles, such as *dignity, equality* or *fairness*, and the judicial writer is again faced with rhetorical choices when deciding which legal *topoi* would be most effective as argumentative premises. Thus, value-based lexis provides linguistic clues to the reconstruction of argument and this approach is applied in very different linguistic and legal contexts of constitutional argumentation to resolve morally complex cases.

While the use of value-based lexis is necessarily dependent on the content of a specific case, some more general observations can be made. The use of value-based lexis is central to how the Constitutional Tribunal of Poland justifies its decisions. It reflects one of the common features of the civil law tradition in which constitutional issues, even if emerging in the context of a specific controversy, are considered to be of public importance. Judicial justifications in such cases invariably include assessment of fundamental values and principles. The judges use value-based lexis strategically to invoke commonly accepted legal values with the goal of gaining general acceptance of their decisions. Analysis of these lexis enables a researcher to track how the value-based lexis forms the bedrock of the court's reasoning. In building its argument, the court applies a value hierarchy, established using an argumentative scheme of balancing and weighing, and applies the principle of proportionality. In contrast, the justification in the case heard before the US Supreme Court that we considered in Chapter 5 does not hinge on value judgment to the extent seen in the Polish case. Instead, the argumentation follows the common law tradition of being largely precedent-based. It aims at undermining the arguments advanced in the earlier precedents. The driving force behind the majority's argumentation in *Dobbs* (2022) is their (negative) evaluation of the reasoning in *Roe* (1973) and *Casey* (1992), justifying the court's departure from its own precedents. In this way, Chapter 5 also contrasts the two types of evaluative language mentioned above.

Finally, Chapter 6 argues that the use and role of evaluative language can be described more systematically if linguistic descriptions are combined with the pragma-dialectical approach to legal justification. Together, the approaches allow us to *describe* how evaluative language is used and, at the same time, to *interpret* and *explain* why it is used at particular points in the text of the justifications. The descriptions no longer start at the micro-level of an utterance (whether in the form of a word, phrase or pattern). Rather, evaluative language is scrutinized and interpreted from the perspective of how it contributes to realizing particular argumentative moves occurring at different stages of justification. Justification itself is viewed as a critical discussion, unfolding in stages that can be described using the ideal model of critical discussion (IM). The IM is especially helpful in showing how evaluative language is used outside the strictly argumentative space of the justification proper. For example, according to the IM, the *confrontation stage* in the Constitutional Tribunal justification uses stance-oriented language to reconstruct legal standpoints in a non-evaluative way and to mark the area of (dis)agreement between the parties and the court.

Apart from enabling functional characterization of evaluative language, seeing evaluation as a discursive and argumentative practice allows us to compare cases originating in different institutional contexts in which the rules of the critical discussion are respected. Explanations for the differences between the use of evaluative language are found in the constraints imposed – regarding the procedural and material starting points – by the rules of procedural and substantive law specific to either the common law system of the US Supreme Court or the civil law system in which Poland's Constitutional Tribunal adjudicates.

Evaluative language is also interpreted in light of Van Eemeren's concept of 'strategic manoeuvring', i.e., the overall strategy adopted by judges to ensure that their argumentation is rhetorically effective and is accepted as sound. In the Chapter 6 case study, addressing a conflict between the values of freedom of worship and animal welfare, strategic manoeuvring was shown at work in the choices made by judges from the 'topical potential' available at particular points in the discourse, their adaptions to 'audience demand' and the 'presentational devices' available at all stages of the critical discussion. The concept of 'strategic manoeuvring', thus, helps to account for the differences in how courts can manoeuvre strategically in their choice of arguments and presentational techniques (including evaluative language) to convince a given legal audience of the acceptability of their decision, even when the decisions in the two cases are similar.

What I hope this book has illustrated are the many ways in which the use of evaluative language is pervasive in legal justification and how the role of modern judicial opinion cannot be fully grasped without coming to terms with the role of evaluative language in communicating judicial decisions. Further, I hope it has illustrated that studying evaluative language can only be effective if it involves making connections across the domains of linguistics, law and argumentation. Evaluative language should never be seen as a single, isolated factor in justifications. Instead, it emerges at the interface between argumentation, persuasion and rhetoric, and, ideally, all these aspects should be taken into account.

Bibliography

Grabowski, Ł., & Groom, N. (2021). Grammar patterns as an exploratory tool for studying formulaicity in English-to-Polish translation: A corpus-based study. In T. Alexsandar & L. Grabowski (Eds.), *Formulaic language* (pp. 171–190). Language Science Press.

Hunston, S. & Sinclair, J. (2000). A local grammar of evaluation. In: S. Hunston & G. Thompson (Eds.),. *Evaluation in text: Authorial stance and the construction of discourse* (pp. 74–101). Oxford UP.

Romano, M. K., & Curry, T. A. (2020). *Creating the law: State Supreme Court opinions and the effect of audiences.* Routledge.

van Eemeren, F. H., Houtlosser, P., & Henkemans, F. (2007). *Argumentative indicators in discourse. A pragma-dialectical study.* Springer.

Feteris, E. T. (2017). *Fundamentals of legal argumentation: A survey of theories on the justification of judicial decisions.* Springer.

Index

abortion 12, 71, 115, 119–20; abortion jurisprudence 8; access to 102, 104, 114–18, 120, 123, 149; as morally sensitive issue 102, 123; unconstitutionality of 105
abstract review 24
abstract values 104, 107, 110, 114, 149, 159–60
acceptability of legal argumentation 16–18, 102, 104, 114, 137–38, 150, 152–54, 156, 169
adjective-centred patterns 34
agreement 72, 158, 160, 168; and alignment 42, 75; expression of 77, 85
alignment 42, 44, 71, 74–75, 77, 101
allowable contributions 131
animal sacrifice 140, 144
appraisal 3–4, 8; appraisal theory 48
argument 5, 9, 17, 22; argument evaluation 16; argument from authority 42; argument of consistency 61; and argumentative move 38; construction and construal of 70; and evaluative language 10–12, 56; lexical semantics of 87; persuasive value of 92; structure of 18
argumentation pattern 138
argumentation pointers 65, 165–66
argumentative discourse x, 16, 33, 38, 40, 44, 48, 70, 73, 77, 90–91, 93, 95, 99, 128–31, 138, 151, 158, 166; activity type 19, 94, 132, 158, 166; and persuasive discourse 75; practice 17, 130, 152, 168; propositions 6
argumentative indicators 18, 165
argumentative move 18, 28, 38, 48, 58, 60–61, 65–66, 69, 132, 159, 165, 167–68
argumentative premises 99, 101, 167
argumentative scheme 16, 123, 131, 138, 167
argumentum ad absurdum 50
attitudinal model 10
attribution 70, 72
audience 17–18, 22, 102, 104, 123; legal audience 11, 103, 159, 168–69; universal audience 110, 149

balancing and weighing 107, 123, 167; *see also* weighing and balancing

Church of the Lukumi Babalu Aye v. City of Hialeah 64, 140
coherence 49; evaluative 91
consequentialist argument 45, 49–50, 129
consistency 49, 61
constitutional review 23–24, 28, 105, 135; object of 143; standard of 136Constitutional Tribunal 39; and abortion 105; adjudication of 22; corpus of 39, 73; and ideal model of critical discussion 133–39; justifications of 27–28; in Polish court system 24; and principle of proportionality 104; rule of law crisis 23, 105; and strategic manoeuvring 158–60; textual structure of **26**; *see also Trybunał Konstytucyjny*
corpus linguistics 5, 163; methods 8–9, 33; research 38
corpus-assisted analysis 123; discourse analysis 40, 103, 123; methods of analysis 99
corpus-based studies 167; corpus-based grammar 33; methods of analysis 99, 166
critical discussion 17, 100, 130, 132, 136, 140, 145; ideal model of 28,

100, 131, 133, 168; result of 157; stages of 139, 148

dialectical goal 131, 143, 150, 157
difference of opinion 7, 27, 82, 94, 100, 130–31, 135–36, 144–45, 166
discussion move 90, 130, 151, 153–54, 158
Dobbs v. Jackson Women's Health Organization 12, 71, 114–23, 168

ethical words 104
European Convention of Human Rights 149
European Court of Human Rights 149
evaluation: act of 43, 45, 70, 77, 93, 101, 164; averred 42; definition of 3–7; and epistemic status 69, 71, 93; face-threatening 46, 53, 165; intensity of 50, 65, 70, 79; ; interpersonal aspects of 42; in judicial discourse and legal argumentation 10–12; in legal linguistics literature 7–10; linguistic expression of 33–35, 37–39; in linguistics and argumentation studies 16–19; two levels of 76–77, 165; *see also* evaluative language
evaluation markers 50, 166
evaluation pointer 43, 77
evaluative embedding 51–52
evaluative intensity 75, 77
evaluative language 5–7; and argumentative moves 132; and critical discussion 139–40, 158–59; functions of 11–12; and lexico-grammatical patterning 99; linguistic study of 10; patterned use of 38; and rhetorical approach 18, 101; and value-based lexis 101, 105, 114, 119
evaluative language choices 131
evaluative polarity 53

First Amendment 58, 145–46, 160
forms of argument 103–4
formulaic language 134, 138, 157

genre 25, 38; genre of judgments 77; genre specificity 75; of judicial justification 7; of legal justification 72, 94
genre theory 17
grammar pattern 33, 63, 93

human dignity 18, 159; as common starting point 149; as general value 104, 111–12, 123

intersubjectivity 6, 42
'introductory it' patterns 37–38

judicial discourse 37, 73, 99, 164; dialogicality of 7; and evaluative language 10–12; and pragma-dialectic theory 130
judicial opinion 10–12, 20–21, 25, 34, 51, 66, 81, 86, 169; justifications of 102
judicial review 23–25, 151; abstract 137

legal argumentation: and acts of evaluation 101; common starting points in 104; dialogical theories of 17; and evaluative language 10–12; pragma-dialectical approach to 130, 158; and status-indicating nouns 74–75, 93; theory of 16, 104, 163
legal argumentation theory 16, 104
legal justification 9, 19, 22, 27, 33–35, 38, 70, 80–81, 93, 129, 158; argumentative discourse of 44, 130; conclusions in 81; and critical discussion 100, 131, 133; functions of 91, 105; genre of 72, 94; textual structure of 83
legitimacy 21, 23, 54, 105, 137
lexico-grammar patterns 6–7, 25, 33, 163–64
logical approach 22, 101

morality 106, 151, 153, 160; public morality 159
move analysis 25, 28

N that pattern 34, 72–74, 77, 83, 86, 94, 156, 165; as a site of contention 166

pattern 33, 37, 40; as evaluation pointer 43
pattern grammar 33, 38–40
Perelman, Chaïm 18
persuasive value 92, 95
pragma-dialectic model 132, 158
pragma-dialectic terms 134, 136

pragma-dialectical approach (PDA) 17, 90; to legal argumentation 130, 168; *see also* pragma-dialectical theory
pragma-dialectical ideal model of a critical discussion (IM) 28
pragma-dialectical theory 17, 130; extended 158; *see also* pragma-dialectics
pragma-dialectics 18
principle of proportionality 104, 123, 136, 158, 167
principles: constitutional principles 102, 157, 160; general principles 123; legal principles 18, 49, 103–4, 129, 132, 138; and values 11, 99, 101–3, 105–7, 123, 141, 159, 167

reasonableness 54–57, 65
religious freedom 140, 146, 154, 158–60
rhetorical approach 17–18, 22, 101–2
rhetorical device 38, 66, 77
rhetorical move 46
rhetorical move structure 25, 28
rhetorical strategies 11, 38, 123
rhetorical techniques 22

semantic sequence 63–64, 66
site of contention 69–70, 72, 93–95, 114, 128, 167
Sketch Engine 39–40, 73, 86
Smith test 146–48, 150, 153–54, 157, 160
stance 3–5, 38, 48, 57, 65–66, 73; attitude and emphasis 8; and evaluation 6–7
stance markers 17, 59; *see also* stance-oriented language
stance-oriented language 158, 168
stancetaking 4, 6–8, 73, 77, 101
standard of review 136, 139, 146, 148
standards of acceptability 130
standpoint 7, 18, 77, 81–82, 129, 136, 151, 165; defending 17, 130; expression of 5, 86, 88, 93, 104
starting point 111, 117, 123, 136, 146, 148–49, 166
status 72, 99; assignment of 72, 93, 165; epistemic status 35, 69–71, 73, 165; evaluation of 93
status nouns 76–78, 80–82, 85–86, 90, 154; choice of 166; as sites of contention 93–95
status-indicating nouns 72, 74–75, 152; *see also* status nouns
status-indicating strategies 72
strategic manoeuvring 17–18, 100, 158–60, 168
strategy 86, 100, 104, 119, 129, 168; rhetorical 123; and value hierarchy 154, 159

teleological–evaluative argument 152
text genre 7, 25
textualist argument 120
topoi 11, 99, 101, 103–6, 111; legal *topoi* 113, 123, 159, 167
Trybunał Konstytucyjny 24, 39

US Supreme Court 23; corpus of 39, 73; and ideal model of critical discussion 140; opinion of 25–28; and Poland's Constitutional Tribunal 7, 20, 65, 93, 99, 102, 132–33, 140; role of 24; and strategic manoeuvring 158–60; structure of **26**

value hierarchy 18, 103, 111, 123, 153–54, 159, 167
value judgment 11, 16, 42, 73, 99, 101, 103–5, 122, 167
value premises 117
value-based language 148–49
value-based lexis 6, 19, 99, 101–3, 105, 114, 119, 123, 167; value-based argumentation 118; value-based nouns 117; *see also* value-laden lexis
value-laden lexis 17, 33, 38, 66, 85

weighing and balancing 138
Word Sketch 86, 88, 91, 107, 109

For Product Safety Concerns and Information please contact our EU
representative GPSR@taylorandfrancis.com
Taylor & Francis Verlag GmbH, Kaufingerstraße 24, 80331 München, Germany

www.ingramcontent.com/pod-product-compliance
Lightning Source LLC
LaVergne TN
LVHW021129300926
849160LV00010B/926

* 9 7 8 1 0 3 2 3 6 6 9 2 0 *